Mad Dogs and Englishness

To Merlin from
Richard —
The Bowie essay is
the best ?

Mad Dogs and Englishness

Popular Music and English Identities

EDITED BY
LEE BROOKS,
MARK DONNELLY AND
RICHARD MILLS

BLOOMSBURY ACADEMIC

NEW YORK • LONDON • OXFORD • NEW DELHI • SYDNEY

BLOOMSBURY ACADEMIC
Bloomsbury Publishing Inc
1385 Broadway, New York, NY 10018, USA
50 Bedford Square, London, WC1B 3DP, UK

BLOOMSBURY, BLOOMSBURY ACADEMIC and the Diana logo
are trademarks of Bloomsbury Publishing Plc

First published in 2017
Paperback edition published 2019

ISBN: HB: 978-1-5013-1125-3
PB: 978-1-5013-5202-7
ePDF: 978-1-5013-1126-0
ePub: 978-1-5013-1127-7

Names: Brooks, Lee. | Donnelly, Mark, 1967- | Mills, Richard, 1964-
Title: Mad dogs and Englishness: popular music and English identities /
edited by Lee Brooks, Mark Donnelly and Richard Mills.
Description: New York, NY: Bloomsbury Academic, 2017. | Includes
bibliographical references and index.
Identifiers: LCCN 2017013601 (print) | LCCN 2017017214 (ebook) |
ISBN 9781501311260 (ePDF) | ISBN 9781501311277 (ePUB) |
ISBN 9781501311253 (hardcover)
Subjects: LCSH: Popular music–England–History and criticism. | National
characteristics, English.
Classification: LCC ML3492 (ebook) | LCC ML3492 .M33 2917 (print) | DDC
781.640942–dc23
LC record available at https://lccn.loc.gov/2017013601

Typeset by Deanta Global Publishing Services, Chennai, India

To find out more about our authors and books visit
www.bloomsbury.com and sign up for our newsletters.

To my Mum for giving me her Billy Fury albums, and Sarah for putting up with me listening to them.
To Paul and Jane, for sharing their records.
And to Dad, Jess, Maud and my elder brother, John, for introducing me to Bowie's music.

CONTENTS

Foreword xiii
Acknowledgements xvi

Introduction: Englishness, whose Englishness? *Lee Brooks and Mark Donnelly* 1

PART ONE English heritage 17

1   'Rosy, Won't You Please Come Home': Family, home and cultural identity in the music of Ray Davies and the Kinks *Carey Fleiner* 19

2   'Rule Britannia is out of bounds': David Bowie and English heritage. *David Bowie Is … (2013) The Next Day (2013)* and *Blackstar (2016) Richard Mills* 36

3   Mod cons: Back to the future with The Jam (1977–79) *Ben Winsworth* 54

4   PJ Harvey and remembering England *Abigail Gardner* 66

PART TWO Spaces of identity 83

5   Adventures in English space and time: Sound as experience in *Doctor Who (An Unearthly Child)* *Dene October* 85

6   Productive boredom and unproductive labour: Cabaret Voltaire in the People's Republic of South Yorkshire *Jon Hackett* 106

7   Flag of convenience? The Union Jack as a contested symbol of Englishness in popular music or a convenient marketing device? *Johnny Hopkins* 125

PART THREE Performing discrepancy 143

8   The poison in the human machine
     Raphael Costambeys-Kempczynski 145

9   'Brand New You're Retro': Tricky as Engpop
     dissident *Christian Lloyd and Shara Rambarran* 162

10   The (un)masked bard: Burial's denied profile and the
     memory of English underground music *Gabriele Marino* 174

11   *Albion Voice*: The Englishness of Bishi *Simon Keegan-Phipps
     and Trish Winter* 193

Index 211

CONTRIBUTORS

Raphael Costambeys-Kempczynski is senior lecturer in media and cultural studies at the Sorbonne Nouvelle in Paris. His research focuses on the performance and reception of Englishness in popular music and he has spoken and published on subjects ranging from David Bowie to The Streets, from the British Invasion to the representation of masculinities in pop culture. Raphael has held the positions of pro-vice-chancellor and deputy vice chancellor of the Sorbonne Nouvelle and is currently vice principal (Campus Life and Student Experience) of the Université Sorbonne Paris Cité. Raphael also works as a journalist and writes and broadcasts on education policies as well as music. He is president of the Editorial Board of The Conversation France and president of the Centre for Enterprise and Entrepreneurship *CréaJ IDF.*

Carey Fleiner is currently senior lecturer in classical and early medieval history and programme leader in classical studies at the University of Winchester. Her formal studies include Roman and medieval history, Latin and classical guitar at the University of Delaware and postgraduate studies elsewhere in Carolingian and Roman history. She has written, spoken and published academic pieces on the Kinks, including *The Kinks: A Thoroughly English Phenomenon* (Rowman and Littlefield 2017). Other publications include a chapter on the portrayal of the emperor Nero in the television programme *Doctor Who* (*Doctor Who and History: A Cultural Perspective*, Carey Fleiner and Dene October, eds., McFarland, forthcoming), the somewhat tempestuous relationship between the emperor Nero and his mother Agrippina the Younger (in *Royal Mothers and their Ruling Children: Wielding Political Authority from Antiquity to the Early Modern Era, Vol. 1,* Carey Fleiner and Elena Woodacre (eds), Palgrave 2016), the reputation of popular musicians in thirteenth-century medieval Europe (*The British Museum Citole: New Perspectives. British Museum Research Publication,* James Robinson and Naomi Speakman (eds), British Museum 2015), and rock and roll in American culture and siblings in rock and roll (*Music in American Life: An Encyclopedia of the Songs, Styles, Songs and Stories that Shaped Our Culture,* Jacqueline Edmonson ed., Greenwood Press 2013).

Abigail Gardner is senior lecturer in music and media at the University of Gloucestershire. She writes on music and ageing, music video and music documentary and produces community film and media. Key publications include *PJ Harvey and Music Video Performance* (Routledge 2015) and *Rock On: Women, Ageing and Popular Music* (Ashgate 2012, with Ros Jennings). She is a founder member of the Centre for Women, Ageing and Media (WAM), an international research hub http://wamuog.co.uk and principal investigator on an Erasmus + European project on diversity and digital storytelling.

Jon Hackett is senior lecturer in film and screen media at St Mary's University, Twickenham. His research interests include film and cultural theory, and popular music culture. He is currently working on a monograph on popular music and monstrosity with Dr Mark Duffett of the University of Chester.

Johnny Hopkins is a senior lecturer in popular music and media industries at Southampton Solent University and has been working in academia for 11 years. He is currently working on his PhD and has delivered papers at various academic conferences. His research interests include popular music and national identity; music PR and marketing; the 1960s counterculture press; punk fanzines; free jazz; independent record shops; soul music and civil rights; the representation of music subcultures on film; moral panics about Teddy Boys; and the UK independent label scene. Alongside this he has over 25 years of experience working as a PR in the music industry. This includes being head of press at Creation Records; launching and developing the careers of Oasis and Kasabian; relaunching the career of Sinead O'Connor; and crisis-managing Graham Coxon's exit from Blur. Other music clients have included Lee 'Scratch' Perry, Billy Childish, Primal Scream, the Jesus and Mary Chain and the photographers Dennis Morris (Sex Pistols, Bob Marley) and Gered Mankowitz (Jimi Hendrix, Rolling Stones) among many others.

Rupa Huq spent a lifetime in universities from her undergraduate days at Cambridge, via PhD studies, followed by lecturing at Manchester and Kingston. In May 2015 she was elected Labour member of Parliament for her home constituency of Ealing Central and Acton, taking the seat from the Conservative Party. Her publications include *Beyond Subculture* (Routledge 2006) and *On the Edge* (Lawrence and Wishart 2013). Since her election she has served on the House of Commons Justice Select Committee and been promoted to shadow home office minister. Her most recent book is the 2016 edited volume *Reading the Riot Act: Reflections on the 2011 urban disorders in England,* a subject she has spoken on in Parliament, particularly focusing on the riots in Ealing. Other subjects that Rupa has brought to the floor of the House of Commons include the teaching of feminism in the school curriculum – a debate that she led in January 2016 produced a change in government policy and the subject's reinstatement on the A-level politics curriculum.

Simon Keegan-Phipps is a senior lecturer in ethnomusicology at the University of Sheffield. His research focuses on the performance of folk and traditional musics of England and the British Isles, specifically in relation to issues of national identity, transmission and participatory practice. He co-authored, with Trish Winter, the book *Performing Englishness: Identity and Politics in a Contemporary Folk Resurgence* (Manchester University Press 2013), and is currently principal investigator on the project 'Digital Folk: Digital Media in Folk Arts Participation', funded by the Arts and Humanities Research Council.

Christian Lloyd is academic director at the Bader International Study Centre, the study abroad campus of Queen's University (Canada) in East Sussex. His most recent research project was the Hendrix flat and museum in London, and his book *Hendrix at Home: A Bluesman in Mayfair* was published in 2016.

Gabriele Marino studied communication sciences at the University of Palermo and has a PhD in Semiotics from the University of Turin, Italy. He deals with musical semiotics, semiotics of online viral phenomena and market research, working with universities, research institutes and private companies. His book *Britney canta Manson e altri capolavori* (2011) is about reviews of imaginary records in rock journalism.

Dene October teaches fan cultures, fashion body identity and doctor who by design at University of the Arts London and is co-editor of the volume *Doctor Who and History* (McFarland 2017) and the author of a monograph on the lost *Doctor Who* episode *Marco Polo* (Black Archive 2018). His work explores many aspects of the cult programme, including fans and computer-mediated discourse ('Hit or Missy: Fan Responses to the Regendering of Missy' in *Doctor Who: Twelfth Night*, I. B. Taurus 2017), public history ('"That's Not Right": Television, History and Education in Doctor Who During the Hartnell Era' in *New Worlds, Terrifying Monsters, Impossible Things: Exploring the Contents and Contexts of Doctor Who*, PopMatters 2016), identity through performance ('Doctor Who? What's He Talking About? Performativity and the First Doctor' in *The Language of Doctor Who: From Shakespeare to Alien Tongues*, Rowman and Littlefield 2014) and memory ('The Day my Doctor Died: A Child's Experience of the First Regeneration' in *Doctor Who at Fifty*, fbi-spy.com 2013). He also writes about David Bowie (who he misses every single day).

Shara Rambarran is an assistant professor of music and cultural studies at the Bader International Study Centre, Queen's University, Canada. Shara gained her PhD in Music at the University of Salford. Her research and teaching interests include popular/critical musicology, post-production, postmodernism, digital media, remixology, music industry, events management, cultural theory, education and law (IPR). She is an editor on the *Journal on the Art of Record Production*, member of the editorial board for the *Journal of Popular Music Education* and has written for *Popular Music, Popular Musicology, Popular Music and Society* and *PopMatters*. Shara is the co-editor of *The Oxford Handbook of Music and Virtuality* (Oxford University Press 2016) and *The Routledge Research Companion to Popular Music Education* (Routledge 2017).

Ben Winsworth is senior lecturer in English literature and popular culture at the University of Orléans in France, where he teaches (among other things) classes on the history and analysis of 'pop', the Beatles and the 1960s, and youth subcultures in the UK. He has published articles and book chapters on James Joyce, John Fowles, Julian Barnes, Graham Swift, Nick Hornby and the Beatles. He is particularly interested in psychoanalysis and literature, football and fiction, and all things related to mod.

Trish Winter is professor of cultural studies and associate director of the Centre for Research in Media and Cultural Studies, University of Sunderland. Her work centres on the investigation of cultural participation using ethnographic and participatory methodologies. She was principal investigator of the research project 'Performing Englishness in New English Folk Music and Dance', funded by the Arts and Humanities Research Council, and she has authored along with Simon Keegan-Phipps *Performing Englishness: Identity and Politics in a Contemporary Folk Resurgence* (Manchester University Press 2013).

Lee Brooks, Mark Donnelly and **Richard Mills** work in the School of Arts and Humanities at St Mary's University, Twickenham. They have extensive experience of teaching courses on popular music cultures. They have also published on subjects including Sixties Britain, The Beatles and Morrissey.

FOREWORD – POP GOES ACADEMIA

Rupa Huq

I recently ended up on a parliamentary delegation to the Holy Land – in itself an eye opener for a girl from the genteel London suburb of Ealing. Together with MPs of all political complexions I met a Christian Palestinian Arab who had done his PhD as an overseas student at Salford University but who had been gone from Blighty for many years, tempted back to his birthplace when peace looked to be on the horizon at the time of the Oslo peace accords in the mid-1990s. Our hosts told us en route to see the professor that while he was fully fluent in English, he might struggle to understand some of our modern vernacular. Many of the phrases he acquired when he learnt English abroad were now quaintly out of date by some twenty years.

Where to start with our modern lexicon? 'Trolling', one of our party piped up from the back of the bus. 'Fake news', another ventured. 'Post-truth politics', I murmured half to myself. At a time when the insurgents have delivered Trump's victory in the United States and seemingly the lunatics have taken over the asylum with the EU referendum result and ensuing chaos in the UK, this book helps us to navigate our way through the complex contours of modern times as Englishness, Britishness and globalization all fight for supremacy, with a European dimension in the mix too – even if Britain is on the way out.

We live in an age which, at the time of writing, appears to be turbulent and unpredictable, even dangerous. Never before has the old adage 'may you live in interesting times' been so appropriate as the *curse* from which it originated in China.

Soundtracking our every move for at least the past sixty years is pop music. This book takes a commendably broad sweep of time in considering pop alongside parallel developments in our global and local sociocultural fabric. It moves through pop's early years, punk, post-punk, electronica and trip hop, as well as the recent passing of Bowie (née David Jones in Brixton before the family suburbanized themselves out to Bromley) and other current developments, with a full awareness that we live in a globalized, interconnected world.

When Ricky Martin performed for President George W. Bush at his inauguration it was read as a significant political nod to the US Latino community. Seeing Bill Clinton pose with his saxophone and Tony Blair with a Fender strat once seemed groundbreakingly significant, signalling that youth culture fans had finally taken hold of the levers of power. This was subsequently bettered by the first Afro-American president, Obama, who was pally with Stevie Wonder. As one of the final actions of his presidency, Obama bestowed on Bruce Springsteen the Presidential Medal of Freedom, declaring, 'I am the President, he is The Boss. Pushing 70, he's still laying down four-hour live sets ... fire-breathing rock and roll.' Obama also awarded the United States' highest ranking honour to Diana Ross, Tom Hanks, Robert De Niro, Robert Redford and basketball star Michael Jordan.

Having David Cameron quote Smiths' lyrics at Prime Minister's Questions in the House of Commons across the dispatch box in a contrived way once looked oddly like progress – though Johnny Marr's tweet forbidding him from doing so again was a delicious moment. This neo-swinging London manifested in 'Cool Britannia', honed by Blair and aped by Cameron, seems to have been stopped in its tracks with the reign of Theresa May. Her easy listening choices on her 2014 *Desert Island Discs* appearance on BBC Radio were very un-rock and roll. How long ago the New Labour era of Tony Blair and Noel Gallagher sharing canapés and fizz in Downing Street now seemed, when the closest to pop that the new prime minister favours is Abba. When she was accused of dithering on the cover of the *Economist* in January 2017 with the slogan 'Theresa Maybe', one wag tweeted 'that has to be the worst Oasis album ever'.

May's indecent haste to salute President Trump so soon after an inauguration at which 'alternative facts' about the size of the crowd at the ceremony were propagated suggests that Britain's post-Brexit desperation to broker trade deals has robbed it of all rationality. Mainstream media gleefully recorded the differences between the calibre of musicians who played for Trump's inauguration (Front of Country Music, Three Doors Down, The Piano Guys) and those who had performed for Obama (as well as Springsteen and Stevie, Beyonce, U2 and Bon Jovi). Lists circulated of those who had refused the opportunity to play the Trump gig, including Charlotte Church, Moby, Elton John and John Legend. The day after the ceremony, names of anti-Trump celebrity protesters were also doing the rounds: Madonna, Katy Perry, Cher and Emma Watson among them. The phrase 'it's not a competition' seems to be lost on the thin-skinned and highly competitive President Trump.

The prospects for Middle East peace mentioned at the beginning of this foreword arguably now look bleaker than ever. But we will be venturing into clairvoyant territory if we try to predict too much of what the future holds. What is more certain is that this book, with its masterful, eclectic collection of essays from some of the brightest and best in academia, is essential reading for anyone who is interested in community, identity, tradition and pop today. It is most warmly recommended by the only MP in the House who has been in the magazine *Private Eye*'s 'Pseuds Corner' for giving a talk on the internationalization of hip-hop at Newcastle University (in my pre-MP days). At a time when we have heard MPs denounce experts, I beg to differ from this prevailing wisdom Mr Speaker.

Enjoy.

ACKNOWLEDGEMENTS

The editors wish to thank the contributors for their cooperation in meeting deadlines, for their patience and for sharing their expertise. We are also grateful to all the speakers and attendees at our 2013 conference on popular music and English identities. Their presentations and comments on papers helped to shape this book's organization and direction at an early stage. We reserve a special mention here for the late Professor Sheila Whiteley whose presence, knowledge and generosity of spirit contributed so much to the event.

We are very grateful to the School of Arts and Humanities at St. Mary's University, Twickenham, for supporting the production of this book. Former colleagues Lance Pettitt and Jessica Jeske were particularly helpful. Chris Durston was instrumental in setting up a course on pop music history where we teach. Current colleagues Allyson Purcell-Davies, Peter Howell, Maria Mellins and Russell Schechter have supported our work along the way. Bloomsbury's editorial team, especially Leah Babb-Rosenfeld and Susan Krogulski, gave us unstinting help and encouragement, even after we missed our first deadline. We would also like to thank the two anonymous readers of our initial proposal.

We owe a particular debt of gratitude to Ian Casey, Ian Chapman, Julie Labalzo-Wright, Alice May, Rob May, Peter Mills and Dan Stone, who shared ideas and books with us. Finally, we would like to thank all our family and friends who helped us to complete this book.

Introduction:
Englishness, whose Englishness?

Lee Brooks and Mark Donnelly

The English enigma

In April 2000 BBC radio broadcast a discussion about Englishness to mark the new century's first St. George's Day (the commemorative day for England's patron saint is 23 April). Listening back to the discussion now reminds us that the only real 'lesson' of history is that things change in unanticipated ways. The programme described a genealogy of Englishness that went back to the mid-eighteenth century, a period when Britain's unusual (and then recent) political stability, intellectual prominence and surging international power required an explanation. Nobody seriously thought that Britain's monarchy was behind the country's changing fortunes, so a collective project to attribute Britain's growing power to supposedly 'national' characteristics, temperaments and values began to take shape. For most of the decades that followed, Britishness and Englishness were used as interchangeable terms in England. Britain, in fact, was regarded as yet one more realization of the supposed English talents for invention and pragmatism, and the folding of Englishness into a wider concept of Britishness was seen to confirm the English preference for modesty over self-assertion. The 'English question' as such remained relatively dormant and was only reactivated when disruptive forces threatened the cohesion of the English-dominated political union.[1] Debating whether the new fact of political devolution in 2000 – by this date separate parliamentary assemblies had been created for Scotland (1999), Wales (1999) and Northern Ireland (1998), but not for England – would produce a more sharply defined sense of Englishness, contributors to the

BBC radio programme concluded that it was unlikely. But what none of them anticipated – and why would they? – were the financial crisis of 2008 and its intensifying effects on the backlash against globalization, the 2014 Scottish independence referendum and a national referendum two years later that called for the UK to leave the European Union. Each of these in its own way has raised the pitch of English nationalist rhetoric. Each of these has led to further questions about what a post-British England might look like, and whether Anglo-Britishness will be reconfigured or replaced within a developing English political community (Nairn 2000: 28; Kenny and Lodge 2009: 222–3). As a result, reflecting on the English question – or what Tom Nairn once called the 'English enigma' – has a degree of political urgency that could not have been predicted twenty years ago (Nairn 1981: 291–305).

Unlike the 1975 referendum, in which English voices sang out most clearly in support of the European political project, the UK's vote to leave the European Union ('Brexit') in the 2016 referendum was overwhelmingly dependent on English votes. This makes it an apposite time to reflect on some of the meanings, readings and imagined futures of Englishness. Brexit has been interpreted by some of its supporters as a mandate for a programme of radical political and cultural change, with a new boss (Theresa May) insistent that she is not just like her old boss (David Cameron). The rhetorical priorities of this programme, along with a rise in incidents of racially motivated hate crime in the weeks and months after the Brexit vote, have brought the referendum's connected themes of nationalism and immigration into yet sharper focus. 'Taking back control' of 'our' country was a powerful slogan for those who wanted to leave the European Union because it could be applied to so many spheres of national life: including control of discursive political space. Indeed, a common complaint from the English nationalist Right – one that has been used to explain its rise in recent years – has been that by endorsing multiculturalism, the country's political leadership have silenced discussion of what it means to be English. However, in the 1990s and 2000s the opposite of this seemed to be true: popular political discourse seemed to be fixated with the question of Englishness. A subgenre of books developed that both reflected on and exemplified how England had for centuries performed itself to itself and told stories about itself to itself (see, e.g. Paxman 1998; Heffer 1999; Nairn 2000, 2002; Colls 2002; Fox 2004; Gill 2005; Irwin 2005; Kumar 2005; Winn 2005; Bragg 2006; Titchmarsh 2007; Featherstone 2009; Kenny 2014; Tombs 2014). These books in various ways critiqued and reworked a repertoire of tropes, symbols and discursive renderings of Englishness that stretched a long way into the past. In some hands this repertoire was used to create a largely essentialist account of English 'national identity and character', or in slightly less rigid terms its 'ethos' or 'cultural genome' (Fox 2004: 2, 400). Others invoked it in an attempt to claim Englishness for politically conservative and ethnically exclusive projects. Simon Heffer's work for the *Daily Telegraph* and the magazine *This England* and Roger Scruton's editorial work for the *Salisbury Review* are good examples of this cultural nationalism in practice. Heffer, Scruton and their ideological allies grounded their preferred version of Englishness on an indigenous cultural tradition that took in Chaucer, Shakespeare, Elgar and Constable among others; they regarded all manifestations of European and/or Marxist-inflected critical and social thought as anathema to English intellectual habits; and they venerated the authority of the principal English institutions – monarchy, Church of England and Common Law (Featherstone 2009: 12–13). Their mobilization of a particular constellation of English symbolic resources was compatible at least with notions of beleaguered Englishness that grew from the 1990s onwards. Reflected politically in the advances of the far-right British National Party (BNP), English Defence League (EDL) and latterly by the United Kingdom Independence Party (UKIP), beleaguered Englishness fed off a sense of resentment at what was taken to be disapproval (or worse, suppression) of English culture and traditions in favour of multiculturalism (Winter and Keegan-Phipps 2013: 140–1). This was why Nick Griffin in his time as BNP leader sought to supplement his organization's race-oriented street politics with an ideology of English folk revival and the recovery of 'home-grown' thinkers like G. K. Chesterton and Hilaire Belloc; and why his successor, Adam Walker, endorsed populist campaigns such as the one to 'protect' Christmas from 'politically correct' local authorities and 'Islamism' (Featherstone 2009: 11–12).[2]

Other writers on Englishness have sought to establish a critical distance from anything resembling ethno-nationalist populism. One way of doing so has been to construct alternative accounts of progressive and cosmopolitan Englishness, usually from left political perspectives (Winter and Keegan-Phipps 2013: 144). Billy Bragg worked this territory in *The Progressive Patriot*, a book that was part memoir, part history, part political polemic (2006). Bragg wanted to reposition the language and symbolism of English patriotism within traditions of radical democracy and socialism, reconfiguring Englishness into something that could inspire a sense of belonging among *all* citizens who shared the nation space, regardless of other identity differences. In some respects it was a timely attempt to disrupt exclusivist and nativist definitions of national identities in the wake of the 7 July 2005 London bombings, and it ran parallel to similar projects undertaken by senior Labour Party figures of the time such as David Blunkett and Frank Field (Kenny and Lodge 2009: 232). But Bragg's fusion of progressive politics and patriotism also drew fire from the Left, where for many internationalism and the salience of class struggle remained irreducible components of political identity (Smith 2006: 198; Tranmer 2009: 198–202). George Orwell and E. P. Thompson had been similarly criticized when they tried to fit together radical politics and a common English identity several decades before Bragg wrote *The Progressive Patriot*. Orwell in particular was regarded as having scrambled his political bearings under the pressure of war when he wrote

The Lion and the Unicorn: Socialism and the English Genius (1941). Here he had argued that while England needed a socialist revolution to win the war, any such revolution had to be compatible with English exceptionalism: its traditions, culture, customs and behavioural quirks. What would never succeed in England, said Orwell, was a revolutionary model that was imported from another country. English 'impulses', he wrote, were against regimentation, Marxism and fascism alike: 'An English Socialist government will transform the nation from top to bottom, but it will still bear all over it the unmistakable marks of our own cilivilsation' (Orwell 1982: 40, 112).

Orwell's faith that English 'genius' would provide a platform for political transformation turned out to be misplaced – unless of course one chooses to read the post-war Labour government's social and economic programme as transformative rather than reformist. More than seventy years on from the end of the Second World War it is still harder to see how Englishness might be the organizational locus of a collective identity that could take on political-institutional expression. As the composition of its population has been reconfigured by migration flows since the end of the war, the degree to which England has to be understood as a site of multiple faith, linguistic and ethnic subjectivities has steadily increased. The rate of population change has accelerated in the past twenty-five years. According to the Office of National Statistics (ONS), England and Wales have continued to become more ethnically diverse since 1991, with minority ethnic groups increasing in size across the censuses of 2001 and 2011.[3] Reading the data from the most recent national census of 2011 confirms the ethnic complexities of England's population, both in terms of the numbers of different ethnic groups that inhabit the country and the extent to which those groups have mixed with one another to produce hybrid ethnicities. This census was also the first to include a question on national identity, reflecting what the ONS describes as 'an increased interest in "national consciousness" and demand from people to acknowledge their national identity'.[4] It found that among the population of England and Wales, there were 57.7 per cent who identified themselves as solely English, while 67.1 per cent described themselves as English either on its own or combined with other identities (people were free to select more than one identity descriptor from the list on the census).[5] This leaves a sizeable proportion of people in the country for whom Englishness is no part of their self-description. There are a number of explanations for this, not least the fact that there are millions of short-term residents in the country at any given time. But we should also recognize that descendants of post-war migrants from South Asia, Africa, the Caribbean and the Arabic-speaking world are liable to find themselves positioned as an unwelcome and disruptive presence in this country – a 'them' who will never be accepted as a 'we' – and who disavow English identities as a result. This is why the development of postcolonial political subject positions, together with the rise of other forms of identity politics from the 1960s onwards, makes it difficult to talk about the politics of English national identity except in populist–nativist or bland terms. As an example of the former, the last two decades have seen attempts to normalize symbols of Englishness, reclaiming them from ethnic nationalists and redirecting them towards a politics of inclusiveness – making them instruments of what Michael Billig called 'banal nationalism' (1995). So, since England hosted the European football championship in 1996 it has become common to see the flag of St George fly from homes, shops and cars whenever England play in international football tournaments. Local authorities, meanwhile, have made efforts to turn St George's Day into an opportunity for celebrating how people of all self-identities inhabit a common civic space, rather than an exclusive display of ethnic particularism. In terms of the latter, English political nationalism often defaults to a 'two-fingered response' to a state that is perceived to promote multiculturalism at the expense of white Englishness (Kenny and Lodge 2009: 227). The lineage here includes the 'Keep Britain White' graffiti that signalled a rejection of post-war policies of encouraging migration from Britain's former colonies, the language used by supporters of Enoch Powell's 'rivers of blood' speech in April 1968, and more recent populist rhetoric about the 'threat' of 'Islamicisation'.[6]

Sounds of Englishness

Popular music rarely features in general academic studies of British or English identities (Morra 2014: 6–10). And yet since it emerged as a cultural and commodified form in the early 1950s – the seven-inch single, the weekly newspaper *New Musical Express,* and the country's first singles chart all appeared in Britain in 1952 (Stanley 2013: 3) – pop music has simultaneously fed off and sustained various iterations of the English imaginary. It was striking, for example, how far English pop music culture, sixty years after the first pop chart in 1952, was integral to the narrative of nation that was staged in the opening ceremony of the London Olympics in 2012. To know England, the ceremony implied, meant understanding the country's relationship to its pop: director Danny Boyle's playlist worked its way from the high-sixties classicism of the Beatles, Rolling Stones and Kinks, through punk, post-punk, rave and electronica, arriving at the more recent sonic hybridity of artists like Tinie Tempah, Dizzee Rascal and Lily Allen.[7] The choice to position this music at the centre of an articulation of London/English identity for a global audience in 2012 showed how far pop's critical reputation had advanced since its formative years. When Frank Sinatra dismissed the new youth-oriented rock and roll of the fifties as 'the martial music of every sideburned delinquent', he at least unwittingly complimented the music's provocative intensity (Birnbaum 2013: 384). But in England, the domestic variant of fifties rock and roll (and pop music generally) tended to be written off as a pale imitation of what US pioneers produced. Liverpool-born jazz singer and writer George Melly criticized home-grown rock and roll for having 'little to do with the fiercely subversive music of the American originals' because English artists of the time largely restricted themselves to performing weak impersonations and cover versions of what they heard from the United States (1989: 52). There was a 'strictly end of the pier' quality to most fifties English pop (Stanley 2013: 17); the form was rooted in light entertainment and a tradition of variety acts – the likes of Jimmy Young and Dickie Valentine. The exception to this was skiffle music, 'the bastard offspring of New Orleans jazz' (Frame 2007: 1), which seemed to offer more creative possibilities in the hands of artists such as Lonnie Donegan, who was the banjo player in Ken Colyer's band, Jazzmen. Donegan, who provided a 'skiffle break' during the intervals of Jazzmen sets, exemplified the hybridity of English musical identities; born in Glasgow to a Scots father and Irish mother, he adopted the name of American blues legend Lonnie Johnson, spoke with a London accent and went on to release a US album, *An Englishman Sings American Folk Songs* in 1957. He inspired a wave of skiffle bands, shaping the do-it-yourself culture in which songwriter Ian Samwell could defy Steve Race's premature elegy for rock and roll in *The Melody Maker* by writing the song 'Move It' – on the top deck of a London bus. Recorded by Cliff Richard and the Drifters in 1958, 'Move It' reached number two in the charts and became perhaps the first credible English rock and roll hit.

In constructing a genealogy of English pop music that connects its formative years to the present, this book demonstrates how pop's temporal orientation can be read in ambiguous ways. One way of thinking the past of English pop music is to emphasize its role within popular modernism, a concept which for Mark Fisher included 'the music press and the more challenging parts of public sector broadcasting ... postpunk, brutalist architecture, Penguin paperbacks and the BBC Radiophonic Workshop' (2014: 22). Pop music in these terms is valued when it is future-oriented, never too far away from its next surge of sonic and lyrical innovation, and immediately responsive to whatever political and social conjunctures it inhabits. English modernist pop was produced within a specific set of socio-political coordinates, finding its feet within the ecology of post-war British social democracy: with its large number of art colleges, pre-tuition fee higher education institutions, the BBC, a network of public libraries and a welfare benefits system that allowed aspiring creative artists to escape a regular paid job for a few years. This was the support infrastructure that in various ways enabled acts such as The Who, Roxy Music, The Slits, Joy Division, Scritti Politti, the Pop Group – as well as producers and independent record label owners like Daniel Miller of Mute Records – the time and space to experiment with form, aesthetics and business distribution models. Pop's capacity to creatively channel its external surroundings also heightened what was at stake in its cultural politics. Perhaps to a greater extent than with other popular cultural forms, pop music's ideological affiliations and politics of representation *mattered* – at least among the core audiences for new material and scenes. Whether the ideas were communicated via the wider discourse surrounding pop (interviews with artists, reviews by music journalists, opinions expressed in fanzines and so on), or through the image, sound and performance of acts themselves, pop pointed to different ways of being oneself within the spaces of England, and it suggested which among these various ways should be valued. For example, punk, Rock Against Racism and Two-Tone records – supported by writers in the *New Musical Express* and the fanzine *Temporary Hoarding* – rejected the white popular nationalism that was a ubiquitous feature of the Queen's silver jubilee celebrations of 1977. As Paul Gilroy argued, it was in these conditions that the Clash's version of Junior Marvin's roots hit 'Police and Thieves' acquired a special status, symbolizing 'the coming together of black and white in opposition to racism' (2002: 162). Similarly, post-punk challenged normative categories of gender and sexual identities, while techno and rave music in the 1980s and 1990s became signifiers for a range of politically oppositional and countercultural positions in England: anti-roads and anti-war protesters, Reclaim the Streets activists, squatters' rights campaigners, free festival goers – all coalescing around opposition to the 1994 Criminal Justice and Public Order Bill.[8] In short, pop music has been able to create imaginaries in which hitherto marginalized, disavowed and 'discrepant' identities – and perhaps identities-yet-to-come – can find a home in England.

From a different temporal direction, pop has also incorporated the backwards-looking perspectives of memory, heritage and nostalgia: 'retromania' for short (Reynolds 2011). Part of what constitutes 'Englishness' in popular music is the way that certain artists choose to invoke traditions within English pop – to write and perform within a lineage that constitutes an English vernacular, the commonly cited template for which was laid down in the mid-1960s. Noel Gallagher recently explained that his 'education as a songwriter' was listening to the Kinks, the Who and the Beatles. Damon Albarn similarly spoke of how he 'studied Ray Davies' (the Kinks' main songwriter) as part of an exploration of his 'musical heritage' (Rachel 2013: 398, 415). As well as regularly citing the formative influence of the Beatles on his work, Paul Weller has said that his lyrics more generally reflected English songwriters' preference for 'picking up on the mundane, the everyday things and putting them into a different setting' (Rachel 2013: 174) – this compositional technique can also be found in the work of artists such as Ian Dury, Andy Partridge, Chris Difford, Suggs, Marc Almond, Morrissey, Neil Tennant, Mike Skinner, Jarvis Cocker and Lily Allen. The notion that there are canonical influences in English pop has been accentuated by the curatorial choices of major museums in the last decade. David Bowie, The Rolling Stones, The Jam and Pink Floyd have all been the sole subject of exhibitions in prestigious institutions like the V&A, Somerset House and the Saatchi Gallery. The fortieth anniversary of punk's 'Year Zero' was commemorated in a series of 'Punk London' retrospectives in 2016 at venues such as the British Library and the Museum of London, and John Lennon's

'New York Years' are the subject of a recent special exhibition at The Beatles Story museum at Albert Dock, Liverpool. The Beatles' home city, moreover, is the new permanent home of the British Music Experience exhibition after its move away from London's O2 entertainment complex. These various ways of giving institutional expression to the idea of a canon of (invariably male, white) artists risk underscoring the hegemonic status of one particular reading of English pop. Such a reading can have the troubling effect of heightening a sense of creative stasis – pop's modernist impulses halted by the gravitational force of its own past – and feeding ideas of national self-superiority about English pop. Another complaint about the 'heritage effect' is that museumification strips popular music of any oppositional and countercultural energies that it might still possess; this was why Joe Corré and his mother, Vivienne Westwood, set fire to '£5 million' worth of punk memorabilia in November 2016 as a riposte to the 'Punk London' commemorative events, which Corré complained 'privatised, packaged and castrated punk' (Ellis-Peterson 2016).[9] Whatever Corré's intention – and there was much speculation about his motives – the destruction of memorabilia on this scale comes across as a symptom of the disease that it professes to resist: the sanctification of popular music as an expression of memory culture. By declaring punk 'dead', Corré acted to 'pastify' it: to position it out of the realm of the now and into a past that has fully passed, where it can be imagined as self-identical to its first iteration, uncorrupted and pristine, certain of its revered status. Acts of anti-nostalgia can become the most nostalgic acts of all.

Although nostalgia is often dismissed as a defeatist longing for better yesterdays – the kind of thing associated with 'old people's talk' (Bonnett 2010: 3) – it can produce more constructive cultural–political consequences. In a special edition of the journal *Memory Studies* in 2010, contributors worked the idea of nostalgia as an activity that might produce useful social effects. In similar fashion, Katharina Niemeyer's recent collection of essays argued that 'nostalgizing' could be understood as a means to 'transform the past' by acts of imagination, in ways that opened up possibilities for inventing different futures (2014: 10, 18). The appearance of the term 'hauntology' in critical writing about pop music in the 2000s functioned in an analogous way to reworkings of ideas about nostalgia. Applied to the work of The Caretaker (James Kirby), Belbury Poly (Jim Jupp), Kode9 (Steve Goodman), Burial (Will Bevan) and various artists who appeared on the Ghost Box Records label, 'hauntology' was a sign for a music that was inhabited by the ghostly traces of earlier soundscapes – English popular music of the 1930s and 1940s, BBC sci-fi productions, public information films, the once-futuristic sounds of a future that never arrived after social democratic projects gave way to 'capitalist realism' (Fisher 2009). Ian Penman prefigured the use of hauntology as a term to describe music in which time was out of joint, in an essay about Tricky's *Maxinquaye* in 1995. Penman discerned how the 'staged reverberations' of samples from *Blade Runner* and Japan's 'Ghosts' in Tricky's 'Aftermath', a song 'that may (or may not) be about a relationship between mother and son', suggested not memory, legacy and continuity, but a condition in which modern technologies had made us all into speaking voids, 'made up only of scraps and citations ... contaminated by other people's memories ... adrift' (1995). Tricky's work produces an aesthetic of liminality, a blurring of source materials to a degree that has been called 'a slurred re-dreaming of musics' (Fisher 2013: 48). His invocation of the past as a source of (re)invention rather than a point of origin was a strategy borne out of cultural–political conviction; it was a way of simultaneously resisting (musical) traditions that meant nothing to him and refusing to be reduced to a singular (racial, national, sexual) identity.

Maxinquaye – as well as the work of Tricky's sometime collaborators Massive Attack – was an important reference point for Burial's first eponymously titled album (2006). As Gabriel Marino argues in this volume, Burial's 'music of musics' should be understood as a kind of 'avant-pastism', an inventory of the early days of dubstep as a way of renewing and injecting new meanings into the genre. But whereas Tricky thwarted music journalists' attempts to reduce him to being representative of the new 'sound of Bristol' in the 1990s, Burial's work was consciously rooted in a sense of place (South London). As Marino explains, Burial's work 'aims at being not only a music *for* London, but the music *of* London; not its accompanying, but its sonic transmutation, its "musicification". Burial aspires to make London *sound*: to turn the matter of which London is made into a different substance' (see Chapter 11). This relationship between music and place – England as a multiplicity of spaces in which music is produced – is another way of thinking about the Englishness of popular music. PJ Harvey's Dorset, Cabaret Voltaire's Sheffield, Bowie and The Jam's sometimes invocation of London's inner and outer suburbs, Bishi's and Ray Davies's differing experiences of the capital city, Oasis's Manchester – memorably described by Dave Haslam as 'the city with the most highly developed musical consciousness in the world' (1999: 139) – are all discussed in the following chapters. These geographic specificities are a reminder of the fictions in play when 'Englishness' or the 'English' are summoned as the basis of political appeals in the present: as Penman observed: 'Truth be told, maybe "nationality" never was such a sure thing to hang a life on: it was always shaky, fragile, limned with the spectres of its own imminent dissolution' (1995).

Mad Dogs and Englishness: Popular music and English identities

In order to reflect the ways in which contributors have connected English pop music to (overlapping) themes of memory, space and identities, this book is divided into three parts. The chapters in part one focus on heritage, traditions and memory cultures within English pop. Carey Fleiner opens this section by discussing the nostalgic imperative of Ray Davies and the Kinks' yearning for the sanctuary of a simpler, more bucolic England. She explains that this evocation of the Homeric concept of nostos in increasing frequency in Davies' work set the band at odds with the aggressive modernism of the 1960s, denying them the popularity of some of their contemporaries. However, more recently it has marked them out as the quintessential standard bearers of a particularly quirky and pastoral version of imagined Englishness. Indeed, Fleiner reflects upon the establishment, by the time of 'Come Dancing' in 1982, of the Kinks at the epicentre of the national embrace of heritage and nostalgia as a safe harbour from the economic, industrial and social tumult that lashed Britain in the 1970s and beyond. She explores the irony that a rejection of this sentiment at home, as 'almost too English', led to a chart-topping reprise of their popularity in America and discusses Davies' own contextualization of this within his latest book *Americana*.

The impact of David Bowie's death in January 2016 prompted Richard Mills to restructure what had been intended as a contemporary examination of the vitality of the artist's late resurgence into a more retrospective discussion of a life's work. However, we should not read this switch of focus as a nostalgic turn, as Mills is at pains to stress his use of the future tense in contextualizing Bowie, even when looking back on *The Next Day* (2013) and *Blackstar* (2016) and when becoming the subject of the V&A's successful *David Bowie is* ... exhibition, as an artist who did so, only in order to point forward. In this chapter, Mills contrasts a Bowie heritage industry, commemorating sites of significance with plaques, and the impulse to romanticize past glories, with Bowie himself who, until the very moment of his death, and beyond, in the form of the continued remix and reappraisal of his work, exists within a constant cycle of reinvention. Within this context we can trace an identity that does not fit comfortably into nostalgic notions of English heritage, but rather, traces an ever evolving performance of influences that draw from a simultaneous conundrum of insularity and internationalism. A similar form of 'radical nostalgia' (or at least a future-oriented use of the past) is discussed by Ben Winsworth. He sets the early history of the Jam in the context of their obsession with, and evocation of 1960s mod style, discussing their use of Union Jack iconography during a period in which the flag and its symbolism had been taken in an alternative direction by the burgeoning punk movement. He links the band's focus on an earlier, arguably, more progressive period with a desire for the projection of a more optimistic, confident Englishness. By contrasting the Jam's use of a brighter, more intact Union flag with Jamie Reid's infamously tattered and torn version, Winsworth identifies Paul Weller as an almost heroic figure, who, by gazing back, is able, through his lyrical and visual choices, to lead a charge forward, beyond the nihilistic, punk inspired crisis of national identity.

In discussing the Englishness of PJ Harvey, Abigail Gardner references wider debates on the nature of memory, national heritage and identity. Gardner focuses upon Harvey's work on *Let England Shake* (2011) and *White Chalk* (2007) and uses the musical tropes, lyrical concerns and associated audio-visual material of these albums to probe the way land, belonging and allegiance have been associated, and most importantly, archived within notions of Englishness. She argues that PJ Harvey's work, particularly, but not exclusively on these albums, records a version of the archived past that, as characterized by Jacques Derrida's view in *Archive Fever* (1995), also articulates a vision for the future. Gardner concludes that this work archives an emotional commitment to land and family ties that draws upon earlier traditions of national identity, and in doing so recontextualizes these signs into her own, archive of Englishness.

The chapters in Part 2 focus on the relationships between space, place and identities. Dene October traces, in the Radiophonic Orchestra's soundscape for *An Unearthly Child*, the first episode of the long-running BBC sci-fi series, *Doctor Who,* an Englishness that is at once familiar in its evocation of a clichéd 1960s London, and otherworldly in its application of a peculiarly British form of avant-garde electronica. October places this innovative sound experience within the context of a BBC still actively pursuing the Reithian commitment to educate, inform and entertain, and a capital city and nation just beginning to countenance ideas of a more fluid construction of identity. In approaching the auditory construction of a liminal time-space, he begins to question traditional ideas of sound playing a supporting role to the visuals, and instead introduces the notion that here, the sound may perform the function of the TARDIS in transporting the audience through time and space. It is in this, at least partial, reordering of the accepted hierarchy of vision and sound that October identifies an Englishness that, like the iconic blue box, is forever materializing and dematerializing.

Jon Hackett discusses themes of industry, machines and labour in Sheffield post-punk music, specifically in relation to the output of Cabaret Voltaire, one of the most well-known bands in Sheffield at the time, and one of the co-founders of the industrial music genre. Starting their life with experimental tape recordings in a loft, securing rehearsal space in Sheffield University's experimental music department and then building their own studio from which to record their avant-rock music and construct accompanying visual collages, Cabaret Voltaire demonstrated an artisanal independence and bloody-mindedness that typifies an ongoing strand in the city's industrial culture. The thesis of Hackett's chapter is that Sheffield's idiosyncratic relation to labour politics and mass production was mediated in the sphere of popular culture through its untimely and at times wilfully perverse popular music. Johnny Hopkins then discusses the uses and meanings of the Union flag as a key signifier of territorial and political space(s) within the visual discourse of popular music. He considers how the flag functioned as an allusion to a past in which British power and influence extended considerably further than the pop charts. He examines the altered iconography of a design classic cut-up, reimagined as a wearable accessory and recontextualized within an extended feedback loop, from the assertion (and revival) of mod style to the new confidence of 'Cool Britannia'. Hopkins also traces a narrative of a banner at once paid homage to and defiled by a timeline of British musicians, led notably by Pete Townshend and the Who. The flag, he argues, can at all times be read as a contested symbol of Englishness and as an irresistible marketing device.

In the final part of the book, contributors examine some 'discrepant' performances of English identities. As Raphael Costambeys-Kempczynski's chapter reminds us, 1977 has been read as the point when punk was at the peak of its cultural power. This was the year when the Sex Pistols released *Never Mind the Bollocks* and when The Clash sang 'White Riot' and 'London's Burning'. It was also the year of the Queen's silver jubilee, leaving the Independent Broadcasting Authority to conclude that the Pistols' single 'God Save the Queen' may have been in breach of good taste and decency and was perhaps even likely to incite crime and disorder. But as punk bands proliferated at this time and often signed record deals, 1977 was also the year when some were already declaring punk to be dead. Through the prism of England at this time, Costambeys-Kempczynski addresses notions of commodification, fracture and authenticity, as well as decency in punk as popular music. He asks us to take a double perspective into consideration: if the establishment viewed punk as 'the poison in the human machine', perhaps from the cultural margins punk's legacy may be seen as just another English dream.

Christian Lloyd and Shara Rambarran examine the Bristolian experimental musician, Tricky, as a dissenting voice at a significant juncture for twentieth-century English identity: the New Labour era. As they explain, *Maxinquaye*, Tricky's 1996 debut album, was released in the context of Tony Blair's attempts to promote a concept of 'Cool Britannia,' a nostalgic, post-imperial ideology that sought to reposition British culture within an increasingly indifferent globalized world by staging a replay of an imaginary 1960s, the last time when Britain pretended to occupy a position of international cultural pre-eminence. Tricky symbolically attacked the centripetal ideology of 'Cool Britannia' by dialogizing his own music in a proliferating strategy of collaborations, production techniques and images. Lloyd and Rambarran use Tricky's music to reinforce the idea that Englishness is always in process from uncertain, often fictional, origins. Ultimately, Tricky's complex, centrifugal performances mean that the national becomes the notional; 'God Save the Queen' is now 'overdubbed' with his 'notional anthems' for contemporary England as the union (perhaps) disperses.

Almost a decade after his identity was revealed, South London 'dubstep' producer Burial (William Bevan) still stands as a mysterious figure. Gabriele Marino's chapter – the first academic contribution devoted to the topic – reconstructs the media quest to undercover the musician's identity, and proposes a global interpretation of the *persona* and his art, from a sociosemiotic standpoint. Tickling the forgotten pleasures of remembering, doubting and investigating, Burial stands as the conscience of English underground electronic music; a secluded bard for these 'days of future past'. Finally, a similar aura of elusiveness and complexity surrounds Bishi's album *Albion Voice*. Tracing its musical, lyrical and visual dimensions, Trish Winter and Simon Keegan-Phipps locate *Albion Voice* in relation to contemporary debates and discourses on Englishness, especially the notion of a postcolonial renegotiation of Englishness as a hybrid identity. Their chapter concludes with a discussion of some of the ambiguities inherent in Bishi's constructions of Englishness. These include a consideration of the slippage between Britishness and Englishness in *Albion Voice*, examination of its metropolitan, London-centric character, and reflection on the significance of femininity in this performance of Englishness as a 'marriage' in which Bishi proposes 'Let West be the husband and East be the wife'. Bishi's creative rearticulations of contemporary English identity, based on her self-description as an outsider who stands between two cultures, are a fitting way to close this book. As Winter and Keegan-Phipps explain, her work can be read as an open exploration of the possibilities of national identity in a contemporary, multicultural England.

Albion Voice is framed by Bishi as an intervention into a vision of popular musical English identity from which, she observes, women and Asians are largely absent. *Albion Voice*, then, can be understood as a reactive exploration of a more cosmopolitan vision of English identity, characterising the artist's own Englishness as an identity with multiple connections and attachments that are both outward looking and, at the same time, rooted and invested in a sense of national belonging.[10]

Notes

1 In British political discourse since the 1970s, the 'English question' has often been rephrased as the 'West Lothian question'. In the debate about Scottish and Welsh devolution in 1977, Tam Dalyell – MP for West Lothian – asked why it would be acceptable after devolution for Scottish and Welsh MPs at Westminster to continue to vote on matters that only affected English constituencies, while English MPs would no longer be able to vote on matters that had been devolved to the Scottish and Welsh assemblies. Following the referendum that rejected Scottish independence in 2014, Prime Minister David Cameron immediately re-raised the question of 'English votes for English laws' – a subject that had featured in the Conservative Party general election manifestos of 2001 and 2005 (Kenny and Lodge 2009: 233). After its election in May 2015, a majority Conservative government announced plans for an English Grand Committee and new parliamentary procedures to deal with laws that only affected England.

2   Attempts to appropriate English folk traditions for extremist politics eventually generated a riposte in the form of 'Folk Against Fascism' (2009). By this point support for Griffin's BNP had grown sharply in places such as Burnley, Dewsbury and Barking, and in the 2009 elections for the European Parliament the party won more than a million votes. For a critical discussion of the place of Chesterton and Belloc in the context of English intellectual reactions to fascism see Dan Stone (2012: 113–47).

3   Office of National Statistics, '2011 Census analysis: Ethnicity and religion of the non-UK born population in England and Wales: 2011' http://www.ons. gov.uk/peoplepopulationandcommunity/culturalidentity/ethnicity (accessed 5 November 2016)

4   http://www.ons.gov.uk/peoplepopulationandcommunity/culturalidentity/ ethnicity/articles/ethnicityandnationalidentityinenglandandwales/2012-12-11#national-identity-in-england-and-wales (accessed 5 November 2016)

5   ibid.

6   On 20 April 1968 senior Conservative politician Enoch Powell made a controversial speech attacking the Labour government's immigration policy and their proposed extension of race relations laws. Powell said that Britain was 'mad, literally mad' to allow some 50,000 dependants of immigrants to enter Britain each year, comparing it to watching a nation heaping up its own 'funeral pyre'. Rejecting his own party's bipartisan approach to immigration and race relations policy, Powell said that he was filled with foreboding at the prospect of social disorder arising from racial divisions: 'Like the Roman, I seem to see the River Tiber flowing with much blood.' He was sacked from his front bench position as Conservative defence spokesperson for departing from party policy, but received widespread public support for his views. For a full text of Powell's speech see *The Telegraph,* 6 November 2007, http://www. telegraph.co.uk/comment/3643823/Enoch-Powells-Rivers-of-Blood-speech. html (accessed 30 December 2016).

7   For a detailed discussion of pop music's place in the London 2012 Opening Ceremony see Morra (2014: 17–30).

8   It was striking that when Margaret Thatcher died in April 2013, pop music was immediately invoked as a resource to make a political point. A 'chart jacking' campaign to make Judy Garland's version of 'Ding Dong The Witch is Dead!' the number one single on the weekend after the former prime minister's death only narrowly failed.

9   'Burn Punk London' was streamed live on 26 November 2016 at https:// burnpunklondon.com/

10 See Chapter 12 in this volume, 207.

References

BBC Radio 4 (2000), In Our Time – Englishness, 20 April.
Birnbaum, L. (2013), *Before Elvis: The Prehistory of Rock and Roll*, Plymouth: Scarecrow Press.

Bracewell, M. (1997), *England is Mine: Pop Life in Albion from Wilde to Goldie*, London: Harper Collins.

Bragg, B. (2006), *The Progressive Patriot: A Search for Belonging*, London: Bantam Press.

Colls, R. (2002), *Identity of England*, Oxford: Oxford University Press.

Ellis-Petersen, H. (2016), 'Malcolm McLaren's son plans £5m punk funeral', *The Guardian*, 25 November.

Featherstone, S. (2009), *Englishness: Twentieth-Century Popular Culture and the Forming of English Identity*, Edinburgh: Edinburgh University Press.

Fisher, M. (2009), *Capitalist Realism: Is There No Alternative?*, Ropley: Zero Books.

Fisher, M. (2013), 'The Metaphysics of Crackle: Afrofuturism and Hauntology', *Dancecult: Journal of Electronic Dance Music Culture*, vol. 5 (2): 42–55, https://dj.dancecult.net/index.php/dancecult/article/viewFile/378/391, (accessed 9 December 2016).

Fox, K. (2004), *Watching the English: The Hidden Rules of English Behaviour*, London: Hodder and Stoughton.

Frame, P. (2007), *The Restless Generation: How rock music changed the face of 1950s Britain*, London: Rogan House.

Gilroy, P. (2002), *There Ain't No Black in the Union Jack: The cultural politics of race and nation*, 2nd edn. London: Routledge.

Haslam, D. (1999), *Manchester England: The story of the pop cult city*, London: Fourth Estate.

Heffer, S. (1999), *Nor Shall My Sword: The Reinvention of England*, London: Weidenfeld and Nicolson.

Irwin, C. (2005), *In Search of Albion*, London: Andre Deutsch.

Kenny, M. and G. Lodge (2009), 'More than one English Question', in M. Perryman (ed.), *Breaking Up Britain: Four Nations after a Union*, 222–39, London: Lawrence and Wishart.

Kenny, M. (2014), *The Politics of English Nationhood*, Oxford: Oxford University Press.

Kumar, K. (2005), *The Making of English Nationality*, Cambridge: Cambridge University Press.

Melly, G. (1989), *Revolt Into Style: The Pop Arts*, 2nd edn. Oxford: Oxford University Press.

Morra, I. (2014), *Britishness, Popular Music and National Identity: The Making of Modern Britain*, Abingdon: Routledge.

Nairn, T. (2000), *After Britain: New Labour and the Return of Scotland*, Cambridge: Granta.

Nairn, T. (2002), *Pariah: Misfortunes of the British Kingdom*, London: Verso.

Niemeyer, K. (ed.) (2014), *Media and nostalgia: yearning for the past, present and future*, Basingstoke: Palgrave Macmillan.

Orwell, G. (1982), *The Lion and the Unicorn: Socialism and the English Genius*, London: Secker and Warburg [1941].

Paxman, J. (2008), *The English: A Portrait of a People*, London: Penguin.

Penman, I. (1995), '[the Phantoms of] TRICKNOLOGY [versus a Politics of Authenticity]',. *The Wire*, no. 133, March. http://www.rocksbackpages.com/Library/Article/-the-phantoms-of--tricknology-versus-a-politics-of-authenticity, (accessed 9 December 2016).

Reviron-Piégay, F. (ed.) (2009), *Englishness Revisited*, Newcastle: Cambridge Scholars Publishing.

Reynolds, S. (2011), *Retromania: pop culture's addiction to its own past*, London: Faber.

Smith, M. (2006), 'Nothing to Reclaim', *Socialist Review*, November. http://socialistreview.org.uk/311/nothing-reclaim (accessed 22 October 2016)

Stanley, B. (2013), *Yeah Yeah Yeah: The Story of Modern Pop*, London: Faber and Faber.

Stone, D. (2012), *Responses to Nazism in Britain, 1933–1939*, 2nd edn. Houndmills: Palgrave

Titchmarsh, A. (2007), *England, Our England*, London: Hodder and Stoughton.

Tombs, R. (2014), *The English and their History*, London: Allen Lane.

Tranmer, J. (2009), 'Reclaiming England for the Left: The Case of Billy Bragg', in F. Reviron-Piégay (ed.), *Englishness Revisited*, 189-204. Newcastle: Cambridge Scholars Publishing.

Winn, C. (2005), *I Never Knew That About England*, London: Ebury Press.

Winter, T. and S. Keegan-Phipps (2013), *Performing Englishness: Identity and politics in a contemporary folk resurgence*, Manchester: Manchester University Press.

PART ONE
English heritage

CHAPTER ONE

'Rosy, Won't You Please Come Home':

Family, home and cultural identity in the music of Ray Davies and the Kinks

Carey Fleiner

Introduction

The image of the Kinks as the most English of the British Invasion bands was a conscious creation on the part of the Kinks' management on the one hand, and a result of Ray Davies's lyrical wit and observation on the other. Formed more or less in 1964 by four young men from London, the Kinks first stormed up the charts with distorted power chords and teenaged angst with 'You Really Got Me', and over the next thirty-two years they drew on their upbringing to create songs about the ordinary and absurd in English life. The image of the Kinks' Englishness outlasted initial gimmicks. It was reinforced by the band's pastoral themes and storytelling songs of the mid-1960s combined with the distinctively 'English' character of the band itself: their witty homeliness, working-class backgrounds and defiance of authority while maintaining a cheeky respect for respectability.

This chapter addresses particular qualities that make the Kinks an *English* band – from obvious signposts to nuanced characteristics that make them appeal to both English and non-English audiences. Their appeal as English comes not from flag-waving or tea-drinking, but rather a combination of social observations, self-deprecating humour and their own obstinate struggles against corporate authority. This chapter considers first the early image of 'Englishness' created by the band's management, and then it looks at the brief trend in the mid-1960s for rock groups to celebrate old-fashioned English music and character. It examines how the Kinks continued to fashion so-called parochial music even as this novelty among mainstream bands wore off, and why their persistence contributed to the band's commercial failure by the end of the decade. The next section considers why the Kinks in fact contribute to a long tradition of 'nostalgia heritage' notable in English music and literature from the late eighteenth and early nineteenth centuries through to the present day, and how their output, which includes references to family, home and working-class solidarity, has created a sense of inclusion between themselves and their fans both in England and overseas. The principal era examined here covers the Kinks' early days of the band's success in 1964 and 1965 and the initial look created for them, and then focuses mainly on their pastoral work between 1966 and 1970.

Much has been written on the Kinks in the past twenty years, both popularly and academically. Following the earliest biographies of the band by Savage (1984) and Rogan (1984), the 1990s saw the publication of diverse works on the band including autobiographies of Ray Davies (1994: 2014) and Dave Davies (1995) and a multivolume fictionalized story of the band by bassist Peter Quaife (2010, 2014). Kitts published a scholarly study of Ray's life and work in 2012; encyclopaedic works on the Kinks' output include those of Hinman (1994, 2004) and Rogan (1998). The band's versatility as well as their inextricable working-class character has made them the subject of studies on the influence of music-hall in popular music and aspects of working-class character in popular music (e.g. Baxter-Moore 2006; Gildart 2012; Simonelli 2013); the influence of family, childhood and growing up in post-war England, and dedicated collections of essays have appeared on their output, character and associations with English life and leisure (e.g. Gildart 2013; Geldart 2003; Sullivan 2002). This is supplemented by a number of recent popular biographies (e.g. Hasted 2011). Finally, there are the myriad interviews, reviews, media articles (print and online), blogs, message boards, fanzines and internet social networking sites – the Kinks are, in a word, well-documented men.

A common theme running through much of this media is the Kinks as an *English* band – without actually defining what is *meant* by 'English'. One should not, however, find fault with this omission: the codification of 'Englishness' (or Britishness) has challenged if not confounded for years philosophers, commentators and politicians ranging from Charles Dickens and Rudyard Kipling, J. B. Priestley and George Orwell, and Kate Fox and Jeremy Paxman through to former (2016) home secretary, now Prime Minister

Theresa May and the Conservative government's determination to codify 'British values' via school curriculum and citizenship tests in the wake of mass immigration into the UK. It becomes further complicated as such behaviour smacks of distasteful displays of patriotism – too American at best and too fascist at worst. That said, the English will grudgingly admit that they like their country and like being English – but they'll reply with understatement when questioned; as Bill Bailey noted in his recent show *Limboland* (2015–16), in response to queries on any experience, accomplishment or health, no matter how good or disastrous, an Englishman will reply, 'Not bad ... given the circumstances.'

Therefore, one must suss out 'Englishness' in a roundabout fashion, not unlike trying to get from Portsmouth to Brighton via the A27. English character does not fit a paradigm; it is shaped instead from an evolving set of cultural institutions on the one hand (Clarke 2009: 89–92), and how those cultural institutions are defined against outsiders on the other. The Kinks' music describes a number of the former, which will be discussed below, including family, particular moral values, self-depreciating humour and an appreciation for the past – without necessarily drowning in nostalgia or desiring to avoid the present by escaping into a rose-tinted past. Ray Davies has noted on a number of occasions in the past few years (e.g. Simpson 2015) that neither he nor the Kinks are about living in the past, as a lazy interpretation of tracks such as 'Days' or the collection of songs on *Face to Face, Something Else,* or *Village Green* might suggest. The Kinks look to the past not for a reconstruction of times lost, but instead for particular emotions that can be brought into the present to cope with current problems (R. Davies 2015b), shaped by common cultural experience. As for the latter, Ray has remarked he has been most aware of his Englishness when he has been away from Britain (R. Davies 2014: 142, 149, 174).

Superficial signposts of Englishness

The Kinks jumped onto the money-go-round in the wake of rising successful bands such as the Beatles and the Rolling Stones. Their original professional management was a pair of young middle-class men called Grenville Collins and Robert Wace. Collins and Wace not only introduced these scruffy, working-class rhythm and blues enthusiasts to a world of debutantes and Noel Coward, but in early 1964 secured the band a commercial recording contract with Pye Records, ultimately bringing them under the auspices of several hardened music professionals: Shel Talmy, who initially produced their records, Larry Page ('The Teenaged Rage'), who managed them along with Wace and Collins, Edward Kassner, who locked them into a draconian publishing contract (R. Davies 1995: 95–7), and Hal Carter, who was charged with improving their image (ibid., 117–21: 139–43).

The band initially struggled in the face of steep competition among all of the wannabes and try-hards of the early 1960s; their performances could be shambolic, and they scrapped like cats both on and off the stage. Their management sought to improve their image to make them stand out: Page, for example, changed their name from the Ravens to Kinks as an attention-getter (especially as they were usually bottom-of-the-bill) (ibid., 102–4). Abandoning the whips and leather that the band had initially draped themselves in, Page shoved them first in matching, stiff green hunting jackets ('evoking Robin Hood!' according to a suit in Joe Penhall's *Sunny Afternoon*; cf. R. Davies 1995: 103–4); after Carter smartened them up, they were taken to a theatre costume shop and acquired their famous Edwardian hunting-pink jackets to show off frilled white shirts ruffled at the wrist and throat. As Ray noted, by the summer of 1964, 'We had started to get a reputation as Dickensian-type characters' (120) – a reputation that preceded their first proper chart hit with 'You Really Got Me.' What started as an act finally clicked as their scrappy yet impishly insolent behaviour gelled with their performance and, especially, the new look. They were photographed at iconic London sites such as Tower Bridge or stood with horses in the park, and these original stage clothes left their mark – even in 2016 Kinks' media still use images from this photo shoot in their copy. Such expectations were not unique to American audiences; Ray spoke in 2015 of sweltering inside those heavy woollen coats in the middle of an Australian summer tour in 1965 (R. Davies 2015a).

The Beatles had primed US Anglomania from late 1963 in anticipation of their February 1964 arrival: American fans adored how different the Fab Four were compared to American pop idols (if not their male classmates) (Perone 2009: 82–3; 84–6; Stark 2006: 20–1: 68; cf. Seago 2000: 123). British bands were irreverent towards adults in a way unlike the sneering American delinquent of *Rebel Without a Cause* or *The Wild One*; instead, they couched their anger against authority with sharp wit rather than grunting hooliganism. British bands also brought to the United States exotic aspects of the Old World: European artiness, mod ennui, adult sophistication and an exotic sexiness lacking in wholesome contemporary American pop and cinema (Perone 2009: 101–6, 115–7; Gildart 2013: 91–3; Clayston 1995: 177). Not only were the Kinks sexy and dangerous (not necessarily mutually exclusive), but they stood out from the delicately feminine, Pierre Cardin–besuited Beatles' Euro sophistication or the Stones' sloppy, leering misogyny. Moreover, neither the Beatles nor the Stones – or most of the British Invasion bands – intentionally played up their Englishness in the early days – if anything, they revelled in their love of American blues, rock and roll, and Motown, aping American singers' accents and sound in their performances (cf. Stark 2009: 133–3). The Kinks were just as keen on American blues, but appeared as quaintly English with their romantic if not Dickensian jackets and Chelsea boots (Perone 2009: 144). This look screamed *English* (if not fancy-dress Victoriana) not only to their countrymen, but also fit the picture of what Americans, the key commercial target of the British Invasion, expected of a land that they knew mainly from James Bond, *Mary Poppins*, and Roger Miller's 'England Swings'. Ray Davies may have had the same sort of art school background as a number of his contemporaries, but the Kinks' working-class attitude further set them apart from the more Euro-centric mod bands. Finally, they also had strong London accents – not only did Ray demand that his girl stay by his side all day and all of the night, but he did so dressed like Heathcliff from *Wuthering Heights* and with a much better cockney accent than Dick Van Dyke.

In addition to creating the Kinks' initial image as English gentlemen, management also cranked up the 'English whimsy' surrounding the band's publicity. Consider, for example, the evolving ersatz eccentricity on the band's LP sleeve notes. On their first LP *Kinks* (1964), for example, every word with a hard 'c' is spelt with a 'k'. Generic reference to Carnaby Street comes into play with Frank Smyth's notes on *Face to Face* (1966), but by 1967 the Kinks' particular Englishness has become singled out as something distinctive: the sleeve notes on the album *Something Else* focus on Ray's imagination specifically.

> Welcome to Daviesland, where all the little kinklings in the magic Kinkdom wear tiny black bowlers, rugby boots, soldier suits, drink half pints of bitter, carry cricket bats and ride in little tube trains. ... Gulliver-like Ray Davies stoops to pluck a small mortal from his musical world – turns him upside-down to see where he was made – and replaces him gently but firmly in that great class society where all men are equal but some are more equal than others.

The increasing tweeness could be attributed to marketers' desire to latch on to the drug-fuelled dream imagery proliferating in the charts in 1967 and 1968 (Faulk 2010: 125), especially as *Something Else* did not sell well, and Ray's sardonic title showed that they were not willingly playing ball with the marketing. The Kinks certainly delivered whimsy on their next LP, *Village Green Preservation Society*, but tracks such as 'Wicked Annabella', 'Animal Farm' and 'Phenomenal Cat' owed more to English fairy tales and Kenneth Graham than to lysergic-acid-fuelled dreams.

Just an English boy on holiday ...

The Kinks may have abandoned the costumes fairly early on (and fought to escape their early image-moulding, as evidenced by 1971s *Muswell Hillbillies*), but this image of them as four stereotypical Victorian Englishmen, however superficial, remained strongly ingrained in American imaginations, especially as the group were banned from touring in or having shown on television filmed performances in the United States for four years (from 1965 to 1969). The combination of the ban and subsequent pressure of touring, recording and composition led Ray to retreat to Torquay in 1965 (the 'English Riviera', best known to Americans as the setting of *Fawlty Towers*). Ray abandoned the holiday as not only was he recognized by staff and clientele, but also he felt snubbed and looked down on by everyone involved. He took as an insult an invitation to a round of golf with several middle-class guests, packed up his family, and returned to London (Kitts 2012: 63; R. Davies 1995: 264). He wrote 'Well Respected Man' as one of the consequences of this holiday; the track is significant because here Ray decided to 'embrace his Englishness' in his lyrics (Hinman 2004: 61, 65; Kitts 2012: 63–7) and to stop imitating American artists in sound and theme. The track itself examines the dreary routine of an apathetic, middle-class man held hostage by routine and appearances of respectability, even as he is infantilized and dependent on his parents' fortune if not control over his life. On the one hand the chorus points out the foibles of respectability, and on the other pokes fun at middle-class expectations.

'Well Respected Man' was followed by two albums and a clutch of singles, 1966's *Face to Face* and 1967's *Something Else by the Kinks*, which further illustrate the Kinks' shift in focus to character-driven songs that drew on themes of ordinary English suburban life. Lyrics across these releases focus on rainy weather, shared phone lines and the joys of owning an allotment; roll-up cigarettes, schoolboy envy, railway commuters; middle-class aspirations, teenaged runaways and the safety of the home and hearth. Musical lines throughout are punctuated by music hall melodies, football-anthem-like choruses and flashes of traditional English folk tunes.

The Kinks certainly were not alone in celebrating being English among rock bands in the 1960s. As the group released songs about Carnaby Street and the fashion chasers, gardening and tea-drinking, so too did other groups: for example, The Small Faces' 'Lazy Sunday Afternoon' presents the lament of the young who want to fit into the neighbourhood with the older generation rather than be looked upon with suspicion; their 'Itchycoo Park' turns 'dreaming spires' and duck ponds into a surrealistic trip (figuratively and literally). Even the Beatles, whose early music and look were derivative of American forms and vocals, sloughed off their Fab Four and touring band personas to become Sgt Pepper's Lonely Hearts Club Band, a nod to Victorian band shells and the music of their grandparents (albeit flavoured with psychedelic imagery and Indian-inspired chants) and took nostalgic trips along Penny Lane and to Strawberry Fields (Green 2005: 261–62). If that did not baffle their fans, the Fab Four celebrated Christmas 1967 by presenting the nation with a satirical home movie aimed at mocking a stalwart British institution: the mystery coach tour (cf. MacDonald 2005: 253–6). The Beatles considered the 'old ways' the domain of the elderly or retired (for example, 1967's 'When I'm 64'), the tracks might be aimed deliberately to please parents (Paul McCartney's father with 'Your Mother Should Know' and 1968's 'Honey Pie'), but often use references to suburban life to criticize the pseudo-cool (cf. Ringo's sardonic assessment of the Mahareshi's Rishikesh: 'It's just like Butlins') or to mock the older generation's grasp on material goods over parental love ('She's Leaving Home' 1967). The Kinks, on the other hand, may have twitted English traditions, but they did not dismiss them as démodé or a source of further generational conflict, but rather as inextricably co-extant. When they urged people to preserve the old ways, they meant it while at the same time acknowledging the humour or absurdity of such ways.

So much so did Ray and the Kinks 'embrace their Englishness' beyond the mid-1960s fad that their management worried that they were *too* English to be commercially viable. Trends moved on as blues-inspired and drug-fuelled psychedelia replaced English suburbia. By 1968, the optimism of the Summer of Love was giving way to the increasing horrors in real life – civil disturbances were endemic around the world in 1968, including protests and violence in the United States, Hungary, Belgrade and Czechoslovakia, and this unrest was reflected in popular culture. The Kinks, however, continued to produce knees-up songs about English life and infused them with traditional English folk-rhythm that, as Ray put it in a recent interview discussing 'Dedicated Follower of Fashion', deliberately embodied English culture (Gross 2014). Nevertheless, such songs, especially from the release of 'Autumn Almanac' were viewed as a tired gimmick, and fans in England dismissed the band as a novelty singles act. While they lost valuable airplay due to lack of commercial viability, the band also appeared, culturally, to be square and to be rejecting the hard line adopted by the counterculture, as the latter themselves rejected the values of the older generation as materialistic and the cause of the West's current problems. English fans were not particularly interested in what seemed to be the Kinks' siding with the older generation, an authority that had been challenged, if not thwarted, by the young in the UK, beginning with the 'Angry Young Men' of 1950s theatre and the satirical movement of the early 1960s; the counterculture wanted revolution, and not to turn back the clock. Choosing to continue with such parochial themes was arguably a daring thing to do – instead of following the trendsetters and psychedelic experimenters, Ray created music that was reflective of his parents' and grandparents' generation. This was the generation he admired: their stories of making do and coping with the horrors of the Depression and the Second World War impressed him not only for their stalwart attitudes, but also for the camaraderie, joy and even humour found in the darkest times (Gross 2014; Simpson 2015) – exactly the attitude needed to cope with current events rather than destruction or conformity (cf. Clarke on Orwell 2009: 103). This stalwart, yet cheerful, 'make-do' characteristic of English life Ray saw lost and forgotten in the new 'classless' society of the 1960s (Dawbarn 1966; R. Davies 1995: 339–49; Simonelli 2013: 57).

The Kinks and their Village Green

As a result, the band produced their most parochially English albums in 1968 and 1969: *The Kinks are the Village Green Preservation Society* and *Arthur: or the Rise and Fall of the British Empire*. *Village Green* is a loose collection of songs with themes of rural gentility and escape ('Village Green', 'Animal Farm'), fairy-tale settings ('Phenomenal Cat', 'Wicked Annabella'), wistful nostalgia of childhood memories ('Do You Remember Walter?' 'Picture Book') and images of England 'gone by' that wouldn't have been out of place in an Ealing comedy ('Village Green Preservation Society', 'Last of the Steam-Powered Trains') (see Miller 2004; Faulk 2010: 115–27). The second, *Arthur: or the Rise and Fall of the British Empire* (1969), not only continued the thematic strand of England, home and family, it was also inspired in part by Ray's sister Rose who had emigrated to Australia with her family a few years previously. *Arthur*'s tracks are more unified than *Village Green* as the work was commissioned as the soundtrack for a BBCTV production that never materialized. English nostalgia, especially for the countryside and the lost empire, is especially strong in the tracks 'Victoria', 'Yes Sir No Sir', 'Have a Cup of Tea', and the sublime 'Shangri-La'. The latter is a sweetly wistful tale of the simple pleasures of owning one's own home and reminds the listener of the English adage that a 'man's home is his castle' – quite the opposite in tone from earlier, more scathing songs about middle-class aspirations ('Mr Pleasant', 'Most Exclusive Residence for Sale') or class entrapment and its pitfalls ('Sunny Afternoon', 'Dead End Street') (Green 2005: 259–60).

It is ingenuous to dismiss the 1960s Kinks as a nostalgic novelty act, however, or as traitors to the cause of the younger generation. The Kinks may have slipped off the commercial music charts and seemed 'uncool' commercially, but as champions of preserving particular English values and behaviour the band became part of a narrative that goes back to the eighteenth century. Clarke discusses a phenomenon in English pastoral writing described originally by Priestley as the 'three Englands' (2009: 89 passim, 103–5). The first of these is the idyllic England pre-industrial revolution, where there are knights and battles, chivalry and milkmaids, and Henry VIII roaring by the fire – this is the England of Walter Scott or Thomas Mallory. This aristocratic ideal is followed by a second idyllic England – the idealization here is of the pastoral settings created from the later nineteenth century in reaction to the scientific and industrial revolutions that saw an influx of rural folk move into urban centres to become factory fodder within a generation or two. While their former agricultural life was a far cry from a fairy tale, the sudden shift from green spaces to overcrowded, grim urban squalor after centuries of agricultural subsistence inspired literature and poetry that mourned for a lost past that people might not have had in the first place – so England's green and rural past became romanticized as a means of working-class escapism, if not social commentary on urban issues and poverty (cf. Perone 2013: 137–41; Green 2005: 257–60). The 'third England' results after the Second World War. Britain pulled together during the war (at least this is the aspect of British life publicized as part of contemporary morale-boosting), and it persists in modern memory of the period (Hobsbawm's so-called 'Golden Age' 1994: cf. Green 2005: 256–7); it is also the era sought during the social and cultural upheaval in the early to mid-1960s through to the current era whenever there is a social or cultural crisis. The search for the 'lost England' and fears for England's past being lost to modern urbanization and industrialization found in the works of such authors as Priestley (especially *English Journey*) and Orwell (Clarke 2009, passim) is echoed similarly by the Kinks' late 1960s output and continued in their early 1970s stage shows and concept albums. Whereas tracks such as '20th Century Man' and 'Acute Paranoia Schizophrenia Blues' warn against the dangers of modern technology, materialism and loss of the old English ways, the Kinks never urged anyone to retreat into the past as a means of escape. Instead, such songs are observations, if not warnings, of the important qualities and quirky eccentricities of family and individual identity that are in danger of being lost. As for those that do insist on living in the past or remaining behind in the village, such as *Preservation's* 'Johnny Thunder' ('Last of the Survivors') or Daisy in 'Village Green', they are rendered in terms of regret rather than envy.

There was certainly much reflection on British heritage in the period between 1965 and the early 1980s: cultural historians such as Bray have noted that it was the deaths of T. S. Eliot and especially Winston Churchill in 1965 that kicked off the whole thought-exercise of what made one British, as the deaths of these two men in particular seemed to signify more than ever the passing of a definitive era in English or British cultural norms and values (Bray 2014: 9). Being *British*, however, especially began to smack of empire, colonialism and oppression, especially from the 1970s: Ray might sing about Victoria and the old days of empire, having grown up with the ghost of the empire hanging over him, but he is by no means wanting it to come back – in 'Victoria' it is the wealthy who enjoy cricket on the village green, and the poor sent off to die for their country. Sandbrook notes how certain contemporary attempts at celebrating the history of imperial Britain backfired when, in 1972, the BBC showed a documentary about the British Empire, part of a larger cultural phenomenon in British popular arts on heritage nostalgia. The programme had the opposite audience response than was expected – instead of stimulating feelings of pride in the past and heritage, viewers took it as a show of British oppression (Sandbrook 2013: 82–3). Around the same time, however, the V&A museum's exhibition 'The Destruction of the Country House' became one of their most popular exhibitions (92–3). As Sandbrook notes, nostalgic heritage in the late 1960s and especially early 1970s, even wrapped up in such cosy accoutrements as James Herriot's novels and sales of Laura Ashley prints, was a means of escapism from the harsher political and economic realities dominating contemporary headlines (Sandbrook 2013: 88–93). Being *English* took on a sense of cosy inclusion: it created the sense of camaraderie and humour in the face of adversity (or expression of anger) and the loyalty to authenticity were characteristics not only inclusive of the English themselves, but familiar and universally appealing to outsiders (Lowenthal 2015: 324–32).

The posh kids always win: Misfits and solidarity

The Kinks' inclusiveness and solidarity against all comers extends the appeal of their Englishness by incorporating into their music themes of family and of working-class solidarity: class identity and appreciation for past values are inextricably linked (Clarke 2009: 103). This self-awareness distinguishes the band and makes them more accessible to a wider audience than contemporary British rock-folks groups of the late 1960s and the 1970s, such as Weather Report or Fairport Convention, which focused more on storytelling, imagery of, and association with England's romanticized historical past (Simonelli 2013: 128–34; Green 2005; Burns 2007, 2010; Ramnarine 2004; cf. Marotta 2006 and Baxter-Moore 2006). Not only does family inspire Ray's lyrics, but songs and performance create an inclusive or familiar relationship between the band and their audience. Music hall, for example, is another very English aspect that permeates the Kinks' music: family singalongs are transformed into the performance hall with rousing, football-chant choruses ('Dead End Street', 'Dedicated Follower of Fashion', 'Autumn Almanac'), strengthening the bond between the performers on the stage and the fans in the audience (Sullivan 2002: 337; Fleiner 2011: 105–8; Faulk 2010: 105–2).

The Kinks' predilection for family and home runs throughout their music, performance and audience engagement. One cannot understate the presence and importance of family in the Kinks' music (Fleiner 2011 and 2017, forthcoming): family had an influence on their musical tastes and styles that were folded into the group's wide-ranging output; family supported their efforts; family lent to them a strong sense of 'us versus them' (Fleiner 2011: 331 and passim) which colours their music and affects the relationship between the group and their fans (Fleiner 2017, forthcoming). Ray has remarked that he did not start out deliberately to write about family and English themes to set the Kinks apart, but rather he had to compose songs in a hurry to feed the demands of the marketing machine, and found his own thoughts and experiences too gloomy as inspiration – hence turning to his own family and what it was about them that made him feel happy (R. Davies 2015b). 'Dead End Street' is a good example: ostensibly about poverty and despair, the song embodies a defiant, uplifting make-do attitude underscored by a cheerful brass section in the singalong, shouted chorus.

Home (and family) as a sanctuary is nevertheless a key theme in the Kinks' output. Ray's cosy home scenes are happiest when they are about making do and memories of family togetherness, rather than thoughts of trying to rise above one's station. 'Have a Cuppa Tea' to solve life's problems; do not worry about debt and loss ('Sunny Afternoon', 'Low Budget') because one came from nothing and will go back to nothing, so make the best of what one has. Even as one dreams of living on an 'Animal Farm' where the domesticated animals gambol and play outside of his window (shades of the idylls of the mythical England dreamt of by urban factory fodder), or dreams of throwing away all of the trappings of civilization and living like the 'Apeman' (expressed musically by a Caribbean accent, steel drums and Calypso beat – replacing staid British Empire with a different sort of Edenic idyll), one may have to settle for a suburban castle ('Shangri-la') and an allotment ('Autumn Almanac'). This is happiness, however, where everyone knows one another ('Almanac' again), and one finds paradise in the predictable and mundane, even as an anonymous 'Face in the Crowd' in the middle of a commuter crowd in a noisy station ('Waterloo Sunset') where 'innocence [prevails] over adversity' (R. Davies quoted by Simpson 2016) and suburbia becomes a paradise (cf. Green 2005: 261–2). Such collective security is in contrast with the scathing tones left to the social climbers of 'Mr Pleasant', 'Most Exclusive Residence for Sale', or 'House in the Country', who neglect the world around them, as in their desire to rise above their station they become too involved with material good and lose sight of, if not control of, their circumstances. The family disrupted results in unhappiness ('Rosy, Won't You Please Come Home' and 'Big Black Smoke'). Finally, there is Ray's depiction of the quick rise to fame and the brutalities of show business into which he, like so many young performers in that era, were thrust: 'Sitting in My Hotel' reflects on the singer's new status as a famous pop star, the feelings of loneliness and isolation, and more important, how his friends from home would mock him for his new appearance and high-maintenance lifestyle. Similarly, the narrator in 'All of My Friends Were There' (1968) realizes that he might be able to hide a half-arsed, hung-over performance from his fans, but that his friends from the old days will see right through the façade and give him well-deserved mockery.

These diverse tracks also reinforce the Kinks' working-class status and, thus, their integrity, which was admired in England and abroad (Simonelli 2013: 55–6): music hall was an entertainment venue, but it was also a platform for working-class authenticity (the opposite being selling out and forgetting one's origins). The idea that music hall is simply silly humour and slapstick itself is ingenuous: music hall comedy could be sharp and cutting-edge; it provided a source of social commentary among the lower classes that was more relevant and respected than editorials found in middle-class broadsheet newspapers (Cleese 2014: 257). The humour of the music hall, as well as in the Kinks' output, has anger and substance behind it: as Orwell noted on Dickens, were he simply a comedy gimmick, no one would have ever taken him seriously (2009: 109).

The Kinks' working-class humour is prevalent in their rebellion against authority: it is an admirable defiance in the face of those more successful and not giving a toss about conforming to commercial pressure. The Kinks not only sang about facing material loss with a shrug and a 'make-do' attitude, but actually lived it: much of their commercial woes were their own doing as they repeatedly clashed heads with management and record labels. While raging against the pop music machine may have cost the Kinks commercially, their persistence has endeared them to both American and to British fans as tenacious underdogs, despite the different cultural responses on opposite sides of the Atlantic to the notion of underdog heroes. Basil Fawlty and Blackadder are popular because they *never* succeed, and the British identify with that sense of stubborn, yet almost optimistic, futility – Americans enjoy the absurd humour, but Britons appreciate the misplaced optimism both characters share: as Bill Bailey noted in his recent (2015–16) stage show, there are more convertible (open-top) cars in Britain than any other country in Europe. American underdogs are losers until the bottom of the ninth inning with the bases loaded and two outs – and everyone knows that the uncoordinated kid is going to hit a winning grand slam against the bullies from the posh school. Such last minute reprieve is not the English way, reminds the quizmaster, as the *Young Ones* are about to face off against the idiotic but wealthy students of Footlights College, Oxbridge, in 'Bambi', 'The posh kids always win.' It is the defiant reaction to the loss that makes us cheer as Vyvyan drops a grenade on the rival cohort – or as Ray asks not for toys but for a job for his dad in 'Father Christmas' (1977): save the baubles for 'the little rich boys'.

Conclusion

Julian Barnes satirizes the marriage between heritage and artificially created national identity in his 1998 novel *England, England*. In the novel, the protagonists decide that the best way to boost the UK's economy is to increase tourism, and what better way to do that than to turn the Isle of Wight into a dedicated theme park of all things Britain? Here they will include all of the landmarks that define England, as well as offer tourists the chance to experience 'the traditions of England's past'. As Allen notes in her discussion of the novel, the protagonists realize that this is not as straightforward as it may seem: can tourists really experience England and Englishness if the inhabitants themselves wrestle with what marks them out as particularly English (Allen 2008: 74–5; cf. Sandbrook on the positive results of the 'Disneyfication' of English heritage, 2013: 92–3)? Postcards for the tourists aren't the 'real England' – in the song 'Village Green' Ray points out the disconnect between the people who grew up to escape the shabbiness of the village and those American tourists who take photographs of the dilapidated houses and comment on the 'pretty scene'. Since the 1980s, popular artists have embraced the old ways and English shabbiness as 'cool'; it is not the landmarks or accessories that make one English, but acknowledging the absurdity beneath the surface. Witness the wild success of Banksy's 2015 summer exhibition *Dismaland* or the popularity of the website-cum-book *Scarfolk Council*, which pokes affectionate fun at 1970s British urban life, health and safety.

There is no denying that the Kinks tended to sing about very English topics: 'Village Green Preservation Society' makes them appear, superficially, as if they are ticking boxes: Sherlock Holmes, little shops and Tudor houses. But even these most *English* things – village greens and restorative cups of tea – have the universal appeal in that they focus the listener's emotions on traditional values or emotions that ought not to be lost to the past and can be recreated in the present if not preserved for the future. The English identify with the Englishness of the Kinks because they are part of the collective culture that the group present through their music and stage shows. Americans and other non-English are at first drawn to the Kinks' Englishness partly because of the exotica of 'the other' and the cultural tradition of what makes being English 'cool'. But beyond the tropes, the Kinks' English character is not necessarily unique to England – the idea of solidarity among a group of followers 'not like anybody else' or rebellion against authority or a collective based on a family, however real or artificial, creates a sense of identification among the audience and a connection between them and the group.

The Kinks were not from a village or the rural countryside; they were suburban kids, growing up poor, with a sense of solidarity with their family and shared experience. Ray was certainly aware of this, and he has recently mused that, for him, North London was his village green (Simpson 2016). It may not have been economically viable in the 1960s to sing about love of one's family and respect for their values, but in the long run, the anti-family sentiment in late-1960s popular music proved to be the anomaly. The Kinks were part of a long narrative tradition that looks back at past sentiment and emotions associated with family and a rural idyll as an era of happiness; they drew on childhood experiences that folded into their shows and output those elements of ordinary events in their lives as sources: fishing with their father, car holidays to the coast, raucous family gatherings that made them the bane of the neighbourhood. By the 1980s and beyond, a number of English acts, comedians and musicians emphasized similar sentiment in their works (Fleiner 2011: 331–2); it continues to thrive at present, if the 'Keep Calm and Carry On' merchandizing juggernaut is any indication. People may still hope to recapture that idyll on their holiday breaks these days, an endeavour aided by an industry now built around remembering the past and growing up in a particular period in Britain. The nostalgia industry thrives and part of its foundation is the sense of inclusion – usually reflected by universal, common experiences that even people of widely diverse ethnic backgrounds are going to share in. Insiders quietly revel in it; outsiders attempt to enjoin with it. The Kinks still disdain the commercialism and potential for the big money. Nagged and begged for years to reunite, Ray and Dave at last performed together again in late 2015: not at the O2 in a well-publicized, merchandised–hyped event, but at Dave's solo show at the Islington Assembly Hall in North London ('My hometown!') where Ray joined him onstage for an encore of 'You Really Got Me' in front of 500 happy if not stunned fans (including this author), looking as if he had just ambled over to the hall from the pub over the road. At the end of the day, the Kinks remain firmly a band that represents England and Englishness in a way the better known and more commercially successful Beatles and Rolling Stones never have. On the eve of 2017, the fiftieth anniversary of the release of 'Waterloo Sunset', the Queen's New Year's Honours List included a knighthood for Ray. He summed up his feelings for a general press release: 'Initially I felt a mixture of surprise, humility, joy and a bit embarrassed but after thinking about it, I accept this for my family and fans as well as everyone who has inspired me to write' (Press Association, 30 December 2016).

References

Allen, N. (2008), *Marginality in the Contemporary British Novel*, London: Bloomsbury.

Baxter-Moore, N. (2006), '"This is Where I Belong" identity social class, and the Nostalgic Englishness of Ray Davies and the Kinks', *Popular Music and Society* 29(2): 145–65.

BBC 2TV. (1984), 'The Young Ones', 8 May.

Bellotti, A. (2014), 'Ham & High: Ray and Dave Davies interview', *Hampstead Theatre Online*, 11 April. Available online: http://www.hampsteadtheatre. com/news/2014/04/ham-and-high-ray-and-dave-davies-interview/ (accessed 21 January 2016).

Burns, R. G. H. (2007), 'Continuity, variation, and authenticity in the English Folk-Rock movement', *Folk Music Journal*, 9(2): 192–218.

Burns, R. G. H. (2010), 'Depicting the "Merrie": Historical imagery in English Folk-Rock', *Music in Art*, 35(1/2), *Rethinking Music in Art: New Directions in Music Iconography*: 105–17.

Bray, C. (2014), *1965: The Year Modern Britain was Born*, London: Simon and Schuster.

Clarke, B. (2008), 'Orwell and Englishness', *The Review of English Studies*, New Series, 57(228): 83–105.

Clayston, A. (1995), *Beat Merchants: The Origins, History, Impact and Rock Legacy of the British Pop Groups*, London: Blandford.

Cleese, J. (2014), *So, Anyway …*, London: Random House.

Davies, D. (1996), *Kink*, New York: Hyperion.

Davies, R. (1995), *X-Ray: The Unauthorized Autobiography*, New York: The Overlook Press.

Davies, R. (2013), *Americana: The Kinks, The Road and the Perfect Riff*, London: Virgin Books.

Davies, R. (2015a), 'After You Really Got Me I thought – how am I going to follow this now?', *The Telegraph*, 5 December. Available online: http://www.telegraph. co.uk/music/artists/ray-davies-after-you-really-got-me-i-thought--how-am-i-going-to/ (accessed 21 January 2016).

Davies, R. (2015b), Guest Speaker, *The Fulcrum Festival: Music and Memory with Ray Davies*, Southampton, University of Southampton.

Fleiner, C. (2011), 'The influence of family and childhood experience on the works of Ray and Dave Davies', *Popular Music and Society* 34(3): 329–50.

Fleiner, C. (2017), *The Kinks: A Thoroughly English Phenomenon*, Lanham: Rowman and Littlefield.

Geldart, M. (2003), 'Persona and voice in the Kinks' Songs of the Late 1960s', *Journal of the Royal Music Association*, 128(2): 200–41.

Gildart, K. (2012), 'From "Dead End Streets" to "Shangri-Las:" negotiating social class and post-war politics with Ray Davies and the Kinks', *Contemporary British History* 26(3): 273–98.

Gildart, K. (2013), *Images of England Through Popular Music: Class, Youth and Rock 'n' Roll, 1955–1976*, London: Palgrave Macmillan.

Grant, P. (2016), 'Grumbly Grimblies, Frozen Dogs and other Boojums: Eccentricity from Chaucer to Carroll in English Psychedelia', Paper given at the PCA/ACA National Conference, Seattle, WA, USA.

Green, N. (2005), 'Songs from the wood and sounds of the suburbs: A folk, rock and punk portrait of England, 1965–1977', *Built Environment*, 31(3): 255–70.

Gross, T. (2014), 'Naive, Yet Revolutionary: Ray Davies on 50 Years of The Kinks', *NPR*, 25 December. Available online: http://www.npr. org/2014/12/25/372906846/naive-yet-revolutionary-ray-davies-on-50-years-of-the-kinks (accessed 23 January 2016).

Hinman, D. (2004), *The Kinks: All Day and All of the Night: Day-by-day Concerts, Recordings, and Broadcasts, 1961–1996*, San Francisco: Backbeat Books.

Hinman, D. (1994), *The Kinks Part One: You Really Got Me: An Illustrated World Discography of the Kinks, 1964–1993*, London: Backbeat Books.

Hobsbawm, E. (1994), *Age of Extremes: The Short Twentieth Century*, London: Michael Joseph.

Kitts, T. (2008), *Ray Davies: Not Like Everybody Else*, London: Routledge.

Lowenthal, D. (2015), *The Past is a Foreign Country – Revisited*. Cambridge: Cambridge University Press.

MacDonald, I. (2005), *Revolution in the Head: The Beatles Records and the Sixties*, 2nd edn. London: Pimlico.

Marotta, J. G. (2002), 'The Loss of Identity and the Myth of Edenic Return in Ray Davies', in T.M. Kitts and M. J. Kraus (eds), *Living on a Thin Line: Crossing Aesthetic Borders with the Kinks*, 68–77. Rumford, RI: Rock and Roll Research Press.

Marten, N. and J. Hudson (1996), *The Kinks: Well Respected Men*, Surrey: Castle Communications Plc.

Orwell, G. (2009), 'Charles Dickens', in J. Paxman (ed.), *Shooting an Elephant and Other Essays*, 31–40, London: Penguin.

Perone, J. E. (2009), *Mods, Rockers, and the Music of the British Invasion*, Westport, CT: Praeger Publishers.

Press Association, '"The Kinks" Ray Davies gushes with "joy and humility" over knighthood', *The Guardian*, 30 December 2016 (accessed 19 February 2017).

Priestley, J. B. (1977), *English Journey*, London: Penguin.

Quaife, P. (2010), *Veritas: Vol. 1*, Hertfordshire: Hiren.

Quaife, P. (2014), Veritas III. Unpublished manuscript.

Ramnarine, T. K. (2004), 'Imperial legacies and the politics of musical creativity', *The World of Music*, 46(1): 91–108.

Rogan, J. (1998), *The Complete Guide to the Music of the Kinks*, London: Omnibus Press.

Rogan, J. (1984), *The Kinks: The Sound and the Fury*, London: Elm Tree.

Sandbrook, D. (2013), *Seasons in the Sun: The Battle for Britain 1974–1979*, London: Penguin.

Savage, J. (1984), *The Kinks: The Official Biography*, London: Faber and Faber.

Seago, A. (2000), '"Where Hamburgers Sizzle on an Open Grill Night and Day"(?): Global Pop Music and Americanization in the Year 2000', *American Studies*, 41(2/3): 119–36.

Simonelli, D. (2013), *Working Class Heroes: Rock Music and British Society in the 1960s and 1970*, Plymouth: Lexington Books.

Simpson, D. (2015), 'Ray Davies: I'm not the godfather of Britpop … more a concerned uncle', *The Guardian Online*, 16 July. Available online: http://www.theguardian.com/music/2015/jul/16/ray-davies-kinks-not-godfather-of-britpop-concerned-uncle (accessed 9 August 2015).

Simpson, D. (2016), 'How We Made Waterloo Sunset', *Guardian Online*, 18 January. Available online: http://www.theguardian.com/music/2016/jan/18/how-we-made-waterloo-sunset-the-kinks-ray-davies-mick-avory (accessed 18 January 2016).

Stark, S. (2005), *Meet the Beatles: A Cultural History of the Band that Shook Youth, Gender, and the World*, New York: Harper Collins.

Sullivan, P. G. (2002), 'Let's have a go at it: The British music hall and the Kinks', in T. M. Kitts and M. J. Kraus (eds), *Living on a Thin Line: Crossing Aesthetic Borders with the Kinks*, 80–99, Rumford, RI: Rock and Roll Research Press.

Discography

The Beatles (1966) Strawberry Fields Forever/Penny Lane, Parlophone [Single]
The Beatles (1967) *Sgt Pepper's Lonely Hearts Club Band, Parlophone* [Album]
The Beatles (1967) She's Leaving Home, *Sgt Pepper's Lonely Hearts Club Band, Parlophone* [Album]
The Beatles (1967) Your Mother Should Know, *Magical Mystery Tour*, Parlophone [Album]
The Beatles (1967) Honey Pie, *The White Album*, Apple [Album]
Blur (1995) *House in the Country*, Food [Single]
The Kinks (1964) You Really Got Me, *Kinks*, Pye Records [Album]
The Kinks (1965) Sunny Afternoon, *Face to Face*, Pye Records [Album]

The Kinks (1965) A Well Respected Man, Pye Records [Single]
The Kinks (1965) Dead End Street/Big Black Smoke, Pye Records [Single]
The Kinks (1966) *Face to Face*, Pye Records [Album]
The Kinks (1966) Dedicated Follower of Fashion, Pye Records [Single]
The Kinks (1966) Most Exclusive Residence For Sale, *Face to Face*, Pye Records [Album]
The Kinks (1966) Rosy Won't You Please Come Home, *Face to Face*, Pye Records [Album]
The Kinks (1967) *Something Else*, Pye Records [Album]
The Kinks (1967) Autumn Almanac, Pye Records [Single]
The Kinks (1967) Mr Pleasant, Pye Records (USA) [Single]
The Kinks (1967) Waterloo Sunset, *Something Else*, Pye Records [Album]
The Kinks (1968) *The Kinks Are The Village Green Preservation Society*, Pye Records [Album]
The Kinks (1968) Animal Farm, *The Kinks Are The Village Green Preservation Society*, Pye Records [Album]
The Kinks (1968) Do You Remember Walter? *The Kinks Are The Village Green Preservation Society*, Pye Records [Album]
The Kinks (1968) Phenomenal Cat, *The Kinks Are The Village Green Preservation Society*, Pye Records [Album]
The Kinks (1968) The Last of the Steam-Powered Trains, *The Kinks Are The Village Green Preservation Society*, Pye Records [Album]
The Kinks (1968) Village Green, *The Kinks Are The Village Green Preservation Society*, Pye Records [Album]
The Kinks (1968) Wicked Annabella, *The Kinks Are The Village Green Preservation Society*, Pye Records [Album]
The Kinks (1969) Shangri-La, *Arthur (Or the decline and Fall of the British Empire)*, Pye Records [Album]
The Kinks (1969) Victoria, *Arthur (Or the decline and Fall of the British Empire)*, Pye Records [Album]
The Kinks (1969) Yes Sir, No Sir, *Arthur (Or the decline and Fall of the British Empire)*, Pye Records [Album]
The Kinks (1970) Apeman, *Lola Versus Powerman and the Moneygoround* Part One, Pye [Album]
The Kinks (1971) *Muswell Hillbillies*, RCA [Album]
The Kinks (1971) Acute Paranoia Schizophrenic Blues, *Muswell Hillbillies*, RCA [Album]
The Kinks (1971) Have a Cuppa Tea, *Muswell Hillbillies*, RCA [Album]
The Kinks (1971) 20th Century Man, *Muswell Hillbillies*, RCA [Album]
The Kinks (1972) Sitting in My Hotel Room, *Everybody's in Show-Biz* [Album]
The Small Faces (1968) Lazy Sunday Afternoon, *Ogden's Nut Gone Flake*, Immediate Records [Album]

CHAPTER TWO

'Rule Britannia is out of bounds':

David Bowie and English heritage. *David Bowie Is ...* (2013) *The Next Day* (2013) and *Blackstar* (2016)

Richard Mills

David Bowie (1947–2016)

Writing in *The Independent* in February 2013, Andy Gill claimed that Bowie's album *The Next Day* was 'the greatest come back in rock history', and he went on to add that the album 'is not just an exercise in nostalgia' as the songs are 'all about today'. The recording 'conveys with apt anxiety or disgust, the fears and concerns of a world riven by conflict and distracted by superficial celebrity' (Gill 2103). Bowie was back, and when he released *Blackstar* in 2016 the consensus of critical opinion was that he had ten to fifteen years more of high quality work still to come: his work promised a late artistic flowering with all the finesse and poise of Picasso, Beckett and Yeats's late work.

Bowie's work on his sixty-ninth birthday on 8 January 2016 was as fresh and off-centre as ever. The future seemed bright and any fears that Bowie might be reduced to the status of nostalgia artist were assuaged. The *David Bowie Is ...* 2013 V&A retrospective of his work, *The Next Day* (2013) and *Blackstar* (2016) disrupted heritage and nostalgic notions of Bowie; the innovative museum curatorship and Bowie's unorthodox final albums had deliberately spurned Derrida's concept of *mal d'archive*: that is, an unhealthy obsession with the past motivated by nostalgia. So, the shock of death two days later was all the more overwhelming as his work was thriving. In retrospect there were clues to his liver cancer: the title *Blackstar* has been construed as a reference to a radial scar on a mammogram that can give a black star or dark star appearance.

As a consequence, this chapter, which set out to be a reading of a thriving artist's late career, has turned into an obituary for his life and work. But as we will see, it rejects concepts of binding nostalgia on his work. I have used the future tense throughout this piece because his work will continue to adapt and change with cover versions by young artists, fan-vids and mash-ups while future generations will perceive his past in a context we can only guess at. When all is said and done, his work cannot be limited by nostalgia, but when we think of his personality, his life and eighteen-month battle against cancer, nostalgia, sentiment and remorse are the only humane and gracious responses. The nostalgia which is present in the three cultural texts under discussion – *David Bowie Is ...*, *The Next Day* and *Blackstar* – function in a similar manner: all three draw 'both the listener and Bowie's persona back to the present and [point] towards the future with the past brought into the present' (Naiman 2015: 318). Naiman goes on to cite Walter Benjamin's writing on the Angel of History, 'A storm is blowing in from Paradise; it has got caught in his wings with such a violence that the angel can no longer close them; The storm irresistibly propels him into the future to which his back is turned'. (Benjamin 1968: 257–8). In a sense, this captures what the three texts have in common: they galvanize the past to make a forward-facing art that interrogates traditional ideas on English heritage culture.

Simon Reynolds has suggested that we are living in a cultural period that is unhealthily fixated on the past. In *Retromania* (2011) he describes how fetishizing 'English Heritage' has become de rigueur in contemporary popular culture. He writes: 'The archival mindset (is) no longer confined within the institution of the museum but seeping out to infect every zone of culture and everyday life – Huyssen contrasted the attitudes of the second half of the century with the first half as a shift from a concern with "present futures" to "present pasts"' (Reynolds 2011: 23). While Reynolds's argument is very cogent, the 2013 V&A retrospective *David Bowie Is ...* , *The Next Day* and *Blackstar* are exceptions which prove the rule. Both are cultural moments which are a weave of past, present and future: Janus-faced art that is open-ended, progressive and which points to the future. The past (the archival impulse), the present (*David Bowie Is …*) and the future (*The Next Day*) coexist.

> The historical object is reborn as such into a present day capable of receiving it, of suddenly 'recognizing' it. This is the famous 'now of recognizability' which has the character of a lightning flash. In the dusty, cluttered corridors of the arcades, where street and interior are one, historical time is broken up into kaleidoscopic distractions and momentary come-ons, myriad displays of ephemera, thresholds for the passage of what Gerard de Nerval calls 'the ghosts of material things'. Here, at a distance from what is normally meant by 'progress'; is the ur-historical, collective redemption of lost time, of the times embedded in the spaces of things. (Benjamin 1999: 7)

In Benjamin's terms, the archival impulse has positive potential in so far as it is coupled with the recognition that cultural identity is 'by definition ambivalent, an imaginary field that is in a constant state of becoming, never fully realized or concretized' (Wiseman-Trowse 2013: 29). David Bowie's work was in danger of being 'concretized' in its staged form as a V&A exhibition, but this *mal d'archive* quicksand has been circumvented by innovative curatorship and David Bowie's shock return to recording in 2014 after a ten-year hiatus. Summarizing Derrida's notion of 'archive fever', Simon Reynolds feels that '*mal d'archive* contains the concept of both illness and evil' (Reynolds 2011: 27). The archive is evil because an obsession with the past is an oppressive and reactionary death-drive for guardians of our national culture and for artists themselves. However, Bowie's work is not bounded by Britannia's death-drive as the V&A curators self-consciously put the stress on the present tense: *David Bowie Is …* and Bowie's return to recording was archly and self-reflexively couched in the future tense, *The Next Day*. In a sense, Bowie's *The Next Day* and *David Bowie Is …* problematize the term 'national culture' suggesting that concepts of national culture have 'thresholds of meaning that must be crossed, erased and translated in the process of cultural production' (Bhabha 1990: 4). Bhabha sees cultural systems as having no 'primordial unity or fixity; that even the same signs can be appropriated, translated, rehistoricised and read anew' (Bhabha 1994: 37). *David Bowie Is …, The Next Day* and *Blackstar* are similar to Benjamin's 'Angel of History': they are productions that predicate the past and the future simultaneously. For instance, the nostalgic and sentimental impulse was part of the cultural zeitgeist before Bowie released his final two albums. In March 2012 his landmark album *The Rise and Fall of Ziggy Stardust and the Spiders from Mars* (1972) was celebrated with a commemorative blue plaque in central London. Former Spandau Ballet star Gary Kemp unveiled the plaque at the spot where the album cover image was photographed. London's Heddon Street (number 23) was becoming a tourist shrine to Bowie fans. That Bowie was in danger of becoming a museum piece is clearly discernible in the years before he released *The Next Day*. The album's release refashioned and problematized the archival impulse. The release of *The Next Day* made the blue plaque a signifier not for a historical heritage act, but for a contemporary performer whose best work lay ahead. The same can be said for a plaque (a red one this time) that was put on the wall of Zizzi's restaurant in Beckenham High Street in 2010. The site was formerly the Three Tuns pub, where Bowie started a creative arts scene that became known as the Beckenham Arts Lab, in 1969.

David Bowie Is ... Retrospective at the Victoria and Albert Museum (2013)

There were concerns that the V&A retrospective of Bowie's career would bottle, label and canonize him as a Britannia museum piece. For an artist who was alive, the V&A exhibition could have been a eulogy to a dead past: archaeology motivated by nostalgia. However, a reading of the exhibition in such a singular way (the museum as mausoleum) would overlook the agency of visitors to create plural meanings from its rich variety of contents. Assistant curator of the exhibition Kathryn Johnson explained how audience interpretation of museum display 'is innately polysemic and open-ended. While curatorial text can carry a particular, carefully considered and researched story, it is a fact that only a small proportion of visitors will read it – however well written. The majority are drawing their own conclusions from primarily visual stimuli' (Johnson 2015: 14). Moreover, *David Bowie Is* ... was conceived as a bold, enlightening and modern show. It exemplifies a curatorial strategy that sought to move museum practices 'away from a didactic, hierarchical model of communication' (Witcomb 2003: 130). Indeed it is the very ambiguity of the exhibition which makes it harmonious with Bowie's enigmatic late work. Katherine Johnson's description of *David Bowie Is* ... underlines the fact that it is an exhibition of a very advanced and contemporary stripe:

> As the design evolved in conversation with curators, it became clear that its authenticity and effectiveness would depend on the degree to which it referenced Bowie's own work. Music and film, as Bowie's key creative outputs, were clearly central to *David Bowie Is*. They had to be fully integrated into the display and given equal status with more traditional objects. Visitors were surrounded by film montages, projection-mapped onto multiple surfaces, and a soundtrack delivered via headphones to individual visitors through Sennheiser's wireless, digital visitor guidance system, guidePORTTM. Using these technologies, the designers created a deeply entertaining and intriguing exhibition environment that appeared in constant movement. (Johnson 2013: 6)

Her illustration of the exhibition's technological variation is fitting for an artist who 'employed a cut-up computer programme for lyrical inspiration, ensuring that the methodology that shaped his seventies liaisons was suitably revised for a new era of technology' (Doggert 2012: 334). Bowie in his late work had adopted his William Burroughs/Brion Gysin cut-up technique for the digital age. The exhibition is a show of tangled and variegated meanings in manner similar to Bowie's last two albums. The newest technology is employed by the curators to create a dynamic and agitated aesthetic.

Entering the exhibition space itself, the viewer is greeted by David Bowie in Kansai Yamamoto's preternaturally shiny red and cardboard-stiff flared suit. The next video installation is of the artists Gilbert and George as 'living sculptures' miming to Flanagan and Allan's *Underneath the Arches*. A chronology of Bowie's twenty-seven studio albums formed the basis of the exhibition, from his pre-fame swinging 1960s R&B bands; and from his first album, *David Bowie* (1967) to *Reality* (2003). Each artistic sidestep was followed respectfully in Bowie's canon. Every album was supported by videos which, more so than for any other artist, are as important as the music: it is again a facet of his artistic legacy that the blank canvas of Bowie's visual imaginings achieves parity with his soundscapes. There is Bowie in a turquoise suit crooning *Life on Mars* Sinatra style; *The Next Day* video with its dolls or South Park trolls with Bowie's face creepily projected; the *DJ* video with Bowie being mobbed by his fans; the *Ashes to Ashes* iconic Pierrot/blue clown designed by Natasha Korniloff; the Union Jack Coat designed by Alexander McQueen and Bowie in 1997 for the *Earthling* album cover; Klaus Nomi lifting Bowie to the microphone (an inverted pyramid suit with only Bowie's head protruding) to sing on Saturday Night Live in 1979; and the modern jazz influenced *The Heart's Filthy Lesson* video, a spiky red-haired Bowie presiding over a weird sadomasochist ritual. In fact, every iconic song is accompanied by video art. *Space Oddity* story boards existential space travel, *Let's Dance* visualizes colonialism and *Sense of Doubt* Cold War alienation. The museum space adheres to a museum format for the most part, each room combines music and video following the Bowie canon. For instance, the Berlin years display Bowie's oil paintings of the Japanese writer Mishima and portraits of Iggy Pop. There is a history of his film appearances on a cinema-size screen, which is on a loop from Bowie's appearance in *The Image* (1967) to his cameo alongside Hugh Jackman in *Prestige* (2006).

It is the final room of the exhibition, however, where the more conventional museum format is transgressed and the space opens into a giant surround sound three-screened concert. Here Bowie sings *Rock 'n' Roll Suicide* at Ziggy Stardust's last outing at the Hammersmith Odeon; a rare film of *Sweet Thing* from the Diamond Dogs tour in Philadelphia and a mullet-haired Bowie in a red suit singing *Bang Bang* on 1987s Glass Spider

Tour. Visitors exited the exhibition via a gift shop that blurred the lines between art and consumerism. Among the items on sale were a Bowie fridge magnet, a Bowie T-shirt, a Bowie button badge, a CD, a V&A *David Bowie Is* poster and a guitar pick adorned with the iconic Aladdin Sane cover. Even the merchandising is off-centre and ingenious, making the souvenirs a Warholesque ironic comment on consumption. The heritage knick-knacks defamiliarize heritage culture because they are bold and go-ahead twenty-first-century objet d'art.

David Bowie Is ... not David Bowie. He is David Jones from Brixton, born on 8 January 1947: appropriately sharing Elvis Presley's birthday. David Bowie is a pop star who realized art was a performance: in his case a performance of traumatic experiences; a performance of madness; and a performance of his influences. He self-consciously used literature, film, poetry and electronica to convey a fractured and damaged self to a late-twentieth-century *fin de siècle* audience. In this sense, he is the natural English successor to the Beatles; but instead of love, peace and sixties countercultural concerns we are offered an artistic performance of alienation, anger and fear: punk for before punk! Popular music has always been a performance of love – *She Loves You, And I Love Her* and *I Want To Hold Your Hand* are real emotions and experience translated into a performance. Bowie does the same, only it is noticeable at this exhibition that it is an artistic performance that avoids such lyrical moon/June romantic clichés; and as such, it is only creative forward-looking curatorship that can do justice to such absorbing art.

Judith Butler writes in *Gender Trouble* that 'in the experience of losing another human being one has loved ... the ego is said to incorporate that other into the very structure of the ego, taking on attributes of the other and sustaining "the other" through "magical acts of imitation"' (Butler 1999: 173). In a sense performance is a structured enactment of sadness and loss: we might think here of John Lennon's songs about losing his mother at an early age (*Julia* or *Mother*), or Bowie's enactments of personal trauma – *Jump they Say* (1993), for instance, a song about his half-brother Terry's suicide. When Bowie's work is viewed as a whole in a museum space, it is apparent that his songs and videos have a common theme: an enactment of this Butleresque concept of sadness and loss. *David Bowie Is* ... an exhibition about the performance of loss, trauma and madness: albeit couched as a contrived performative act by a canny showbiz trouper. This does not make this subject matter any less touching. In fact, the alienation of Major Tom impacts on a visceral level; we feel the detachment and stasis more powerfully than the outpouring of angst and emotion of an 'authentic' act like Nirvana. The *David Bowie Is* exhibition is a bravura performance. Bowie's 'acts of magical imitation' show that collaboration (and influence) is the key to his legacy; and this exhibition is pioneering and inventive as it is a series of forward-looking, postmodernist, performative pieces which use the past to look forward.

The Next Day (2013)

Sean Redmond, in the manner of Walter Benjamin, writes that he simultaneously experiences Bowie in the past, present and future.

> I also ask why his new work in 2013 recasts or reignites that relationship, encouraging me to question: who am I now? I am watching for the first time the video to Bowie's new single, Where are we now?, released on the day of his sixty-sixth birthday (8 January 2013). Within seconds of hearing the first vibrato chords of this wistful song and of seeing the memorial images of the Berlin in which Bowie did some of his finest work, I find myself in a flood of tears. The video has acted as a 'memory text', activated a 'structure of feeling' that has thrown up all sorts of nostalgic impressions, affects, and ultimately taken me right back to a heightened moment of personalised time, of enchanted plentitude, as this question begins to fall from my wet lips. ... Who was I then?' (Redmond 2013: 382)

Redmond goes on to describe Bowie as a forward-looking artist. He describes *The Next Day* as a forward-looking Heraclitean fire, 'When Bowie sings of walking the dead, I see myself in a crowd of zombies, undistinguishable from everyone else, crossing Bösebrücke, to an uncertain future. And yet Bowie and I are not yet completely used up. As the lyrics go on to suggest, we still live, we live with a remarkable fire burning within us' (Redmond 2013: 380). David Cavanagh agrees with Sean Redmond that *The Next Day* is forward looking. The single that was released on 18 January 2013, 'Where Are We Now',

> was a classic case of misdirection. It's nostalgia, by the simple expedient of identifying a handful of Berlin landmarks, Bowie ensured that the public would be primed to expect melancholia, old haunts, fading memories and bygones. They'd be tantalised by the prospect of this legendary enigmatic man looking back over his 66 years in a mood of regret (or maybe pride) and phrasing his mortality in verses of honesty and disclosure. ... One of the album's characters is 22. Another is 17. Another could be as young as 14. Far from concerning itself with Bowie's demise, two songs openly wish death on others. (Cavanagh 2015: 128–9)

Cavanagh is echoing Benjamin, recognizing that Bowie's *The Next Day* is the 'now of recognizability', an artist who has 'come back because clearly he has plenty to say, and new ways of saying it, and couldn't keep silent any longer' (Cavanagh 2015: 129). As we have seen, Bowie's 'late style' was commercially successful but at the same time was perplexing enough to challenge the listener, something also managed by Beckett, Picasso and Yeats, each of whom produced late works that were commercial and artistic successes:

The idea of 'late style' was originally formulated by the cultural critic Theodor Adorno while seeking to understand the final works of Beethoven. For Adorno, the autonomy of the work of art is threatened by the dominant logic of consumer society. Music and other art works should seek to challenge the demand that it be easily understood, resisting attempts to reduce culture to the demands of the marketplace. The standardisation and homogenisation of culture is the main thrust of the dominant market society. For Adorno, more 'authentic' works of art would arrest the listener into active engagement with the artwork rather than the sleep-like trance required by commercialism. (Stevenson 2015: 287)

In a manner similar to Stevenson's analysis, Bowie's 'late style' disrupts 'heritage' concepts of national identity. *The Next Day* is not bounded by nostalgia; the album is proactive and progressive in its subject matter: mortality, violence and fear. It is a piece of work that shows that an acknowledgement of the past does not necessarily mean that an artist is ossified by the memory of an important artistic legacy – 'Becoming is an anti-memory,' as Deleuze and Guattari noted (1987: 16). Indeed, although the term 'museum' recurs throughout the critical lexis on Bowie in this period, reviews of *The Next Day* noted how Bowie himself was acutely aware that his late albums should be contemporary rather than feed off his own artistic past. Emily MacKay, for example, wrote in the *NME*:

> Tony Visconti says that while making 'The Next Day', Bowie was smiling all the time, happy to be back in the studio, and had told him 'I just want to make records'. This album is, foremost, about songcraft. Rather than reinventing Bowie, it absorbs his past and moves it on, hungry for more (and indeed, Visconti has hinted that more is to come). It demands that you listen to it in this moment, not that you give it an easy ride because this is the man who made 'Heroes'; and its songs more than live up to the demand. When Bowie sang this song he sounded as if he was too busy and having too much fun to worry about the dying of any light, it seemed like there's many more next days to come. (MacKay 2013)

After his death, the track *The Stars (Are Out Tonight)* takes on a new meaning – that Bowie's work would continue to live and resonate after Bowie (the dead star was gone). The song is about the legacy of the dead and the lyrics imply that Bowie's posthumous fame will outshine his acclaim while alive. Bowie uses 'star' imagery to point forward, the juxtaposition of 'memory' (dead ones) and 'living' (the future tense) symbolizing memory looking forward, 'an anti-memory' in the Deleuzian sense.

Bowie's entire career has always already been a retrospective, a reflective mediation on itself – right from, or almost from, the very start. 'Do you remember a guy that's been/In such an early song?' Bowie asked in the first line of Ashes to Ashes. His reference to Major Tom, from 1969s Space Oddity, positioned the new song, Ashes to Ashes – released in 1980, 33 years before the V&A retrospective – as an already nostalgic look back into history. Its lyrics carry a sense of reckoning, of final confession. … But then, Space Oddity, by the 22-year-old Bowie, was already a mournful farewell from a pilot facing his last hours alone … and sending a final message to his wife. Hallo Spaceboy (1996) revisited the character for a third time, but the spaceman's adventures had always been elegiac, already over, ever since 1969. (Brooker 2013: 390)

However, there is a caveat to Brooker's analysis; Bowie uses nostalgia to look forward. Bowie's *The Next Day* single prepared the listeners to expect a 'heritage' album, with Bowie being nostalgic about his own legacy. But in fact he made an album that is the opposite. It is progressive and subverts heritage: even the cover is a white inset brutally placed on top of the cover image of *Heroes*. Bold black letters on a white background function as an artistic minimalism that obfuscates the past iconic album. The inset blocks Bowie's face, but leaves enough of the iconic album visible so as to make it recognizable, but not enough of the original cover is visible to allow the spectator to wallow in nostalgia. The past is blocked out revealing and allowing only a partial, fractured nostalgic glance. Like the single, the past is used to evoke interest in the future. Bowie's English heritage impulse is creative and daring, leading to future expectation and not a wallowing retrospective conservatism. *The Next Day* is an axe which breaks the ice of deadening nostalgia. *The Next Day* rejects English heritage and puts Englishness in an international context. The archival impulse is there, but in a manner similar to *David Bowie Is* … the impulse is deliberately transgressed to position the work in a contemporary context.

Blackstar and *Lazarus* videos: 'Look at me I'm in heaven'

Bowie's choreography in the *Blackstar* and *Lazarus* videos is similar to the minimalist stagecraft of Beckett's late plays (for instance, *Play* (1962) consists of three characters immersed up to their necks in large funeral urns). Bowie's hospital bed scene and his retreat into a wardrobe in the video *Lazarus* are reminiscent of Beckett's whittled down essentialist stagecraft. The image of Bowie disappearing into the darkness accompanied by a thumping primordial guitar chord is one of the most affecting and emotional pieces of theatre in the Bowie canon. The dancing is convulsive in this final shot: a feature it shares with the spasmodic dancing figures in *Blackstar*. The final two videos demonstrate Bowie's refusal to be a nostalgic

English heritage artist. As we have seen, Bowie's final videos are in the tradition of late Beckett, and the lyrics are in the bleak elegiac tradition of Yeats's 'Last Poems'. For instance, Yeats wrote the poem 'The Black Tower' a week before he died on 21 January 1939: 'Black Tower', 'Blackstar', both are titles which ominously rhyme. In fact, Bowie's and Yeats's last artistic acts have significant commonalities. In a manner similar to Yeats, Bowie is angry at death and the response of both the artists is to put self-presentation and self-reflexive performativity into their last texts. The moment when the critical images delineate the point where human consciousness is about to be dissolved is couched as a final postmodernist, performative and ironic act: the temptation to convey nostalgia is suppressed and both artists use self-conscious imagery that questions the authenticity of performance. Of course the imagery is bleak, but it is structured and managed in such a constructed and self-aware manner that our expectations are confounded. The imagery is melancholy, but is more nuanced than simple backward-looking sentimentality. The artists' lives may be over, but the work is designed to be forward-looking and transgressive concerning death, grief and mourning. In Yeats's poem the dead stand (2001: 169), while Bowie's title 'Lazarus' is concerned with resurrection. Bowie's final artistic act eschews over-emotionalism: tropes that less imaginative artists would fall into. Both 'Black Tower' and 'Blackstar' use the word 'black' as an obvious symbol of death. In the 'Blackstar' video, there is a black skull on Bowie's writing desk, which demonstrates Bowie and Yeats's use of the uncanny and of occult imagery in their later work. Yeats was a member of The Order of the Golden Dawn and Bowie explicitly cited two members of The Golden Dawn, Alastair Crowley and Madame Blavatsky, throughout his career. At the end of their lives both artists use the occult to be socially transgressive and to look forward: their final artistic acts are obsessed with the symbolism of the dead rising.

Bowie is not bounded by heritage culture in death because his passing was managed, postmodernist and ironic. Lazarus is a staged self-conscious performance. It is a self-reflexive memento mori of recognition of the skull beneath the skin, but a reminder of mortality that is artistically radical and which rejects mawkishness. Even the bluebird lyrics of the song, imagery which is potentially clichéd and sentimental, seem aesthetically challenging when combined with the spartan choreography. The effect is sorrowful but without evoking a pining for the past. The *Blackstar* video also evokes the past without lapsing into heritage nostalgia. Bowie's last work is bold, modern, anti-romantic and pioneering: Jude Rogers writes that Blackstar is 'also the term for the transitional state between a collapsed star and a singularity (a state of infinite value) in physics – which makes sense if Bowie is placing himself as the collapsed star, and the singularity the state he will enter after his death' (Rogers 2016).

Kathryn Johnson has written that Bowie uses music as a 'medium' to 'direct' fans and critics: 'It is clear that the richness of meaning in Bowie's creative output is also the result of his deep interest in music as a medium. He continually observes, reflects on and directs the dialogic relationship between the musician, the music and listeners' (2015: 14–15). In *Blackstar* and *Lazarus* Bowie is managing grief to direct fans away from nostalgia and towards the future, to artworks such as Yeats's 'Last Poems', Beckett's last plays, his own last songs: all works that will transcend the social context and milieu of their own production. Cole Moreton wrote a piece in the *Independent on Sunday*, six days after Bowie's death that was motivated by nostalgia and progression in equal measure. He describes how when Bowie was diagnosed with liver cancer, he visited London in the summer of 2014 with his wife Iman and daughter Lexi. Bowie used the trip to visit his old haunts: the site that was once Beckenham Arts Lab, his first primary school, his family home in Brixton and Plaistow Grove where he grew up. Although an emotional goodbye, this sentiment does not dominate his final music. The last two albums and their videos are enterprising and original works of art. Of course Bowie looks back with a certain amount of regret, but the work does not lapse into a pining reminiscence. Instead 'he made art from the experience: the beautiful disturbing last album *Blackstar*' (Moreton 2016: 24). Moreton describes Bowie's recent work as an ahistorical now that may galvanize the past for images and ideas, but it is a past that is wedded to the moment:

> 'I can't give everything away,' he sings on the last song of the last album *Blackstar* and in that sense we have not lost so much. The music, the words, the images, the ideas, all remain. The flowers will wilt, the candles go out, the notes fade, but one sentence keeps coming back at the end of this pilgrimage, which is perhaps a message for all of us who care, even the Girl with the Mousy Hair: 'Don't copy me, go out and create yourselves.' (2016: 25)

For Bowie, the emphasis in the lyrics is on future creative endeavours. Bowie's final work is a two-headed Janus god. He builds progressive art on fragments of his past work. 'The past as it really was may be a delusion, yet we can try to understand why we fashioned it in our image' (Wegman 2012: 44). Bowie uses his artistic legacy to make it new. His work recognizes the subjectivity of interpretations of his artistic canon. So, the final videos are a bricolage of past and present: 'Yet the fiction of a real past has undeniable heuristic value, and may well bring out the best in us' (Wegman, 2012: 48). *Lazarus* and *Blackstar* and late Bowie texts are littered with allusions to the past: a dead Major Tom, bejewelled skulls, the Berlin place names in 'Where Are We Now?', Donny McClaslin's saxophone is reminiscent of *Aladdin Sane* and *Low*. Bowie is not completely wiping the slate clean with these albums but they are palimpsestic texts which, like the cover of *The Next Day*, still bear traces of earlier forms. *The Next Day* blocks out Bowie's *Heroes*' cover with a minimalist white square. The past is visible but it is problematized by the present subjectivity of the artist. This is the achievement of Bowie's last works. He looks back without falling into the trap of *mal d'archive*. English heritage is disturbed and is *recognized* as fragmented and partial truth. As Bowie writes, 'All art is unstable. Its meaning is not necessarily that implied by the author. There is no authoritative voice. There are only multiple readings' (*1. Outside*, 1995: sleevenotes).

Blackstar (2016)

The musical style of *Blackstar* defamiliarizes retrospective organizing principles. As we have seen the cover art of *The Next Day* references the past but points to the future. *Blackstar* also blurs the rose-tinted revisionist gaze by its musical invention. Both albums 'situate recollection as action, a performance of historiography that contributes to the construction of the star text through a laborious interpretive and communal relationship to the various meaning associated with that text' (Palmer 2013). The music and iconography of Bowie's last albums are a bricolage or collection that 'resists chronology or linearity' (Palmer 2013). The musical action of *Blackstar* pushes forward but there are many references to the past: the song *Sue (or a Season of Crime)* has an industrial sound reminiscent of *Hallo Spaceboy* from 1995s *1. Outside* album. The electronic drum beats are a reminder of his drum and bass album, *Earthling* (1997). The last song on the album, *I Can't Give Everything Away*, steals the saxophone sound from *Low* (1977). Other songs such as *Dollar Days* are very difficult to place in the context of Bowie's past work, the lyrics of the song are a rejection of nostalgia. Critchley writing about *Dollar Days* summarizes Friedrich Hölderin stating that Bowie believed 'in ways of seeing that put the past to shame' (Critchley 2016: 173). The music too is progressive, the modern jazz saxophone stylings of Donny McClasin give the album a space-age jazz feel and a traumatic hauntology in the style of 1960s jazz works such as Miles Davies's minimalist *In A Silent Way* (1969) and John Coltrane's galactic free-jazz album *Interstellar Space* (1967). The jazz is melodic and minimalist avant-garde, the cover is enigmatically and simply a symbol ★ and Bowie and Visconti revealed that their current listening was Kendrick Lamar's *To Pimp A Butterfly* (2015). This is not the artistic palette of a typical heritage artist: the album is 'recollection as action'.

Heritage culture, Bowie's Englishness and a Diamond Dog who is 'happily mongrelized'

Englishness has always informed Bowie's work, from Anthony Newley's London accent on the first Deram recording, the first album, *David*

Bowie (1967), to the Union Jack Alexander McQueen coat that Bowie is wearing on the cover for *Earthling*. But English heritage is blurred by internationalism and plurality. Bowie is an artist whose identity is 'happily mongrelised, interdependent, impure, mixed up' (Kearney 1996: 152). David Bowie is an English artist whose work is a bricolage of different international influences. Although English identity and English heritage are essential spokes on Bowie's cultural wheel, Bowie's work problematizes English heritage culture by his internationalism. His first album *David Bowie* (1967), with songs such as 'London Boys', 'The Laughing Gnome' and 'Love You Till Tuesday', is in the English vaudeville and Anthony Newly tradition: light entertainment, whimsical songs sung in a faux cockney accent. In fact, many Bowie commentators have suggested that Bowie was destined to be an English mainstream entertainer before his reinvention as Ziggy Stardust. Bowie's early years were in many ways typified by the song 'Little Bombardier' which, according to biographer David Buckley, tells the story of 'Frankie, a demobbed soldier who drank his money' and the song is 'set in a bygone age' of nostalgic Englishness and the 'comedy cockney' of *She's Got Medals* (Buckley 2005: 31–2). Throughout his career Bowie sang in a distinctive South London accent, but his Berlin years, his New York influences, his Japonism (Kabuki theatre, Kansa Yamamoto costumes), the 'China Girl' single, Pierrot costumes in the 'Ashes to Ashes' video, Nagisa Oshima's 'Merry Christmas Mr. Lawrence' and American Rhythm and Blues, all demonstrate that Bowie's was an English identity that was constantly in a process of renegotiation and change. His identity was a kaleidoscopic mess of different cultural strains. Bowie's global cultural interests meant that he greatly influences Western culture, for instance, 'Bowie acted as a lightning rod for Japonism in Western popular culture dress, repositioning the image of the masculine body through incorporation of *onnagata* costuming into his Ziggy Stardust stage wear' (Thian 2015: 142). As Bowie's career took off his Englishness became global; he was an intercontinental rock star who never lost his music hall tradition. So, Bowie began his artistic life as an English heritage performer. Buckley writes that

> Bowie's influences came from the music hall, light entertainment and the theatre as well as from Anglo-American popular music. ... Bowie also made sure he sounded like where he came from. In the era in which the distinctly parochial was making its first impact in the charts with the MS, Mike Sarne, Lionel Bart, Tommy Steele and, of course, Anthony Newley, Bowie's voice was of South London. (Buckley 2005: 28)

In a sense, Bowie's cultural identity and art combined English with borrowed American musical forms, as well as American hip linguistic idioms. The *Ziggy Stardust* album, for instance, was full of American colloquialisms; in the song 'Five Years', Bowie used 'Cadillac' instead of 'car', 'cop' instead of 'policeman', 'bobby' or 'copper' , 'news guy' instead of 'newsreader' (Buckley 2005: 130).

In fact, Bowie's work is reminder that national identity is a hybrid that only exists in a very specific (and very ephemeral) cultural and historical context. Benedict Anderson writes that a homogenous national culture or sense of self is the product of eighteenth-century 'dusk of religious modes of thought' (Anderson 1991: 178). To Anderson, 'rationalist secularism brought with it its own modern darkness' (ibid). Bowie's Englishness is a nineteenth- and twentieth-century imagined and mythological state embodied by an intermingling of different global influences that reimagines the museum culture. Anderson suggests that 'museums and the museumizing imagination are both profoundly political' (ibid). He demonstrates that 'the new nation state of Indonesia learned from its immediate ancestor, the colonial Netherlands East Indies. The present proliferation of museums around Southeast Asia suggests a general process of political inheriting at work' (ibid). In a sense English heritage culture is a *mal d'archive*, but not when the subject of an exhibition is a self-reflexive artist who combines past and future in a radical mix. Bowie's final two albums and the V&A exhibition are profound renegotiations of English heritage culture. Bowie's music and image each have an ambiguity about national certitude that is challenging and progressive:

> A network can be destroyed by noises that attack and transform it, if the codes in place are unable to normalize and repress them. Although the new order is not contained in the structure of the old, it is nonetheless not a product of chance. It is created by the substitution of new differences for the old differences. Noise is the source of these mutations in the structuring codes. For despite the death it contains, noise carries order within itself; it carries new information. This may seem strange. But noise does in fact create a meaning: first, because the interruption of a message signifies the interdiction of the transmitted meaning, signifies censorship and rarity; and second, because the very absence of meaning in pure noise or in the meaningless repetition of a message, by unchanneling auditory sensations, frees the listener's imagination. The absence of meaning is in this case the presence of all meanings, absolute ambiguity, a construction outside meaning. The presence of noise makes sense, makes meaning. It makes possible the creation of a new order on another level of organization, of a new code in another network. (Attali 2011: 33)

In a sense, the electronic and concrete music of Karlheinz Stockhausen's *Hymnen,* which was first performed in Cologne on 30 November 1967 (making its debut at the same time as Bowie released his first album) prefigures Bowie's artistic and cultural odyssey. *Hymnen* consists of recordings of national anthems from around the world. There are four movements, or Regions, as Stockhausen refers to them. Region I (dedicated to Pierre Boulez) has two anthems: The Internationale and La Marseillaise. Region II has four anthems: the German anthem, a group of African anthems, the opening of the Russian anthem, plus a recorded moment where past and present join together. Region III (dedicated to John Cage) has three anthems: the continuation of the Russian anthem, the American anthem and the Spanish anthem. Region IV (dedicated to Luciano Berio) has one anthem: the Swiss anthem final chord that turns into an imaginary anthem of a utopian dream. Described by Ian MacDonald as 'a mordant satire on nationalism' (MacDonald 2008: 291) the piece demonstrates that the V&A exhibition, *The Next Day* and *Blackstar* are all cultural texts that are examples of progressive and disruptive art that is constantly ch-ch-ch-changing. Bowie's music can be understood in the context of the classical minimalist tradition of Steve Reich, John Cage and the electronic collage of *Hymnen,* as well as popular entertainers such as Anthony Newley and his beloved 1950s rock and roll. As Thian demonstrates his costumes are internationalist, the semiotics of which interrogate the absolutes of national boundaries in the manner of Baudrillard's description of how the in-between spaces in airports, 'compress the near and the far, the local and the global, into some kind of random and incoherent pastiche' (Baudrillard 1983: 163). Sean Mayes observed that the soles of Bowie's shoes were so clean because 'he never sets foot in the street. It's all hotels, limousines, sterilized airports' (Mayes 2016: 13). In other words, Bowie's identity is indeterminate; he is at 'home' while constantly travelling.

Bowie's psyche is a hybridized international and English identity. Bowie's lyrics at their best inherit Burroughs's cut-up technique experiments and have the melancholy death symbolism of late Yeats. His stagecraft and the choreography of his videos is a mélange of Beckettian minimalism, kabuki theatre and mime. He has built his career on a leading-edge forward movement, but as we have seen, 'occasionally he's attempted to grab the second hand and swing, Harold Lloyd-like back in time' (Jones 2012: 182). Bowie's art constantly exploits artistic self-referencing without surrendering to a collapse of creative invention. 'For me it's just a question of finding there's little steam left in the last thing that I did to keep me happy as a writer' (Thomas 2015: 143). In, sum, then, Bowie's bricolage of 'high' and 'low' culture is predicated on a plural English identity: an Englishness that is of its time, but not of its time: an English heritage culture which is reaching both back and far forward.

References

Anderson, B. (1983), *Imagined Communities*, London: Verso.

Attali, J. (1989), *Noise: The Political economy of Music*, Minneapolis: University of Minnesota Press.

Baudrillard, W. (1983), *Simulations*, New York: Semiotexte, Inc.

Benjamin, W. (1999), *The Arcades Project*, trans. H. Eiland and K. McLaughlin, London: Belknap Press [1940].

Benjamin, W. (1968), *Illuminations*, H. Arendt (ed.), trans. H. Zohn, New York: Harcourt, Brace and World.

Brooker, W. (2013), 'Look Back at that Man: David Bowie in Retrospect', *Celebrity Studies*, 4(3): 390–2.

Buckley, D. (1999), *Strange Fascination: David Bowie. The Definitive Story*, London: Virgin, 2005.

Butler, J. (1999), *Gender Trouble*, New York: Routledge.

Bhabha, H. K. (1994), *The Location of Culture*, London: Routledge.

Cavanagh, D. (2015), 'The Next Day', *Uncut*, June.

Critchley, S. (2016), *On Bowie*, London: Serpents Tail.

Doggett, P. (2012), *The Man Who Sold The World*, London: Vintage.

Deleuze, G. and F. Guattari (1987), *A Thousand Plateaus: Capitalism and Schizophrenia*, Minneapolis: University of Minnesota Press.

Gill, A. (2013), 'The Starman pulls off the greatest comeback in rock history with The Next Day'. *The Independent*, 25 February. Available online: http://www.independent.co.uk/arts-entertainment/music/reviews/david-bowie-album-review-track-by-track-the-starman-pulls-off-the-greatest-comeback-album-in-8510608.html.

Goddard, S. (2013), *Ziggyology*, London: Ebury.

Hackett, J. (2015), 'Art, artifice and androgyny: Roxy Music's dandy modernism'. *Subverting Fashion: Clothing Cultures*, 2(2): 167–78.

Jones, D. (2012), *When Ziggy Played Guitar: David Bowie And Four Minutes That Shook The World*, London: Random.

Johnson, K. (2015), 'David Bowie Is', in E. Devereux, A. Dillane and M. J. Power (eds), *David Bowie: Critical Perspectives*, 1–19, New York: Routledge.

Kearney, R. (2016), *Postnationalist Ireland: Politics, Culture, Philosophy*, London: Routledge, 1996.

Mayes, S. (2016), *Life On Tour With Bowie*, London: Music Press Books.

Mills, R. (2016), The Last Word, *BBC Radio 4*, 15 January.

Mackay, E. (2013), 'The Next Day' – Album Review, *NME*. Available online: http://www.nme.com/reviews/david-bowie/14183.

MacDonald, I. (2008), *Revolution in the Head: The Beatles' Records and the Sixties*, London: Vintage.

Moreton, C. (2016), 'David Bowie: Retracing the icon's journey from post-war Brixton to superstardom', *The Independent on Sunday*, 16 January.

Naiman, T. (2015), 'Where are We Now? Walls and Memory in David Bowie's Berlins', in T. Cinque, C. Moore, S. Redmond (eds), *Enchanting David Bowie. Space/Time/Body/Memory*, 305–23. London: Bloomsbury.

Palmer, L. (2013), 'Recollecting David Bowie: The Next Day and late-career stardom', *Celebrity Studies*, 4(3): 384–6.

Petridis, A. (2013), 'The Next Day – Album Review'. *The Guardian*. Available Online: http://www.theguardian.com/music/2013/feb/25/david-bowie-next-day-review.

Redmond, S. (2013), 'Who am I now? Remembering the enchanted dogs of David Bowie', *Celebrity Studies* 4(3): 380–3.

Reynolds, S. (2011), *Retromania: Pop Culture's Addiction To Its Own Past*, London: Faber and Faber.

Rogers, J. (2016), 'The Final Mysteries of David Bowie's *Blackstar* – Elvis, Crowley and "The Village of Ormen",' *The Guardian*. http://www.theguardian.com/

music/2016/jan/21/final-mysteries-david-bowie-blackstar-elvis-crowley-villa-of-ormen.

Stevenson, N. (2006), *David Bowie: Fame, Sound and Vision*, London: Polity Press.

Thian, M. H. (2015), 'David Bowie and Japonism in fashion in the 1970s', in E. Devereux, A. Dillane and M. J. Power (eds), *David Bowie: Critical Perspectives*, 128–47, London: Routledge.

Thomas, D. (2015[1983]), 'The Face Interview', in S. Egan (ed.), *Interviews and Encounters: Bowie and Bowie*, 140–59, London: Souvenir Press.

Trynka, P. (2011), *Starman. David Bowie: The Definitive Biography*, London: Sphere.

Wegman, R. C. (2012), *Historical Musicology: Is It Still Possible?*, Abingdon: Routledge.

Wiseman-Trowse, N. (2013), *Nick Drake: Dreaming England*, London: Reaktion Books.

Witcomb, A. (2003), *Re-imagining the museum: beyond the mausoleum*, London: Routledge.

Yeats, W. B. (1991), *The Major Works*, Oxford: Oxford University Press.

Young, R. (2010), *Electric Eden: Unearthing Britain's Visionary Music*, London: Faber and Faber.

Discography

The Beatles (1963) I Want To Hold Your Hand, Parlophone [Single]
The Beatles (1963) She Loves You, Parlophone [Single]
The Beatles (1968) Julia, *The White Album*, Apple [Album]
David Bowie (1967) *David Bowie*, Deram [Album]
David Bowie (1967) Laughing Gnome, *David Bowie*, Deram [Album]
David Bowie (1967) Little Bombardier, *David Bowie*, Deram [Album]
David Bowie (1967) London Boys, *David Bowie*, Deram [Album]
David Bowie (1967) Love You Till Tuesday, *David Bowie*, Deram [Album]
David Bowie (1967) She's Got Medals, *David Bowie*, Deram [Album]
David Bowie (1969) *Space Oddity*, Philips [Album]
David Bowie (1969) Space Oddity, Space *Oddity*, Philips [Album]
David Bowie (1971) *Hunky Dory*, RCA Records [Album]
David Bowie (1971) Life on Mars? *Hunky Dory*, RCA Records [Album]
David Bowie (1971) Quicksand, *Hunky Dory*, RCA Records [Album]
David Bowie (1972) *The Rise and Fall of Ziggy Stardust and the Spiders from Mars*, RCA Records [Album]
David Bowie (1972) Five Years, *The Rise and Fall of Ziggy Stardust and the Spiders from Mars*, RCA Records [Album]
David Bowie (1972) Rock 'n' Roll Suicide, *The Rise and Fall of Ziggy Stardust and the Spiders from Mars*, RCA Records [Album]
David Bowie (1973) *Aladdin Sane*, RCA Records [Album]
David Bowie (1974) *Diamond Dogs*, RCA Records [Album]
David Bowie (1974) Sweet Thing, *Diamond Dogs*, RCA Records [Album]
David Bowie (1977) *Low*, RCA Records [Album]
David Bowie (1977) *Heroes*, RCA Records [Album]

David Bowie (1977) Sense of Doubt, *Heroes*, RCA Records [Album]
David Bowie (1980) *Scary Monsters (And Super Creeps)*, RCA Records [Album]
David Bowie (1980) Ashes to Ashes, *Scary Monsters (And Super Creeps)*, RCA
    Records [Album]
David Bowie (1983) *Let's Dance*, EMI [Album]
David Bowie (1983) China Girl, *Let's Dance*, EMI [Album]
David Bowie (1987) *Never Let Me Down*, EMI [Album]
David Bowie (1987) Bang Bang, *Never Let Me Down*, EMI [Album]
David Bowie (1993) *Black Tie White Noise*, Savage [Album]
David Bowie (1993) Jump They Say, *Black Tie White Noise*, Savage [Album]
David Bowie (1995) *1. Outside*, BMG/Arista/RCA [Album]
David Bowie (1995) The Heart's Filthy Lesson, *1. Outside*, BMG/Arista/RCA
    [Album]
David Bowie (1997) *Earthling*, BMG/Arista/RCA [Album]
David Bowie (1997) Hallo Spaceboy, *Earthling*, BMG/Arista/RCA [Album]
David Bowie (2003) *Reality*, ISO. Columbia [Album]
David Bowie (2013) *The Next Day*, ISO. Columbia [Album]
David Bowie (2013) Where Are We Now? *The Next Day*, ISO. Columbia [Album]
David Bowie (2013) The Stars (Are Out Tonight), *The Next Day*, ISO. Columbia
    [Album]
David Bowie (2016) *Blackstar*, ISO. Columbia. Sony. RCA [Album]
David Bowie (2016) Blackstar, *Blackstar*, ISO. Columbia. Sony. RCA [Album]
David Bowie (2016) Dollar Days, *Blackstar*, ISO. Columbia. Sony. RCA [Album]
David Bowie (2016) I Can Give Everything Away, *Blackstar*, ISO. Columbia. Sony.
    RCA [Album]
David Bowie (2016) Lazarus, *Blackstar*, ISO. Columbia. Sony. RCA [Album]
David Bowie (2016) Sue (or a Season of Crime), *Blackstar*, ISO. Columbia. Sony.
    RCA [Album]
John Coltrane (1974) *Interstellar Space*, Impulse! [Album]
Miles Davies (1969) *In a Silent Way*, Columbia [Album]
Flanagan and Allen (1932) Underneath the Arches
Kendrick Lamar (2015) *To Pimp A Butterfly*, Top Dawg. Aftermath. Interscope
    [Album]
John Lennon (1970) *John Lennon/Plastic Ono Band*, Apple [Album]
John Lennon (1970) Mother, *John Lennon/Plastic Ono Band*, Apple [Album]
Karlheinz Stockhausen (1966–7) *Hymnen*

CHAPTER THREE

Mod Cons:

Back to the future with The Jam (1977–79)

Ben Winsworth

Although the Jam rode to prominence on the tattered coat tails – or rather tartan bum flaps – of punk, they had a sense of unity and cohesion (in both a visual and musical sense) that marked them out as being different. Paul Weller, like many of his generation, was fired up by the cultural explosion of punk, inspired by the performances of the Sex Pistols and the Clash at the 100 Club, and yet ultimately disillusioned at the way the movement unfolded. Looking back on 1976–77, he felt that the period had been 'totally romanticised', that most punks were 'bullshitters', and that the musical and cultural revolution it promised failed to materialize:

> And being 17 or 18, and being arrogant, I thought I knew what it should have been about: a real street movement, the first working class musical movement that our generation had had. We'd read all about the Sixties, but it was the first time for us that something similar had happened. That's what I wanted it to be. (Heatley 1995: 15)

Weller's hope that punk would match the energy and influence of 1960s pop/youth culture says as much about his true origins as it does about his disappointment with a contemporary scene within which the Jam occupied a rather ambivalent position. Punk gave the Jam a means of playing to a young audience, allowed them to integrate themselves into a live circuit where their raw sound and aggressive lyrics found favour, even if their being labelled revivalists by Caroline Coon in *Melody Maker* (Hewitt 1983: 35) and a retro band by *Sniffin' Glue* (Perry 2000) disqualified them from being fully paid-up members of the punk union. Not, perhaps, that they would have wanted to join.

Although an appellation most famously denied by Weller on a piece of cardboard that he wore around his neck in a pub – 'How can I be a fucking revivalist when I'm only 18?' (Hewitt 1983: 35) – there was something a little disingenuous in the gesture. Photographs from the October 1976 gig at Soho market clearly show the Jam suited up in a way that appears more backward than forward-looking, and certainly strikes a conservative pose in comparison with the emerging punk style already starting to manifest itself through various media channels. John Lydon's attire for the Sex Pistols' first TV appearance on Granada's *So it Goes,* in August of the same year, is a more potent representation of late-1976 zeitgeist than the mohair being promoted by the Jam in Soho. Similarly, while the fast-paced energy of their early songs and Weller's South London market boy vocal delivery chimed in with the rough and ready nature of punk, the lyrics, as well as the appearance of 1960s soul and R&B standards in their repertoire, also made them a musical oddity, if not at odds with the new 'in crowd'.

Punk clearly provided a context in which the Jam could break out of Woking, build up a national fan base, and secure an all-important record contract. At the same time, as Weller recalled in 1995, the Jam were creating their own scene: 'What we and our audiences were about was more the real spirit of punk' (Hewitt 2008: 80), although that spirit clearly had more mod in the depths of its soul. For the boy raised on a diet rich in the music and style of the 1960s, who turned his back on the mainstream and who rode a Lambretta in the mid-1970s (Nicholls 1984: 15), punk was never going to be enough in itself, however much inspiration he took from it, and however much he tried to bend it to his own vision of a musical revolution. While the Jam supported the Clash on 'The White Riot Tour' in May 1977 as a means of promoting their first album, they were uneasy bedfellows, Weller burning a copy of *Sniffin' Glue* on stage and announcing to Steve Clarke in *New Musical Express* (after the tour quickly ended) that the band would all be voting Conservative in the next election because this 'change-the-world thing is becoming a bit too trendy' (Clarke 1977: 28–9). It is more than likely that he was rebelling against the dominance of a movement that he felt had let him down and failed to fulfil his expectations, rather than expressing an authentic political stance. It also pointed to something of the way in which the Jam would work to reconstruct an image and identity of Britain that punk seemed hell-bent on destroying, even if that way was not yet clearly defined, and even if the damage and destruction that punk reflected was already deeply ingrained in the threadbare fabric of the nation.

The controversial lyrics of 'Time for Truth' on the *In The City* album, released in April 1977, with their criticism of 'Uncle' Jim Callaghan and regret that the British Empire had been turned into 'manure', did little to ease the suspicion that the Jam were moving further to the political right. But powerful attacks on the police – both here and on the title track – perhaps give a better indication of Weller's true sentiments: the Labour government had failed, it had let people – especially young people – down, it was corrupt and complicit with the police brutality that helped it to maintain power by reframing acts of resistance as criminality. In a similar way to his antagonism towards punk, Weller – like the angry teenager he was – was reacting in a highly charged manner against his political fathers, borrowing the expletive bravado of the former to attack the latter: 'Why don't you fuck off?' However, rather than throwing in the towel and following the road to destruction and anarchy that the Sex Pistols advocated, the Jam's attitude was expressive of the desire to provoke a positive reaction to the economic, cultural and political malaise of the 1970s. The pro-empire sentiments, although uncomfortable and disturbing, can best be understood as a further expression of dissatisfaction with the present, at the same time as they are mixed with a sense of Kinks-like regret for a happier, if only half-imaginary, past. While certainly not apolitical, nor unaware of the decline and decay around them, many of their early songs were looking for a different reaction – a new idea, a 'young idea' ('In the City') – one which they found, paradoxically, through engaging with an earlier youth subculture and style. The title of the album and single is more than a passing nod to the Who song of the same name released on the 'B' side of 'I'm A Boy' in August 1966.

'Art School' is interesting in this context for the way it considers the contemporary scene to have the same potential to influence a new direction, a new identity, as these creative institutions had had in the previous decade. However, the lyrics also warn indirectly that punk, for all its brio and bravado, lacks any real clarity or direction. Underlining that this is the *new* art school might also be interpreted as an attack on the old art school graduates (like Malcolm McLaren, Jamie Reid and Vivienne Westwood) for manipulating young punks as part of a wider situationist-influenced experiment (Savage 2005: 23–36). It is with a degree of youthful arrogance that Weller assumes the responsibility to reawaken the listener to the idea of finding oneself through a more clearly defined individual style and – at the same time – a way of life that does not conform to normative frameworks. Anything that one feels to be right, wearing the clothes one chooses while ignoring the laughter of the jealous or ignorant, is the more authentic way to go, and works as a corrective to the fuzzier distortions of a tabloid distilled punk. At the same time, of course, 'Art School' reintroduced aspects of the mod aesthetic and philosophy into the mid–late 1970s equation.

This is something also witnessed in 'Away From The Numbers', a track that applies the mod term 'numbers' to the popular punk collective: a crowded, contemporary (sub)culture already in danger of being diluted and/

or dissipated by mainstream fashion, rather like the original mods. However, for Paul Weller and the Jam, reawakening the sound and spirit of the mid-1960s was paradoxically a way of breaking free, of moving forward, not escaping from reality, which (as the lyrics note) is so much harder than living in the cosy world of English escapism and apathy, a world that Weller felt punk was quickly adapting itself to. Furthermore, this return to mod – an identity strengthened and confirmed on the next two albums – rather than being simply a rejection of punk in favour of revivalism, was more an attempt to harness the original positivity and energy of both movements within the self-confidence and optimism of a new modernism and carry it into the future as an antidote to contemporary nihilism. As Steve Clarke noted in the *NME*: 'The Jam have taken what they want from the past and fused it with a Seventies' street consciousness while totally eschewing the blind negativity which has, until now, been *de rigeur*' (Clarke 1977: 28–9).

It is perhaps for this reason that they adopted the habit of draping Union Jacks over their amplifiers during live performances. Although this led to them being tagged as conservative with both a small and capital 'c', the gesture is better understood as a reaction to the torn and tattered flags designed by punk artist Jamie Reid. Reid's publicity poster for 'Anarchy in the UK' – the Sex Pistols' infamous first single released in November 1976 – quickly established itself as one of the iconographic focal points of the punk movement. Ripped apart to reflect a spirit of national breakdown, the Union Jack is revealed to be an empty symbol, a façade behind which there is only blankness, a void perceived through the tears in the soiled and dirty material. Held together by safety pins and bulldog clips, acknowledging the presence of punk as a consequence of – and comment upon – the pitiful state of a Britain that is anything but Great, it offers little else than cold comfort and only a tenuous promise of cohesion. The blackmail note style of lettering places the Sex Pistols and Anarchy at the centre of Reid's bleak vision of the UK, in the same way that the Pistols became central to the punk subculture itself. Paul Weller and the Jam, however, were not going to be held to ransom, even though Weller had respect for the way in which the Sex Pistols in their early days awoke and terrorized a soporific music industry.

The Union Jack first made its presence felt in 1960s mod culture via the stylistic transformation of the High Numbers into the Who. Pete Townshend's legendary red, white and blue jacket and guitar amp decoration was a pop art gesture of appropriation and transformation that liberated the flag from its more military and monarchical associations. Bringing the Union Jack out of the historical past and into the present moment as a vector for the mod style turned it into a symbol for the celebration of the 'NOW', as well as a potent signifier of social mobility: the flag – the nation itself – equally belonged to a new generation who wanted to get around, get beyond, and get over the Second World War and its austere aftermath (Weight 2013: 131–2). The adoption of the Royal Air Force (RAF) roundel can be understood in this way too. Repossession and contextual recreation of these old symbols was also an expression of pride in English/British, popular/youth culture that was – if only for a brief moment – starting to supersede and define itself against an American equivalent manifest in the UK through the maintenance and preservation of mid–late 1950s rock and roll influences by certain groups within the new decade. To some extent the tension between the mods and rockers can be read as a symptom of this evolution, with the old refusing to die while the young were struggling (yet generally succeeding) in being born through the assertion of a new identity: Gramsci's monsters and morbid symptoms transformed into beach fights and folk devils (Cohen 2011).

The Jam's recycling of the Union Jack in a variety of manifestations throughout their early and mid-career was a deliberate identification with the optimistic, upwardly mobile ideology of mod, and thus a rejection of the 'no future' pessimism of punk. Through forging direct links with the past, they were trying to re-establish a sense of pride in the popular cultural achievements that made Britain great, but not in an overtly political or nationalistic sense. Instead they wanted to create a musical platform from which constructive – rather than purely destructive – criticism could be levelled against Britain's past and present. The positivism of mod mixed with the intensity and stripped-down musical simplicity of punk – itself an echo of 1960s mod and garage bands – seemed the perfect solution to the more self-destructive aspects of the latter. Richard Weight (132013: 243–77) chronicles the interesting stylistic transitions and influences between mod and punk, even if at the time the similarities were perhaps not so evident as they are now with the benefit of hindsight. However, Weight is definitely onto something when he suggests that the mod influence within punk – clearly represented by bands like the Jam – helped to make punk 'ultimately more meaningful to young Britons with little knowledge of, or interest in, the intellectual radicals who fostered it from 1972 to 1976' (Weight 2013: 244). 'All Around The World' – the Jam's second single (July 1977) – sounds like a manifesto clearly pointing out where the band are going to in this respect. Why say destroy, asks Weller, arguing that it is better to find a 'new' direction out of the legacies of the past. The refrain of 'All around the world' sounds like a direct contact call to other early mod revivalists and/or disillusioned youths who were also starting to turn their backs on punk and look for musical and stylistic inspiration in the past.

A new direction through linking up with the 1960s was further established by the Jam in their second album, *This is The Modern World*. Released in November 1977, the title itself brings together past and present – mod and modern – as a way of moving forwards beyond the stagnation of punk. The album cover shows Bruce Foxton and Rick Buckler (wearing a Union Jack button badge) staring out into the future, while Paul Weller's self-made and self-conscious mod arrow jumper (and Who badge) is suggestive of the dual direction in which the Jam were travelling. Standing under the shadow of Westway flyover, built during the 1960s and opened in 1970, also creates a visual link between the past and the present and – like the tower blocks from the Silchester estate – is a concrete memorial to an earlier more visionary modern world, at the same time as it also stands as a stark reminder of everything that is wrong with the 1970s. Like the cars in 'London Traffic' the political and cultural scene of 1977 has become congested and the inspirational creativity and vision of the 1960s halted by the harsh reality of economic decline. The title track also plays on the idea of mod/modern: the 1960s is a place that Weller has discovered, the modern/modernist world is one that has given him purpose and self-confidence, the determination to find his own way and realize the dream of recreating – rather than simply repeating – mod in his own time. Weller's bold and arrogant declaration of self-knowledge and purpose transcends the need for self-justification, allowing artist and group to dismiss the criticisms that had been levelled against them. Although Weller states that he will not 'preview' where his direction is headed, in many ways this is exactly what he does throughout the album, albeit in a sometimes indirect and imperfect manner.

This is The Modern World finds the Jam testing out their reworking of mod and picking up where 'Away From The Numbers' left off in the previous album. Many of the songs deal with observing, looking, watching ('Life From A Window'); with distancing oneself from the crowd ('The Combine'); and with the way in which the state attempts to dictate and manipulate its citizens ('Standards'). Behind all of this we can detect a call for authenticity and originality, if only faintly at times, possibly due to the sometimes disjointed feel of the track listing and one or two less committed compositions. There is also a sense of anxiety and insecurity that haunts the album in places (perhaps as a result of the well-known dip in Weller's creative form at this period): moments where the 'hate', 'murder', 'paranoia' and general fear referred to throughout 'In the Street Today' (and elsewhere) threaten to overwhelm the more confident assertions being made about the kids wanting 'action'. None the less a new perception of the world, one that cuts through the blasé vision of a tired punkocracy, is being persistently advocated together with the creation of a new, individual identity and standpoint built out of the stylistics and attitude of mod. 'Here Comes the Weekend' speaks for itself in this context, encouraging kids to do something positive with their time at the end of the working week, rather than bum around like the 'London Girl' who is lost, unemployed and unwashed! In the climax to the song, Bruce Foxton does not condemn her, but hopes that she finds the answers to the questions that the Jam are resolving for themselves and other directionless young punks.

All Mod Cons, released in November 1978, built on the work of *This is The Modern World*, the title once again playfully signalling Weller's true allegiance, as well as being an ironic and insightful anticipation of the way in which the mod revival – still in its infancy – would eventually be hijacked by the media and transformed into money-making fashion rather than a mode of being. Although the Jam were a significant component in this revival, and one of the bands around which a new breed of mods coalesced, Weller was keen to distance himself from the more superficial aspects of the movement. Mod was a serious business, a way of life: the iconography of the album's inner sleeve established the Jam's credentials as a committed band fully aware of mod history, but also promoted them as mod activists in the present. 'Bif, Bang, Pow' by the Creation, a ska record, a cappuccino served in a retro glass cup and saucer, are some of the items that figure in the collage, but they interact with contemporary postcards of London and Jam parka patches conceived in the style of the Who's maximum R&B posters, one of which features the Union Jack. On the other side, the lyrics printed over a diagram of a scooter perform a similar interplay between past and present. The colour transformation of the mod target on the label of the vinyl disc and the Immediate Records typography is another visual blending of the 'then' and 'now' out of which the album as a whole gains its force. Once again the iconographic elisions that are taking place here represent the new direction, one fuelled from an earlier power source and described by Charles Shaar Murray in the *NME* as 'Weller's reaffirmation of a specific mod consciousness'. For those with short memories, or those who were too young to remember the mid-1960s, Shaar Murray offers a brief history lesson: 'Remember the mod ideal: it was a working class consciousness that stressed independence, fun and fashion without loss of integrity or descent into elitism of consumerism' (Shaar Murray 1978: 43).

The working-class consciousness manifests itself here in the cover version of the Kinks' 'David Watts', a tune that feeds energy into the equally acute social observations found in 'Mr Clean', almost an 'adult version' of the Ray Davies original in its bitter invective directed towards the Oxbridge educated, *Times*-reading, upper-middle-class elite. It also anticipates 'The Eton Rifles' in voicing disdain for those who maintain the rigidity of the class system to suit their own prerogatives. Like the first wave of mods, Weller was attempting to resist social imposition through regenerating a sense of working class pride, confidence and solidarity in his own reworking of the original subculture: delivering an ideology and attitude through which a new identity – and it *was* new for many listeners in 1978 – could be discovered and thought about. This was something more realistic and realizable than the dead-end fantasies of 'Billy Hunt' who dreams of being Clark Kent, James Bond or the Bionic Man, and far removed from the thug mentality of National Front supporters and small-time criminals haunting tube stations late at night. Like the music of the Who (circa 1965), the Jam in their first two albums wrote songs about working-class life, boosted by the equally class-conscious energy and anger of punk in its early days, an anger that was also balanced by more self-reflective compositions about what to do and where to go with the identity that one's social position conferred. On *All Mod Cons* that same territory is extended both lyrically and musically as Weller integrates psychedelic influences into an album which pushes even further the experience of listening into something beyond the purely recreational and into areas where ideas about the re-creation of the self can be explored.

Weller has often commented upon how awful he found the music of the early–mid-1970s, and although he first embraced punk as a welcome kick up the loon pants of glam and prog rock it did not fully compensate for the musical and cultural rupture that the Jam were working to cure. In so doing they were tracing a line back to something that had been lost in British music sometime around 1968, when psychedelia gave way to full-blown hippiedom. Interestingly enough, one of the records that Weller selected on *Desert Island Discs* in 2007 was James Brown's 'Don't be a Dropout', in many ways a subtext to the Jam's rejection of punk and their own attempt to create a 'youth explosion' as punk itself was imploding in the wake of the Sex Pistols' long drawn out demise. While the brief title track to *All Mod Cons* shared many sentiments with the yet-to-be-released *The Great Rock and Roll Swindle,* especially in exposing the cynical and exploitative nature of the music industry, Weller quickly carried on with the mod-like task of observing the way of the world and engaging the listener to get to grips with the present. 'To Be Someone (Didn't We Have A Nice Time?)' is almost an antidote to the title track in unashamedly celebrating working-class fantasies about making good as a footballer, film star or pop star. While it acknowledges the ephemeral nature of celebrity and is clearly a lyrical transference of some of Paul Weller's own concerns and fears, the cautionary tale ultimately suggests that this singer will be sticking to his guns and will not turn out to be one of the lost and forgotten 'bastard sons': something borne out as the thematic concerns of the album unfold.

'In the Crowd' is the third Weller song to warn of the dangers of conformity, consumerism and media manipulation, and the *Revolver*-like backward guitar fade-out is an alternative psychedelic space running counter to the crowd in its provision of an aural context where the true self can be freely experienced. In 'Don't Be a Dropout', James Brown sings about the importance of getting an education, something that Weller received via the music of an earlier generation, allowing him to craft his songs and identity out of an interplay between the mid-1960s and late 1970s and inject them with a proactive countercultural philosophy that invites the listener to tune in and turn on, but not drop out. In the same way that 'English Rose' finds the patriotic and romantic narrator returning to his homeland and his love, so Weller maintains the tradition of English pop/rock through continually returning to explore it and so use the themes and ideas found there as a source of inspiration for his own 'lost' generation. Herein lies a musical and cultural heritage to be proud of, one that provides the foundation for a better future – rather than no future – and one that also supplies the critical acumen to examine questions concerning the nature of Englishness and both national and individual identity with clear sightedness.

Originally conceived as an album based on the lives of three friends growing up and growing apart politically as the result of a civil war, leaving one on the political left, one on the right and one in the middle, *Setting Sons* (November 1979) still displays aspects of this vague idea, but is more tied together by the themes and ideas explored through the artwork and the individual songs rather than the original narrative concept. On the back cover and inner sleeve, the Union Jack is once more in evidence, this time as the fabric of a deckchair guarded by a British bulldog on (of all places) Brighton beach. The setting is probably another ironic nod towards the mod revival, now at the height of fashion since the release of Franc Roddam's *Quadrophenia* in September of the same year. However, Andrew Douglas's front cover photograph of Benjamin Clemens's 1919 sculpture 'The St. John's Ambulance Bearers' offers a much deeper register in warning of the conflicts and consequences that can arise from blind allegiance to the flag, and the dangers inherent in nationalistic politics. Both the sculpture and its reproduction also pay homage to those who resisted, and who continue to resist, war and the ideology of Empire, further images of which are found on the inner sleeve collage made up of a First World War infantry uniform, what look like several small illustrations from Britain's colonial past, and a medal half buried in the mud. The Pears' soap advertisement carries suggestions of home 'under an English heaven' (Keynes 1970: 43), a false impression related to the political 'soft-soaping' that Weller is trying to wash away. The contrast between the images on the front and back of the album cover (and the record liner) offers a way of thinking beyond the more jingoistic aspects of national identity, and beyond the vacuous use of the Union Jack as decoration or fashion, towards a historical understanding that takes account of the crimes committed under what Weller ironically refers to as the flag of democracy in 'Little Boy Soldiers'. While acknowledging the imperialistic past, there is also a way in which *Setting Sons* is working to disengage the Union Jack from its more negative, nationalistic, 'Queen and country' associations, and to reclaim it in an act of sabotage that recalls something of the ways in which the original mods used it and identified with it.

The historical analysis of 'Little Boy Soldiers' is matched by contemporary observation, with Weller writing about class war in 'The Eton Rifles', where the elite are portrayed as both the inheritors and benefactors of the 'Rule Britannia' spirit that he wishes to expunge from the Union Jack. The fact that David Cameron, an old Etonian himself, listed the track as one of his favourite songs during an interview on the BBC Radio 4 broadcast, *The Jam Generation* (March 2008), shows how its message occasionally misfired, with the song being adopted by the very privileged subjects who it attacked. It was just this kind of cultural appropriation and establishment sentiment that Paul Weller was writing against: 'Which part of it didn't he get? It wasn't intended as a fucking jolly drinking song for the cadet corps' (Wilson 2008). At the same time the song is also critical of the new Left for protesting outside the House of Commons, for composing revolutionary anthems while sleeping with the enemy and – worst of all – for running away and abandoning the very people they were supposed to be fighting for when faced with the reality of physically violent clashes. The working classes, it seems, would have to fend for themselves.

Many early reviews remark that Paul Weller matches Ray Davies in his observations of English life and – as 'The Eton Rifles' suggests – he offers lyrical snapshots of all classes in the social panorama that binds *Setting Sons*, and many other Jam albums, together. Middle-class characters like the unfortunate Smithers-Jones, who is made redundant after years of sacrificing himself for his 'sun tanned boss', are also victims of the ruling classes. 'Private Hell' narrates the alienation and isolation of a middle-aged and (supposedly) middle-class housewife in a boring, loveless marriage, whose children have moved away, never keep in touch, and just do not care because they too are all living similarly lonely and depressing lives. 'Burning Sky' is an epistolary song in which the narrator laments losing touch with his old friends, but his work in the financial sector has changed his priorities and led him to abandon his formerly held values and dreams. 'Burning Sky' obviously represents the self-serving capitalist system, in which the cold indifference of the 'greedy' to the mortals living in the 'little' world recalls 'Big Sky' on *The Kinks are The Village Green Preservation Society* (1968). Once again such a thematic identification underlines how Weller, like his artistic predecessors, was motivated by a desire to alter the perception of the record buying public and get them to think more deeply about the world and the structures that contain and control them.

'Burning Sky' paints a pessimistic picture, but it can also be read in positive terms as a statement of intent designed to clarify the vision of the listener. Weller seeks to elucidate, educate and motivate through upping the intellectual register and in so doing encourage those who have identified with the sentiments and ideas expressed on the album to become more forward-looking: to be realists, but also modernist dreamers in the anticipation of a better present and future. There may be no direct answers given, but there is a provision of material and knowledge from out of which answers can be found. Invested as it is with vignettes of working-class life and hierarchical injustice, *Setting Sons* offers what we might call a bleak condition of England album, but one in which those who inhabit Weller's 'Wasteland' are being armed through a social and political awareness to question and challenge the kind of repressive 'system' that is attacked in 'Saturday's Kids'. Here in their fourth album, the Jam place their socialist cards face up on the table in a record that continues to show them urging for a new reaction, a new direction – both musically and politically – re-energizing pop through a contemporary reworking of mod that is helping to repair some of the damage and despair expressed in Jamie Reid's 'Anarchy in the UK' poster. While both Reid and Weller are suggesting that symbols like the Union Jack can only have any real meaning if we continue to question what it is that they represent, it is the Jam who are more active and urgent in their efforts to find a way to put the flag back together again and help repair something of the crisis of national identity that characterized Britain and the popular music scene in the aftermath of punk.

References

BBC Radio 4, (2007), Desert Island Discs, 16 December. Available online: http://www.bbc.co.uk/programmes/b008gh41.

BBC Radio 4, (2008), The Jam Generation, 4 March.

Clarke, S. (1977), 'All Change and Back to 1964 … The Jam', *New Musical Express*, 7 May.

Cohen, S. (2011), *Folk Devils and Moral Panics The Creation of the Mods and Rockers*, Oxford: Routledge Classics [1972].

Heatley, M. (ed.) (1996), *Paul Weller in His Own Words*, London: Omnibus Press.

Hewitt, P. (1983), *The Jam: A Beat Concerto*, London: Riot Stories/Omnibus Press.

Hewitt, P. (2008), *Paul Weller: The Changing Man*, London: Corgi.

Keynes, J. (ed.) (1970), *The Poetical Works of Rupert Brooke*, London: Faber and Faber [1946].

Nicholls, M. (1984), *About the Young Idea: The Story of The Jam*, London: Proteus Books.

Perry, M. (2009), *Sniffin' Glue: And Other Rock 'n' Roll Habits*, London: Omnibus Press.

Savage, J. (2005), *England's Dreaming Sex Pistols and Punk Rock*, London: Faber and Faber.

Shaar Murray, C. (1978), 'All Mod Cons The Jam', *New Musical Express*, 28 October.

Weight, R. (2013), *Mod A Very British Style*, London: The Bodley Head.

Wilson, J. (2008), 'Chasing the Blues Away', *The New Statesman*, 15 May. Available online: http://www.newstatesman.com/music/2008/05/paul-weller-jam-album-song.

Discography

Thomas Arne (1740) Rule, Britannia!

The Beatles (1966) *Revolver,* Parlophone [Album]

James Brown (1966) Don't Be A Drop-Out, King [Single]

The Creation (1966) Bif, Bang, Pow, Sonet [Single]

The Jam (1977) *This is the Modern World,* Polydor Records [Album]

The Jam (1977) All Around the World, *This is the Modern World,* Polydor Records [Album]

The Jam (1977) Here Comes the Weekend, *This is the Modern World,* Polydor Records [Album]

The Jam (1977) Life From a Window, *This is the Modern World,* Polydor Records [Album]

The Jam (1977) London Girl, *This is the Modern World,* Polydor Records [Album]

The Jam (1977) Standards, *This is the Modern World,* Polydor Records [Album]

The Jam (1977) The Combine, *This is the Modern World,* Polydor Records [Album]

The Jam (1977) *In the City,* Polydor Records [Album]

The Jam (1977) Art School, *In the City,* Polydor Records [Album]

The Jam (1977) Away From The Numbers, *In the City,* Polydor Records [Album]

The Jam (1978) English Rose, *All Mod Cons,* Polydor Records [Album]

The Jam (1978) *All Mod Cons, Polydor Records* [Album]

The Jam (1978) Billy Hunt, *All Mod Cons,* Polydor Records [Album]

The Jam (1978) In the Crowd, *All Mod Cons,* Polydor Records [Album]

The Jam (1978) Mr Clean, *All Mod Cons,* Polydor Records [Album]

The Jam (1978) To Be Someone (Didn't We Have A Nice Time?), *All Mod Cons,* Polydor Records [Album]

The Jam (1979) *Setting Sons,* Polydor Records [Album]

The Jam (1979) Burning Sky, *Setting Sons,* Polydor Records [Album]

The Jam (1979) Little Boy Soldiers, *Setting Sons,* Polydor Records [Album]

The Jam (1979) Private Hell, *Setting Sons,* Polydor Records [Album]

The Jam (1979) Saturday's Kids, *Setting Sons,* Polydor Records [Album]

The Jam (1979) Smithers-Jones, *Setting Sons,* Polydor Records [Album]

The Jam (1979) The Eton Rifles, Polydor Records [Single]

The Kinks (1967) David Watts, Reprise [Single]

The Kinks (1968) *The Kinks Are the Village Green Preservation Society,* Pye [Album]

The Kinks (1968) Big Sky, *The Kinks Are the Village Green Preservation Society,* Pye [Album]

Sex Pistols (1977) Anarchy in the U.K., EMI [Single]

Sex Pistols (1979) *The Great Rock 'n' Roll Swindle,* Virgin Records [Album]

The Who (1966) I'm A Boy, Reaction Records [Single]

CHAPTER FOUR

PJ Harvey and remembering England

Abigail Gardner

Introduction

PJ Harvey is an English musician who has, to date, enjoyed a career spanning nearly a quarter of a century. She comes from Dorset, a rural county in the south-west of England, where she still lives. This fact is important because it locates her in a particular rural and potentially 'pastoral' place, one that is far away from the metropolitan, from Thomas Hardy's 'madding crowd'. This chapter focuses on *White Chalk* (2007) and *Let England Shake* (2011) to argue that they are her 'English' albums, a claim that rests not only on their musical temperament, lyrical concerns or audio-visual representation, but also on the nature of how they remember England, especially when this collides with narratives of war and home. Remembering is often selective and selection is part of the archiving process. What we leave in or out of the archive dictates in turn what is or is not remembered. In these two albums, Harvey presents a version of Englishness that adds to contemporary discourses on (and memories of) national identity by foregrounding the forgotten, the rural, the disappointed; by narrating tales of love and war that are not those of victory or triumph but of longing and loss.

For clarity of navigation, throughout the chapter a music video or short film will be written in capitals (WHITE CHALK), the album titles will be in italics (*White Chalk*) and a song track from an album will be within quotation marks ('White Chalk').

Harvey has been recording since the early 1990s, has won the UK Mercury Prize twice and might be considered to be one of the country's most long-standing and important musicians. Her 2011 work, *Let England Shake*, on land and nation cemented her musical and intellectual reputation. She has been awarded an MBE, an honorary degree from Goldsmiths, University of London, has conducted poetry readings at the British Museum and guest edited on BBC Radio 4; she has been taken into the folds of the intellectual elite. It is even tempting to start thinking about her as a 'national treasure', whereby she is rehabilitated from the wilds of the independent music shores to take part in a shared cultural life.

This chapter interrogates how and why this has happened and argues that it is, in part, due to her narration of Englishness and what aspects of it are remembered. To map this out, the discussion entails an analysis of the development over Harvey's recent career (2007–11) and of audio-visual aspects of her work that might be construed as 'English', particularly in relation to locality and land (Aughey 2007). One of the questions asked here is whether these aspects might be seen to culminate in her more recent work at a time when nation and identity may be considered to be pertinent political and cultural themes. In this sense, the chapter asks whether her albums are part of an archiving process that contributes to a reframing of Englishness.

Harvey the archivist

In an other work (Gardner 2015), I have argued that Harvey is an archivist, in that she collects, curates and presents alternative versions and visions of the past, predominantly those of past femininities. Sifting through what is presented to her from the past, she has reinhabited them and reconfigured them, questioning their legacies with irony and camp humour. In a similar fashion she does the same in *White Chalk* and *Let England Shake*, the first of which is concerned with matrilineal histories and rural place, the second where she presents a tapestry of Englishness that has as its metanarrative an idea of nation as configured through loss, war and remembrance. Harvey's lyrical concerns in these two albums centre not only on land and belonging, but also on how that land and allegiance to it are archived and remembered. In *Let England Shake* in particular, Englishness is defined in relation to land and war and, crucially, what is recorded (literally, through the audio archiving that is the record) becomes Harvey's archive of Englishness. It is a radical reimagining of England at a time when its mythology and status were under debate. What she does on this album, the process of setting down on record, the audio inscription, is in line with Derrida's (1996) view in *Archive Fever* that the archive is not always about the past but can be about the future. It records what we are agreeing to remember of the past, specifically that of a mythologized pastoral England.

Harvey's stories people the land with voices that have been marginalized or under-explored. We hear laments from wounded soldiers (2011), young women abandoned by their lovers (2007), we see, in Seamus Murphy's films, young gamekeepers, elderly men and women. Harvey rescues these ordinary accounts and pastes them onto the received trope of Englishness that are the stock imagery of an old and pastoral England, across meadows, beaches, fields, oak trees and milestones. These two albums fit into a wider compulsion across contemporary British popular culture to retrieve from history the voices of those previously unheard and to focus on the emotional weight they have. The BBC's 2016–17 year of popular music memories ('My Generation') is one example of the mediation of musical memories and emotional attachment. Emotion has featured in academic work on media in general (Doveling, von Scheve and Konijn 2010; Gorton 2009; Garde-Hansen and Gorton 2013) and is visible in recent additions to the popular music canon (Juslin and Sloboda 2010; Hesmondhalgh 2013). Harvey's albums express a narrative of Englishness that articulates the emotional ties to family and land that are themselves emergent from older archives of Englishness such as musical expressions, melodic structures, military archives, all of which Harvey has consulted and reinterpreted, producing in turn her own archive of Englishness.

Harvey emerged onto the UK 'independent' or 'indie' music scene in the early 1990s and has, to date, produced nine solo studio albums. 'Indie' is a term whose 'exact definition and boundaries are open to dispute' (Leonard 2007: 4). It has been, and continues to be, a topic of debate across popular music, both in academia and within industry discourses and Moore's (2003) oft-cited paper positions it as a construct characterized by 'rawness' (Frith and Horne 1988: 88) and unmediated communication. It has become allied to a white masculinity (Bannister 2006b; Leach 2001) despite its historical link to 'difference' (Bannister 2006a: 58) and countercultural possibilities, particularly with providing space for women to perform and produce (Leonard 2007). A seam through all of these conversations is the notion of 'authenticity'. This term, itself much debated, arguably determines how punk and folk music have been discursively situated within a polarity, at the opposite end of which sits 'pop' (Hesmondhalgh 1999: 56). Throughout the 1990s and early 2000s, Harvey mined a seam of gothic blues and garage punk so that both her early output and later albums might be corralled into such generic parameters. However, keen to cross musical genres, her Mercury Prize winning 2001 album *Stories from the City, Stories from the Sea* experimented with a fuller sound. Six years later, she released, *White Chalk* (2007), which was pared down, piano-led and, arguably, more versed within a folk tradition. *Let England Shake* (2011) continued this line of creative direction.

These two albums herald a shift towards a consideration of country (side) and belonging that work as audio-visual renditions of a radical pastoralism. That is, Harvey uses musical and visual tropes of rural and imagined England as material upon which to stage narratives that foreground the place of land and countryside within personal stories of gendered (2007) and national (2011) identity. In their work on popular music and place, Connell and Gibson articulate how the term 'nation' is a contested concept 'that provides the basis for debates in society about cultural difference, uniqueness and attachments to territory' (Connell and Gibson 2003: 123). Their last assertion that national identity is tied up with relationships to land plays the biggest role in Harvey's two 'English' albums.

Finding England

The idea of 'Englishness' and England has become ripe for reconsideration within the academy as writers on popular culture trace out emerging imaginations of Englishness with respect to identity and place (Bunting 2009), politics (Kenny 2014) and popular culture (Featherstone 2009). But England as a geographical place and as a national or regional identity has figured less in popular music accounts, partly because, as Moy suggests, it remains 'problematic' (Moy 2007: 56). These problems are to do with definitions, absences and appropriations. Aughey (2007) has argued that 'Englishness' as a term has been fraught with political tensions because concerns with the soil (often conflated with continuity) lie at odds with a progressive politics and this is very clearly marked in folk music, which as Winter and Keegan-Phipps note, is enjoying a 'resurgence' (2013). Their ethnographic and musicological study notes that while the 1980s saw the start of a body of work on Englishness as a 'scholarly ... political and a cultural, concern' (2013: 3), there has been little investigation into Englishness and folk music, which they address. *White Chalk* and *Let England Shake* are not folk albums, but they borrow some of the genre's idioms, instrumentation and melodic structures. Arguably, this is because folk music has a stronger bond with English national identity than the blues-rock of Harvey's earlier work; she is 'coming home' in a sense. It is possible to read these albums and particularly *Let England Shake* as part of the 'resurgent' Englishness that Winter and Keegan-Phipps claim for English folk music, so that the albums are read as indicative of 'an English cultural sensibility or sense of English national identity rather than nationalism' (Winter and Keegan-Phipps 2013: 132). However, delineating such boundaries is difficult, and Winter and Keegan-Phipps note that there have been cases where folk music has been appropriated by the Far Right, which in turn has been countered by movements such as Folk Against Fascism.

Let England Shake utilizes English folk idiom to present an album that mixes such traditions with diverse interjections of reggae and Bulgarian choirs to offer a sound palette that suggests the fluidity and diversity of nation. In a review for *The Guardian*, Alexis Petridis noted how its 'guitars [were] wreathed in echo', how it used 'muzzy electric piano' and 'smears of brass', all leading to an album whose take on Englishness was, he argued, 'muted, misty and ambiguous' (2011). Throughout the album there is an ambiguity of narratorial position that makes it difficult to discern a sympathetic identificatory standpoint, although it offers the listener an insight into what belonging and partisanship might feel like as Harvey sings disparagingly about Europeans and claims allegiance to England in the rhetoric of the patriot. This ambiguity did not stop the album being conflated with a Far Right agenda. The short film for *Let England Shake* was posted up for around eight months from April 2012 on a nationalist website, where below an image of the Cross of St George, seemingly rendered in blood against snow, under the title 'Let England Shake', Harvey's film sat among anti-Semitic, anti-Muslim and white supremacist posts and adverts. With links to Far Right parties and organizations across Europe, the presence of Harvey's name on the site is illustrative of the tensions that folk music, in particular, has had as a consequence of its embrace by the Far Right. There is much therefore at stake in the term, 'Englishness'. It is perhaps not surprising that it was the image of 'Punch' from the film that took pride of place on the Birmingham Nationalist blog spot. Perhaps what connected Punch to this site was that this eponymous bruiser was a cipher for a specific British masculinity, pugilistic and peculiar to England, and for nationalist rhetoric it indicated how this past might be fighting back. The blog is now removed and its presence and subsequent absence indicate the tussle of what, and what is not 'English'.

Harvey: English rural

If there is a problem with defining Englishness in general, and how it might be situated within popular music more specifically, then there is a real problem when we get to trying to attach the label to Harvey. She has always made a play in her lyrics and music video performances of not 'fitting' in (see MANSIZE, 1993; 50ft QUEENIE, 1993) and this is apparent when we start to consider her as an English artist in relation to other musicians whose national identity has been marked in their work or representation.

Throughout her career up to 2011, her national identity has been incidental, neither key to her representation nor to her lyrical concerns or musical influences. She has been positioned within a transatlantic canon, alongside other Anglo-American female musicians such as Courtney Love or Tori Amos (Whiteley 2001; Burns and Lafrance 2000) indicating that her work has been considered as part of a broader, international genre of 'indie' rather than an alliance to any specific national musical or aesthetic heritage.

Harvey is not an 'English artist' in the way, for example that Kate Bush is (Moy 2007) and I want to use Bush as a benchmark to frame this section on Harvey as English rural. Moy argues that Bush's accent, delivery, lyrics and instrumentation are specifically and uniquely 'English' (2007: 61). Harvey's back catalogue certainly does not match this, and it is only in recent work (2007, 2011) where she has turned to instruments that might be coded as potentially, but not exclusively, English (the autoharp, the Mellotron). This she does to evoke versions of Englishness and to refer back to musical traditions that she adds to. Neither can she be allied to Bush's version of English 'eccentricity'. This derives, in Bush's case, from working within a musical and aesthetic tradition that derives partly from a middle-class progressive rock or psychedelic lineage, whose discourse has been typified by a reification of theatricality and whimsy (Hegarty and Halliwell 2011; Reynolds and Press 2005: 57; Whiteley 2003) and partly from romanticism, a discourse deployed within popular music to foreground creativity and genius (Negus and Pickering 2002).

She is not an 'English' artist in the way that the Kinks or Ian Dury, the Jam, Paul Weller or the Libertines are, and she is not part of a 'long lineage of mythically English bands and performers' (Moy 2007: 57). She is not concerned with the minutiae of suburbia, concentrating on the travails of suburban love and frustration and so cannot be conflated with that constructed sense of 'Englishness' that was subsumed under the 'Britishness' that was Britpop, where 'nostalgic images of small-town and suburban working-class life grounded the music in specific locales' (Connell and Gibson 2003: 125). Her work does not 'fit' with a retro Britpop that was largely underpinned by a constructed English masculinity, premised in turn on nostalgia for the 1960s (Bennett and Stratton 2010). Being neither Northern, nor Southern, nor male, she sat outside the narratives of Englishness that have appeared across British popular music culture in the mid-1990s. Within the available constructs of national identity that had appeared within the British popular music industry, there was nowhere where she fitted, and there was nothing about her music, influences, lyrical concerns, or instrumentation that could be identified as particularly 'English'.

Harvey therefore is an English artist by default, not an artist whose work has carried with it specific markers of Englishness that have surfaced in popular music discourses. Her identity, as such as it has been referred to in reviews and interviews with her, has placed her as a regional artist, located within a specific rural place. Any reference to identity in terms of location or provenance has been not on 'country' but on 'county', specifically on Dorset, her home. This largely agricultural country in the southwest of England has figured more, particularly in press representation. Kitty Empire (2011a) positions *Let England Shake* as 'an agrarian polemic' and Harvey is arguably positioned as being rooted in a 'Deep England', a 'Southern Metaphor' of England (Winter and Keegan-Phipps 2013: 116) signified by 'Dorset' and 'farm'. There is again an implied eccentricity in this affiliation to a rural place (that chimes with how Kate Bush has recently been mediated in sections of the UK press, e.g. Harmsworth 2014; McNulty 2014), which is associated with her refusal to conform to norms or rock stardom (Moy 2007) and remain located in the rural.

Authenticity is bound up in the idea of this rural space (Moy 2007: 37; Connell and Gibson 2003). It is allied to the pastoral and coded as idyllic (see Winter and Keegan-Phipps 2013), lying, as it does, as opposite to the urban and its troubles, and most often associated with a conservatism that sees it as unchanging and to be preserved as such (Aughey 2007). In this respect, the rural that has been referred to within academic debates on the folk resurgence across England and on Englishness within the broader cultural sphere, is reliant upon the notion of the Pastoral. This is a long-standing literary conceit, which has its echoes within classical and popular music and which appears too in contemporaneous media reviews of the videos for the album (Newman 2011). Literary theorist Gifford (1999) identifies three interwoven strands of the pastoral within literature whereby it – and 'it' refers to an idealized rural space (forest, wood, meadow for example) – has one of three dominant functions.

The first function of the pastoral, seen in Renaissance drama and poetry particularly, is where it acts as an imaginative space outside of the ordinary, beyond the boundaries of the urban, the real and the possible and thereby offers a retreat from the urban. Upon return from it, the protagonist is afforded a sense of renewal. Gifford's second framing of the term is to note it as a conventional rural setting and the third is a pejorative one that critiques the second – where ideas of nature as benign and rural idyll come under scrutiny. The pastoral has surfaced within the English creative arts and English classical and folk music, from William Morris's Arts and Crafts Movement and Cecil Sharpe's English Folk Song and Dance Society, which might be corralled into what Moy terms the 'English pastoral project' (2007: 61), some of which was defined by a desire to collect and protect a national culture against a European (most notably a German) one. What characterizes the English pastoral in classical music is the use of a sonic palette that is the opposite of the mathematical baroque and classical German. Moy argues that the English pastoral, as illustrated by Vaughan Williams, is 'a more impressionistic terrain often expressed through "washes" of sound' (2007: 61) with the use of strings and wind rather than brass. Across Europe, composers such as Béla Bartók were also looking to folk music for inspiration, and utilizing folk melodies in their work. Recourse to the 'folk' has therefore been a form of a retreat to the pastoral, done to regain and renew, and Moy argues that this is apparent in Kate Bush's work and in progressive and psychedelic English rock (2007: 61).

Harvey's work on *White Chalk* and *Let England Shake* is not pastoral in the sense of using the English countryside as an idyllic place of retreat and return, despite the urban commentators' reading of it (Newman 2011); rather she, and Murphy, utilize rural landscapes pejoratively. In both albums, the natural (English) world is used as a setting for disappointment, death and war. It rots bones ('White Chalk'), its tree branches are home to body parts ('These Are the Words that Maketh Murder') and its milestones are the stage for doomed love affairs ('The Devil'). This is not a picturesque pastoral in any way. The farm workers that we see in Murphy's films (THE WORDS THAT MAKETH MURDER) may stride across a field swathed in the mists of dawn but as they do, Harvey sings about how (she) has seen and done things that she regrets. Bell ringers may be filmed in their belfry but as they ring out their bells, they are accompanied by Harvey singing about soldiers burying their dead ('In the Dark Places'). Writing from a rural perspective, Harvey is reinvesting the pastoral with the reality of the repercussions of war upon those who live there.

It is in the representing and repeopling of this rural English space that what is key to understanding Harvey's work as related to Englishness emerges. Most crucially, what is important is not how Harvey might be conceived of as 'English', rather it is what she has to say about how we might remember Englishness that positions her work as a contribution to articulations of Englishness, since it is in the remembering that the construction of both the present and the future notions of such an identity are formed. Harvey uses this space as somewhere to review and consider the past, and in *White Chalk* she focuses on women's relationships to men, to each other, to children in an audio-visual language and instrumentation that is, arguably, more influenced by English folk song writing traditions than previous work. It is what she does with this format that marks her out as important and as a commentator on Englishness as presented in folk narrative and myth. *White Chalk* sees her upsetting the English rural idyll by ushering in narratives of death and violence.

White Chalk: Harvey's return of the native

England's Jurassic Coast is known for harbouring dinosaur bones. Stretching across its southern counties Dorset and Devon, it has been famous since Victorian times for its fossils, its prehistoric possibilities. The cliffs of the Jurassic Coast are white and sheer, and they crumble regularly down onto the pebble beaches into the sea. The white chalk within these cliffs appears across the hills of Dorset and it is within these hills that Harvey in *White Chalk* sings that her bones will rot. The track is from an album of the same name, released in 2007, and it heralded the start of Harvey's mining of Englishness.

White Chalk acts as a transitional piece, whereby she moves from the concerns of previous work where desire, sexuality and home are apparent, towards a more explicit concern with home and connection to the land and nation. In the 1990s and up to *Stories From the City*, Harvey was interrogating different modes of femininity, working out how to fit into its templates and picking through archives of its imagery to try on and reformulate what gendered identity might be (Burns and Lafrance 2002; Gardner 2015). In *White Chalk* she is still concerned with love and loss but importantly the land upon which these narratives play out becomes predominant. Her lyrics begin to use language from the rural English past, 'milestone' is referred to in 'The Devil' and 'Dorset' is named in the title track.

This marks a contrast with the references to San Diego, New York, Mexico, Brooklyn and the Empire State Building that appeared across *Stories from the City, Stories from the Sea*, particularly in the track 'Beautiful Feeling'. The album cover for *Stories* had Harvey looking out at the viewer from behind dark sunglasses on a neon-lit city street.

In stark contrast to this, *White Chalk*'s album cover sees her dressed in a full-length, white, Victorian-era dress. It has puffed sleeves, a bustle, is tight across the torso and Harvey is sat on a chair, with her hands neatly folded on her lap, her hair a mass of black curls, looking straight at the camera. She is staring out from the past as she replays it. Harvey, like Cindy Sherman, has used photography and music video performances (Gardner 2015) to perform stereotypes of the feminine. Like Sherman, she draws on a familiar archive of culture and 'stag[es] stereotypic figures from the image repertoire of femininity, fairy tales, or horror films' (Bronfen 1998: 416, 418). Harvey mines this history of the silent Victorian feminine to foreground the allure of the archive and one's performance within it. She looks back at this particular archive of feminine imagery and re-represents it in a way that forces a rethinking, that may, as Butler (1993) argues, challenge our conventional reading of what gendered identity might be. Here she is presenting a version of femininity that is both familiar and strange. We can understand that this is an old photograph of a young woman taken possibly around a century ago; Harvey's image, staged as this photographed Victorian, bears the imprint of the real or, as Hirsch describes it, in a work on family photography and loss, 'the photograph gives the illusion of being a simple transcription of the real' (2002: 7).

But we know that this is a fake, that Harvey is playing around with what the past might be and who might have inhabited it. By investing herself in this past, she manages to bring it back 'in the form of a ghostly revenant, emphasising, at the same time, its immutable and irreversible pastness and irretrievability' (2002: 20). This version of femininity is long gone but its existence in the form of a recognizable photograph of somebody's ancestor renders it somehow readable within the parameters of the conventions of the family photograph. Without the context of stories, narratives that knit the family story together through the photographic album, this photo, de-serialized and de-contextualized, becomes at the same time a young woman who is both known and unknown to us. Harvey has put herself into a family photograph album and then emptied it of content and context, foregrounding how heritage, lineage and our pasts are at once strange and familiar.

Videos for the album also mined this seam of upright Victorian femininity, repressed and corseted, with an image of Harvey in a black version of the album cover dress sitting at an upright piano that accompanied the video for 'When under Ether'. Live performances of the album saw her dressed similarly, with Victorian lamps and decorations adorning the piano she played. Harvey is not an accomplished pianist and she learnt the instrument for the album in order to refresh her approach and come up with new sounds. In contrast to the electric guitar, which had been her instrument of choice up until then, the piano is strongly coded as feminine (Bayton 2007). The Victorian lady was expected to be accomplished on it. But the gap between her and the piano in the video THE DEVIL is telling; it is the gap between her artistry and the presentation of herself as feminine. This particular version of the feminine, one from the nineteenth century, is 'strange' to her, and, as she sings of insanity, pining and the Devil, she performs stereotypes of the literary nineteenth-century female: the mad woman in the attic, the pining gothic heroine. She adds herself into an English Victorian archive, and we might consider that this is a reflection on where she sits in relation to 'rooted' musical practices and regional memory. It is part of her heritage and yet she is temporally removed from it. She becomes the ghost, the governess, the Victorian upright, uptight. Revisiting Victoriana in lyrics and visual aesthetics, she travels back in time, making herself present where she was absent. Harvey's performances are conversations with the past, specifically with visualized memories of archetypes of femininity and have to be understood in relation to what they say of the past, about the weight of history and the ways in which she controls and commands her own archive.

A ghostly Englishness is implied through these visuals and the vocal technique that characterized the album, which was a departure from the guitar led 'indie rock' that she had arguably worked within prior to this. Her image evokes a lost femininity, and the lyrics circulate around loss; of grandmothers ('To Talk to You'), unborn children ('When under Ether'), of childhood ('White Chalk') and of love ('The Devil'). The instrumentation underpins this sense of loss; all of the tracks on the album are piano-led bar one, the title track, and the piano is treated with reverb and echo to make it sound old. She uses a Mellotron, which is a synthesized keyboard that had been used in progressive rock in the 1970s by bands like King Crimson and The Moody Blues. This ties her back to a previous English genre that, in turn, was fascinated by earlier English myths and legends. The zither (or autoharp) appears too, and figures more predominantly in *Let England Shake*, as does the banjo. These two instruments are rare in Anglo-American popular music, and are more commonly featured in folk music on both sides of the Atlantic and foreground the sense that Harvey is returning to some form of musical roots. These roots are further emphasized by references to inanimate objects and landmarks such as oak trees (in 'Grow, Grow, Grow'), white cliffs ('White Chalk') and milestones ('The Devil'), all three of which prioritize a sense of rural and a historical landscape, one within which Harvey locates her *White Chalk* protagonists. These white chalk cliffs of Dorset act as a backdrop not just to her own life, from childhood to death, but evoke a sense of the ancient; they have paths cut through them that are 1,500 years old. They are markers of both place and nation representing the specific (Dorset) and England (the oak tree).

Set against these backdrops, the stories that Harvey tells remain focused on the women's experiences of love and violence. They are connected by a strong sense of female lineage; the protagonist in 'To Talk to You' yearns for her grandmother, women grieve for their lost children, their own lost childhood and others' childhoods before them. The album therefore treads similar ground to Harvey's previous work around gender, desire and loss, but what marks it out as different is its focus on place and the past. Harvey is starting to consider how home and history act not merely as stages for her narratives, but drive them. This concern is manifest throughout the album that came after *White Chalk*, whose very title is an exhortation to radicalize, to review, to literally 'shake' things up. Harvey uses the past, its archives and myths, its language, as the pastoral. She uses it in an anti-nostalgic way that also manages to comment on nostalgia: Harvey's pasts are not a place to retreat to in opposition to an anxiety-fuelled present; they were just as troubled.

Remembering England: Shaking England beyond nostalgia

The nostalgic mindset conceives of a time somewhere in the past that was comprehensible, unlike the incoherence that plagues the present (Lowenthal 1985: 40), and so it operates in a similar fashion to the pastoral but in time, not space. However, Harvey's pasts are fraught with loss and suffering too and so she upsets the past as nostalgic pastoral. It is worth considering how she treats the past through Borges' concept of 'once upon a time', since it offers a creative reading of the phrase that maps well onto what she does. Aughey details how Borges reads the phrase as a mask of the present and not as a mirror of the past, in that it obstructs and veils rather than narrates; it is 'not even the remotest of historical moments but [is] a current state of mind' (2007: 83). *Let England Shake*'s tales from Gallipoli and the Anzac trenches ('The Colour of the Earth') and from other wars where young men encountered hells from which some of them did not return, offer both specific and ambiguous 'once upon a times' and, in so doing, seek to question what England and Englishness might mean. *Let England Shake* was emblematic of a broader political/cultural race to claim such an identity and is partly responsible for that album's success; it won the prestigious UK music industry's Mercury Prize. But Harvey's rendition of nation is far from jingoistic. On the contrary, her stories of England, the place and its people are those of the forgotten, the ordinary and the universal, of national identity as felt and, in particular, of how it is remembered. We see images of letters possibly written home from the First World War trenches (THE GLORIOUS LAND) and Harvey herself conducted a great deal of archival research for the album. This is her attempt to overwrite the 'arche', to commence and command with different voices, to offer up alternative archives and untold stories.

It is important to note that *Let England Shake* was released in 2011, a year that saw summer riots scarring England's urban centres and dead soldiers arriving back from Afghanistan in body bags. It was a year when England fought its enemies abroad and itself at home. Harvey's album was well-timed to fit into a moment when the nation was asking questions of itself; what its role was, what its limits were, who felt 'at home' in it and who did not. It resonated at a time when England was being shaken, upset by internal and external conflict. Harvey's album that referred to war and home, nation and loss, was afforded a high level of publicity and promotion. She had appeared the year before on a current affairs television programme, *The Andrew Marr Show* (18 April 2010), where she discussed the war in Iraq and her research for the album. She sang 'The Words that Maketh Murder' in the studio to Marr and the incumbent UK prime minister, Gordon Brown, also a guest on the show. Harvey was appearing alongside the political elite and her work seemed to matter.

In a year in which London and other major cities erupted into riots, music journalist Kitty Empire saw in this album a serendipitous resonance, a 'once upon a now' that accords with Smith's view on remembering the past which 'does not necessarily indicate a desire to return there. Remembering the past should instead be seen as a way to express valid desires and concerns about the present' (Smith 2000, in Wilson 2005: 26). Seen thus, Harvey's work is similar in spirit to Bikhu Parekh's (2000) political view of national identity in relation to history, in which its history should be acknowledged not for the purpose of nostalgia but for the purpose of imagination; 'not [to] inspire collective loyalty alone but also [to] inspire critical reflection on that loyalty' (Aughey 2007: 115). *Let England Shake* is an imaginative and critical reflection on war and homeland. The spaces that we see and imagine in *Let England Shake* are an England of fogs, graveyards, the Thames, the white cliffs of Dover, ploughed fields and dead sea-captains. This is arguably an 'old' England, a collage of historical and politically important landscapes and literary characters that have peopled prose, poetry and song over many centuries. However, Harvey uses this heritage as a background on which she maps tales of war and brutality and sutures into that map songs of soldiers reminiscing about 'home'.

The lyrics are first-person narratives of soldiers returning and wanting to return; it is apparent that although England is the home for many of the narrators of the songs on the album, it is the concept of 'home' that Harvey is playing with. Home is a place of sensory belonging (Featherstone 2009: 73) as well as of a cultural and mythical allegiance; the lyrics conjure up a history that can be smelt and felt, and Harvey's depictions of wartime are visceral and evocative. *Let England Shake* sits a long way from the city; her lyrics and the majority of Murphy's images are of the land. She details its beauty and how it comes to define home, while indicating how the enormity of consequences for those men involved in battle are inconsequential to the locations on which those battles are played out. In Harvey's world, land, the countryside, is both beauty, home, identity but also impassively indifferent to their lives and deaths.

The album was recorded in a nineteenth-century church, in Eype, a small village on the Dorset coast (adding further to the authenticity of place and intent), and includes many descriptions of land in the album – of birds, insects, fields and forests, rivers, oceans and descriptions of how that land smells. There are 'lingering panoramic shots of the countryside' (Winter and Keegan-Phipps 2013: 116) interspersed with those that inhabit them – huntsmen, gamekeepers, ramblers, Punch and Judy shows, campanologists (IN THE DARK PLACES). Churches appear; we see spires in one film (BATTLESHIP HILL), and Harvey stands inside a church, wearing a black headscarf, autoharp in hand, against the hymn numbers on the hymn rack. Interwoven through these 'icons of timeless English rurality' (Winter and Keegan-Phipps 2013: 116) are images, too, of the urban and the abandoned; there are shots of bingo players, young men in hoodies, derelict fairgrounds and Punch and Judy shows, adding up to a heterogeneous snapshot of contemporary England seen through Murphy's photographic lens and adding to the sense of the 'land' as diverse and belonging to all. His shots of old, young, black and white, assert that Englishness, and England, is open to all. They add to the sense of radicalism that one might see Harvey as promoting by adding images of the urban and multicultural England to which Aughey was referring as the England of progressive politics and the future.

This might be reflected, too, in the use of samples that Harvey deploys on the album as they come from 1950s America, reggae and Eastern Europe. She weaves in Eddie Cochran's famous refrain from 'Summertime Blues' about taking problems to the United Nations, uses The Four Lads' 'Istanbul', samples Niney The Observer's 1971 reggae track 'Blood and Fire' as well as fragments of Bulgarian and Kurdish choral pieces, and uses the autoharp, an instrument more commonly associated with American folk music, especially the Carter Family. Harvey's work has been an amalgam of influences benefitting from networks of cultural flow (Connell and Gibson 2003:18). In this way, she maps out the differences within Englishness that are a mirror of a contemporary national identity, a patchwork of diasporic and transatlantic conversations, journeys and relationships.

Empire (2011b) also uses the phrase 'haunted psychogeography' and, without going into a discussion on how this might be linked to nostalgia or its repression, it is apparent that rural England as a place is crucial to a sense of self driving the narratives throughout the album either as point of physical return or as place of perceived continuity. It might be somewhat of a leap, then, to argue that Harvey's use of the rural, an England of fog and fields might in any way be radical when the rural and its championing have been owned by such conservative agendas. But Harvey reignites the rural with a common claim, that its present and past, her version of English heritage, is for all, so that this album and its films become part of a radical folk tradition which has at its core distrust for capital, monopoly, homogeneity along with a pride of place (see Winter and Keegan-Phipps, 2013).

Conclusion

These are Harvey's 'English' albums. They 'facilitate a reframing and re-imagining' (Adams, 2008: 469) of Englishness through acts of remembrance that foreground loss, yearning and violence. In both albums, Harvey deconstructs the fabric of constructed pasts drawn from shared cultural archives of Englishness as pastoral, of Englishness as triumphant, and plays with ubiquitous imagery to rework that fabric. *White Chalk* is Harvey's musical 'return of the native'. It signalled a lyrical embrace of home and, in its simplicity and musical sparseness, reconfigured narratives of the lives led in that home to question rural idyll and the myth of the pastoral. It remembered England as a place of rural violence and misery, of disappointment and death, of thwarted female passion. This remembering was fully realized in *Let England Shake*, which is characterized by a radical pastoralism. Harvey remembers England as a place of emotional belonging, and we hear the voices of those who have sat on the margins of official histories of war and nation. In particular, the album encapsulated contemporaneous anxieties about 'England' that tapped into a broader cultural and political unease about Englishness; what it might be and who might have claim to it. Both albums celebrate land. They sing of soil, chalk and earth. They are grounded. They are Harvey's readings of the importance of place to memory, and these places are, by default, an England whose pastoral myths she reframes.

Bibliography

Adams, R. (2008), 'The Englishness of English Punk: Sex Pistols, Subcultures and Nostalgia', *Popular Music and Society*, 31(4): 469–88.

Aughey, A. (2007), *The Politics of Englishness*, Manchester: Manchester University Press.

Bannister, M. (2006a), '"Loaded": Indie Guitar Rock, Canonism White Masculinities', *Popular Music*, 25(1): 77–95.

Bannister, M. (2006b), *White Boys, White Noise: Masculinities and 1980s Indie Guitar Rock*, Aldershot and Burlington, VT: Ashgate.

Bayton, M. (2007), 'Women and the Electric Guitar' in S. Whiteley (ed.), *Sexing the Groove: Popular Music and Gender*, 37–49, London: Routledge.

Bennett, A. and J. Stratton (2010), *Britpop and the English Music Tradition*, Farnham: Ashgate.

Bronfen, E. (1998), *The Knotted Subject: Hysteria and its Discontents*, Princeton, NJ: Princeton University Press.

Bunting, M. (2009), *The Plot: A Biography of an English Acre*, London: Granta Publications.

Burns, L. and M. Lafrance (2002), *Disruptive Divas: Feminism, Identity and Popular Music*, New York: Routledge.

Butler, J. (1993), *Bodies That Matter: On the Discursive Limits of 'Sex'*, London: Routledge.

Connell, J. and C. Gibson (2003), *Sound Tracks: Popular Music, Identity and Place*, London: Routledge.

Dale, P. (2012), *Anyone Can Do it: Empowerment, Tradition and the Punk Underground*, Farnham: Ashgate.

Derrida, J. (1996), *Archive Fever: A Freudian Impression*, trans. E. Prenowitz, Chicago: University of Chicago Press.

Doveling, K., C. von Scheve and E.A. Konijn (eds) (2010), *The Routledge Handbook of Emotions and Mass Media*, London: Routledge.

Empire, K. (2011a), 'Best Albums of 2011, No 1: Harvey – Let England Shake'. *The Guardian*, 16 December. http://www.guardian.co.uk/music/musicblog/2011/dec/16/pj-harvey-let-england-shake.

Empire, K. (2011b), 'Harvey: Let England Shake – Review'. *The Guardian*, 13 February. http://www.guardian.co.uk/music/2011/feb/13/pj-harvey-let-england-shake.

Featherstone, S. (2009), *Englishness: Twentieth Century Popular Culture and the Forming of English Identity*, Edinburgh: Edinburgh University Press.

Garde-Hansen, J. (2011), *Media and Memory*, Edinburgh: Edinburgh University Press.

Garde-Hansen, J. and K. Gorton (2013), *Emotion Online: theorizing affect on the internet*, Basingstoke: Palgrave Macmillan.

Gardner, A. (2015), *Harvey and Music Video Performance*, Farnham: Ashgate.

Gifford, T. (1999), *Pastoral*, London: Routledge.

Gorton, K. (2009), *Media Audiences: Television, Meaning and Emotion*, Edinburgh: Edinburgh University Press.

Harmsworth, A. (2014), 'Kate Bush comeback: Hit-starved fans are demanding refunds'. *Metro*, 27 August. http://metro.co.uk/2014/08/27/kate-bush-comeback-hit-starved-fans-are-demanding-refunds-4848306/#ixzz3sbKA1PYS.

Hegarty, P. and M. Halliwell (2011), *Beyond and Before: Progressive Rock since the 1960s*, New York: Bloomsbury.

Hesmondhalgh, D. (2013), *Why Music Matters*, Chichester: Wiley-Blackwell.

Hirsch, M. (2002), *Family Frames: Photography, Narrative and Postmemory*, Cambridge, Mass: Harvard University Press.

Juslin, P. N. and J. A. Sloboda (eds) (2010), *Handbook of Music and Emotion: theory, research, applications*, Oxford: Oxford University Press.

Kenny, M. (2014), *The Politics of Nationhood in England: Class, Culture and Governance after Devolution*, Oxford: Oxford University Press.

Kuhn, A. (2002), *Family Secrets: Acts of Memory and Imagination*, London: Verso.

Leach, E. (2001), 'Vicars of "Wannabe": authenticity and the Spice Girls', *Popular Music*, 20(2): 143–67.

Leonard, M. (2007), *Gender in the Music Industry: Rock, Discourse and Girl Power*, Aldershot: Ashgate.

Lowenthal, D. (1985), *The Past is a Foreign Country*, Cambridge: Cambridge University Press.

McNulty, B. (2014), 'Kate Bush: The last of the Great British Eccentrics is truly bonkers', *The Telegraph*, 28 August, (accessed 26 November 2015). http://www.telegraph.co.uk/culture/music/rockandpopmusic/11059176/Kate-Bush-The-last-of-the-Great-British-Eccentrics-is-truly-bonkers.html.

Moy, R. (2007), *Kate Bush and Hounds of Love*, Aldershot: Ashgate.

Negus, K. and M. Pickering (2002), 'Creativity, Communication and Musical Experience', in D. Hesmondhalgh and K. Negus (eds), *Popular Music Studies*, 178–90, London: Arnold.

Newman, J. (2011), 'Indie Music Month Video Premiere: Harvey, 'The Colour Of The Earth'. *MTV news*, 20 March, 2011, (accessed 8 April 2016). http://www.mtv.com/news/2297597/pj-harvey-colour-of-the-earth-video/.

Parekh, B. (2000), 'Defining British National Identity', *The Political Quarterly*, 71(1): 4–14.

Petridis, A. (2011), 'PJ Harvey: Let England Shake – review'. *The Guardian*, 10 February 2011. http://www.guardian.co.uk/music/2011/feb/10/pj-harvey-let-england-shake-review.

Reynolds, S. and J. Press (2005), *The Sex Revolts: Gender, Rebellion and Rock and Roll*, London: Serpents' Press.

Whiteley, S. (2000), *Women and Popular Music: Sexuality, Identity and Subjectivity*, London: Routledge.

Wilson, J. L. (2005), *Nostalgia: Sanctuary of Meaning*, London: Bucknell University Press.

Winter, T. and S. Keegan-Phipps (2013), *Performing Englishness, Identity and Politics in a Contemporary Folk Resurgence*, Manchester: Manchester University Press.

Wiseman-Trowse, N. (2013), *Nick Drake: Dreaming England*, London: Reaktion.

Web sources

http://birminghamnationalist2.blogspot.co.uk/search?q=let+england+shake&x=44&y=16
(removed)
http://www.seamusmurphy.com/

Discography

PJ Harvey (2000) *Stories from the City, Stories from the Sea*, Universal Island Records [Album]

PJ Harvey (2007) *White Chalk*, Island Records [Album]

PJ Harvey (2011) *Let England Shake*, Island Records [Album]

Film and Videography

MANSIZE (1993) [Video] Dir. Maria Mochnacz

50FT QUEENIE (1993) [Video] Dir. Maria Mochnacz

WHEN UNDER ETHER (2007) [Video] Dir. Maria Mochnacz

THE DEVIL (2007) [Video] Dir. Maria Mochnacz
Let England Shake: 12 Short Films by Seamus Murphy (2011) (Films) Dir. Seamus
    Murphy
Let England Shake (2011) [Short Film] Dir. Seamus Murphy
The Last Living Rose (2011) [Short Film] Dir. Seamus Murphy
The Words that Maketh Murder (2011) [Short Film] Dir. Seamus Murphy
In the Dark Places (2011) [Short Film] Dir. Seamus Murphy
Battleship Hill (2011) [Short Film] Dir. Seamus Murphy

PART TWO

Spaces of identity

CHAPTER FIVE

Adventures in English space and time:

Sound as experience in *Doctor Who (An Unearthly Child)*

Dene October[1]

In *An Unearthly Child*, Susan Foreman, mysterious granddaughter of the Doctor and eponymous subject of the title, lets it be known, 'I like England in the Twentieth Century.' Her taste includes listening to popular music, which she plays on her modern portable transistor radio, an appropriate auditory register for an adolescent girl marking her identification with 1960s London. Perhaps the first naïve viewers of *Doctor Who* could also identify with this attempt to dematerialize the visual in favour of the aural, to seek *soundscape* as an escape from the flat monochrome and humdrum visual representations of Englishness. This chapter embraces the opportunity for experiential submersion into the aural space of *Doctor Who*, offering it as a challenge to a detached visual–critical analysis.

Hearing has received less philosophical attention than seeing (Metz 1980), the latter of which is traditionally associated with somatic detachment and rationality, the very objective distance through which hearing is then described and understood. The modernist tradition, in preserving 'consciousness ... from doubt' (Lyotard 1992: 74), reifies the materiality of the object, insisting on a critical distance between the viewer and the viewed. Commentary typically seeks to understand rather than experience the essence of the sonic, muting it with cultural universalism, contextualizing it through 'quasi visual conventions' (Voegelin 2011: 26–7), thus compromising the subjective individual experience.

The question of where sound is produced has been answered by scientific and philosophical traditions attempting to describe it as a quality of the medium or the object heard. Pasnau rejects this insisting sound is not an intrinsic feature 'of our sensory experiences' (1999: 309), thereby marking the distinction between the sensory receptors of taste, touch and smell, and the '*locational* modalities' (1999: 313) of sight and sound: 'How do we manage to hear an orchestra,' Pasnau asks, 'if not by the sound of the performance?' (1999: 317). For Voegelin, a subjective immersion in sound is the only way to fully hear it since sound 'sits in my ear' (2011: xi). A philosophy of sonic art must be willing to share time and space with the sound object, as a rejection of detachment and objectivity. Such an engagement offers 'no real conclusions but only strategies for engagement and efforts of interpretation' (Voegelin 2011: xiii). To become immersed in the acoustic space of *Doctor Who* is to speculate on its physical and psychic actualizing of subjectivity and to interpret always *with an eye* on the rationalizing tyranny of visual and linguistic modes, a style of writing that may sneer at self-aware visual metaphors while struggling *to see beyond them*.[2]

Audiences are responsive to sonic manipulation partially because of their adeptness with negotiating sound on a daily basis (Tagg 1999), filtering out the vast amounts of unimportant background noise and paying 'selective attention' (Fox 2012) to that which requires conscious decision-making. Sound has a profound effect on us, more than we are normally consciously aware of, a fact exploited by film music and sound effects (Hendy 2013). Donnelly (2005) argues that sound plays an important role in disciplining the audience into the authority of the narrative. Film music is meant to be unheard, serving the diegesis 'in a manner which renders it inaudible' (Smith 1996: 230). Television, much more than film, is a product and practice of the everyday, one we trace a first musical encounter to (Deaville 2011b: 1), and will continue to spend a great deal of time engaging with[3] in the creation of what Burlingame calls 'the soundtrack of our lives' (Burlingame 1996: 1). Media theorists like Fiske (1987) argue that television transmits cultural values through a shared language which viewers are rehearsed into 'decoding'. Yet music is only *one* of television's languages, communicating both of itself and in collaboration with other modes, in various roles (Rodman 2010: 4), enabling both the programme producer and consumer access to a range of tools for meaning production. Television music allows for more discreet subjective positioning and is increasingly experienced in solitary settings[4] where contingencies of experience must invariably include solipsistic behaviours and attitudes.

Yet there is a growing recognition of the integrity of sound in visual arts. Rather than a mere appendage to the image, music is 'an essential element of the realisation of the concept as a whole' (Tarkovsky 2000: 158). Listening is generative of the audio-imaginary and, freed from a service role, can be studied as an affective architecture demanding imaginative connections from the listener. A sonic sensibility in criticism should highlight this, illuminating 'the unseen aspects of visuality, augmenting rather than opposing a visual philosophy' refocusing philosophical problems around subjectivity ... 'via the notion of interpretative fantasies', connecting 'the experience of sound with the notion of virtuality and possible worlds that are not linked to the logic and rational of a visual reality' (Voegelin 2011: xiii–xiv). The commitment to the notion of *Doctor Who* as soundscape is therefore a commitment to the inner space-time journey that sound augments, always conscious of, while not ignoring, the consensus visual-linguistic interpretation that sound also supports. The problem with sound subsumed into the visual, without such an intervention, is it 'invites our bodies to meet the work after its mediation through language and documentation, rather than before' (Voegelin 2011: 26).

The time-space of 1960s London, England

In evaluating 1960s London as a time-place, and setting this into a contest between visual and aural representations, I have been conscious of marking distinctions between place and space, before attempting, that is, to posit notions of sonic environments. In this regard, whereas I have used space to refer 'to the structural, geometrical qualities of a physical environment, place is the notion that includes the dimensions of lived experience, interaction and use of a space by its inhabitants'.[5] [6] Space, inhabited and situated experientially,[7] is always *becoming* as place, materializing in *performative* interactions. The place of London in *Doctor Who* is literally created in the studio space, through the fourth wall of which viewers are relocated immaterially into other rendered spaces, before being returned to the re-material place. Space is cultural, historical and social and this mediates how it is experienced bodily, yet it is also *material*, experienced phenomenologically, through visual, tactile, olfactory and aural interactions, interactions which meet this mediation, as contingencies of subjective experience. Technologies promote the notion of space over place[8] and there is certainly nothing controversial about the notion of the *screen* as a window to third space through which consumer agency is called upon to rematerialize London as a space of alien diversity and possibilities, but this is a convenient visual analogy that overlooks the role of sound in rendering space, dematerializing and rematerializing it.

In the post-war years, English identity drew on a complicated and contradictory set of myths, practices and representations. War had helped cement the notion of a monolithic and unchanging national identity by rallying 'a specifically English set of values against attack' (Giles and Middleton 1995: 6) but in its shadow, the country was faced with increased economic competition, a decline in international sway, and having to cede political control to many of its colonies. Unrestricted immigration, where people from former colonies were regarded as neither subjects nor aliens, was accompanied by introspective disputes over 'Englishness' and 'Britishness', the collapse of class consensus, the 'generation gap' and the onset of a more diplomatic era in international affairs where culture took on greater prominence as a primary export.

This was the context for *Doctor Who*, the first episode of which is set in a London junkyard where the detritus of empire, so out of authentic time and place, acquires its modern value as nostalgic curio. Slotted into the schedules between the football results and *Juke Box Jury*, the programme filtered the identity crises and emerging liberalism through its fictional tropes, serving as a mirror to modern Britain and perhaps 'showing how the nation ... thinks it ought to be' (Pless 2012: 359). International viewers discerned recognizable emblems of Englishness, as well as understanding the show as 'the last dilettante farewell of a ruling class culture' (Skillen quoted in Tulloch and Alvarado 1983: 35). Domestically, TARDIS journeys to fictional landscapes may have offered a convenient escape from complications to the naïve view of England as pastoral Eden, while the Doctor himself was the figure of the eccentric gentleman who alluded to the romanticism of the English poet and wanderer in 'representing the freedom and adventure of a life on the open road' (Giles and Middleton 1995: 22).

The programme's cultural heritage permits the conflated observation 'very British, very BBC' (Tulloch and Alvarado 1983: 35), particularly given John Reith's continued influence on the channel – Reith was formerly general manager and director-general of the BBC – and his interpretation of its charter to educate and entertain 'fully in the spirit of Matthew Arnold' (Kumar quoted in Tulloch and Alvarado 1983: 37). Globally, the BBC was well established as an authoritative British national institution but its paternal position had begun to change with the onset of independent commercial television. Thus *Doctor Who* had to deal with the reality of competition for viewers, compounded by budget practicalities 'which helped shape it from the very beginning' (Potter 2007: 161). Sydney Newman, the Head of Drama who initiated the programme and set the guidelines, made commercial use of his experience with ITV, but also espoused Reithian values. The programme would steer responsibly clear of American sensationalism (Bignell 2007: 46) but not fail to reflect the interests of modern audiences. When the early reports strayed from his brief, Newman put his foot down: 'I don't like this much. It all reads silly and condescending. It doesn't get across the basis of ... educational experience.'[9]

Sound and modernism(s)

The post-Reithian context for creativity within the institution meant that BBC production teams and specialist services were positioned between conservative and experimental impulses. The Radiophonic Workshop fitted the Reithian ideal of how national broadcasting should expand the cultural horizons of the public, yet pursued techniques which threatened the hegemony of British music tradition,[10] as embodied in particular by the BBC's conservative Music Department. By the mid-century, the avant-garde was well established in Paris, with the manipulation of existing sounds of *musique concrete*, and in Cologne, with the pure electronic sounds of *elekrtonishe Musik*. What united the French and German modernists was the principle that electronic music was too important to put in the service of film (Niebur 2010: 5). Early pioneers, like Daphne Oran, pushed for the development of an English studio similar to the Continental models, setting up clandestine laboratories (Stevens 2010: 188) after her 'day-job', and was eventually hired as the Workshop's first studio manager when it opened in 1958. But while state-run radio stations, such as *Radiodiffusion-Télévision Française*, *Westdeutscher Rundfunk* and *Radio Italia*, provided the facilities and funds for pure research, the Workshop was created solely as subordinate to the needs of the radio and television product, and Oran quickly left.

The Workshop responded equally to a lack of facilities for musical experimentation as to the practical needs of providing modern sound effects for radio drama.[11] Yet despite its service position, the Workshop inspired criticism and suspicion from Light Music, the latter fearing attempts by 'charlatans' (Niebur 2010: 44), to create music from sound effects, while conservative music critics such as Reginald Smith called experimentalists the 'lunatic fringe' (Toop 2011). The BBC found itself in the odd position of celebrating the Workshop's innovatory sound effects while downplaying its relationship with music. Although some of the techniques are similar, 'radiophonic sound is not an art in itself'[12] it announced at a press conference to promote the Workshop's opening. Such an apologetic attitude did little to raise the profile of electronic pioneers like Tristran Cary and Daphne Oram, the latter completely overlooked in favour of Karlheinz Stockhausen as the first composer to use world music samples (Stevens 2010: 188). On the other hand, it is perhaps the case, as Niebur argues, that the fierce opposition of the Music Department was instrumental in radiophonic composers forging 'a path of their own, unconnected to the trends and fashions of the larger BBC music community' (Niebur 2010: 119).

In bridging the experimental and the commercial, the Workshop recognized the limits of abstract work. Maddalena Fagandini, for example, composed her famous interval signals in recognition of a 'general listener'. Her work was so popular that George Martin, future producer for the Beatles, backed one piece with an orchestra and had a hit with the single *Time Beat* by a performer listed as 'Ray Cathode'. This shift to tonality was accompanied by a growing demand for radiophonic sound and in the first year of *Doctor Who*, the Workshop fulfilled 150 commitments (Niebur 2010: 93), some classified as *effects* while others were more clearly 'musical'. But it is in combining the abstract *musique concrete* sounds with rhythmic patterns and tonality that the Workshop created a unique sound that would not only influence pop music (Niebur 2010: 95–6) but indeed make electronic sound accessible as a particularly British alternative to the high modernism of the Continent.

Nevertheless, the experimentalism of the Workshop was frustrated by the BBC's rigid institutionalism, politics, class hierarchy and claims to cultural consensus. The BBC provided necessary space, labour and equipment – most of which was specifically invented or 'recycled' from other BBC departments – affording the Workshop the means to experiment with electronic sound not available to individuals and smaller organizations. The Workshop also benefited from the peculiar mix of skills that the BBC staff and structure provided. Delia Derbyshire's background in mathematics and music enabled compositional complexity while Brian Hodgson's technical experience was useful in producing new sounds from electronic equipment. Despite the focus on 'knob-twiddling',[13] operations at the Workshop were initially staffed by one studio manager, responsible for creativity, and one engineer, whose responsibility was maintenance. In reality skills crossed over, Hodgson being one example of an engineer turned composer, but the dichotomy spoke not only about the grading scale of BBC jobs, but also, arguably, reflected wider class distinctions.[14] It was also a source of strain in staffing consistency. Similarly, the cultural anxiety towards electronic music, partially borne out by the observation that its dissonance was an effective signifier of environmental detachment (madness, alienation, and a sense of the unknown), and amplified by an elitist concern for standards of taste, led to interruptions in Workshop operations as staff were frequently rotated on the basis that too much electronic noise could lead to mental instability (Niebur 2010: 36–7).

Internal politics also meant 'bureaucratic struggles over equipment purchase' (Toop 2011) with debates, for example, about limiting its role to producing effects, rather than music. Initially the Workshop depended on borrowing from other departments, which typically included basic oscillators and old tape recorders. Everyday objects included combs, rubber bands and paper. The more expensive tools included test equipment, such as tone generators – used to output square waves, and sine waves – equalizers (tone controls), a white noise generator and a 'wobbulator'[15] – a frequency modulating oscillator.[16] The equipment, which often required customizing, 'tended to be test equipment'[17] and was temperamental. There were no synthesizers – these were only invented in 1963, by RCA, and not used outside that organization until later in the decade. Electronic music was either generated from electronic sources or, to employ a more recent term, 'sampled' from recordings, recorded and then 'treated' (manipulated and enhanced). These tools frequently 'starred' in media coverage, which furnished fetishized lists of equipment (Niebur 2010: 110–11), reinforcing the BBC policy of authorial anonymity and echoing public ambivalence towards the scientific.

The focus on modern equipment also reinforced the distinction between effects and music, one that the Workshop sought to blur in creating 'musically inspired sound design' (Donnelly 2007: 201). For Buhler (2001), music is but one element of film soundscape, the proper study of which must include effects and dialogue. The soundscape of *Doctor Who* included 'electronic sound effects, which were labelled "special sound" and included such things as alien speech, spaceships' engines, and any other aurally unusual element' (Niebur 2010: 101–2) that might be required, and incidental music, the latter either composed or from library stock, used primarily for non-diegetic functions. Yet it was in the blurring of the realist distinctions between diegetic and non-diegetic sound, effect and music, that a 'more unified electronic atmosphere' (Niebur 2010: 102) was able to work in the background and on the subconscious, rendering soundscapes that might be properly qualified as 'musical'. Ironically BBC politics had ensured that the Workshop did not fall under the music budget (Donnelly 2007: 198), so the Workshop was called upon to create music from effects for the budget-starved programme. By the 1970s, as new producers looked to place their own signature on the programme, special effects were foregrounded in a more conventional way as the language for weapons, spacecrafts and the like.

Clearly this sonic architecture can be understood as supporting the visual and narratory requirements of the programme as well as adding important layers in the production of meaning. The argument that soundscapes are generative of aural subjective immersion already finds some support in addressing the soundtrack as an experience in itself. Koldau (2012) has discussed how the soundtrack serves as a souvenir of the cinematic experience. Since many early *Doctor Who* stories were wiped as part of an economy drive by the BBC, the soundtrack is all that remains in some instances. These soundtracks 'often demonstrate not only how well music works for the series, but also how well the soundtracks work as objects within themselves, without the missing visuals' (Donnelly 2007: 190). Many of the BBC's DVD releases contain extras which give the opportunity to listen to the score without the full soundtrack; this appreciation of *Doctor Who* as sound has also meant that the full soundscape treatment – including theme music – is recognized as an important aspect of the audio drama experience.

The soundscape of *An Unearthly Child*

An Unearthly Child aired in the late afternoon of 23 November 1963, its haunting dissonant *soundscape* at once augmenting the *viewer* experience, immersive and generative of the *aural-imaginary*. The auditory space enhanced the visual and narrative elements, compensated for low budgets and the cramped space in Studio D at Lime Grove, struck terror in the hearts of the young (Fuller 2010) and destabilized the consensus world view already shaken in the aftermath of Kennedy's assassination the day before. For some, it was an experience that would be deferred and mediated by word-of-mouth when a national blackout left the viewing population at 4.4 million (the launch episode was repeated a week later, prior to the second instalment). In either case, the reception was an *uncanny* one, immediately memorable and oddly familiar.

The strange familiarity of the first transmission is experienced as an eerie echo of the programme's conceit at offsetting the ordinary against the mysterious. The seeming banality of 1960s London cloaked the enigma of the exiled travellers, while the iconography (originally, the Doctor's ship was to be invisible, but Newman wanted something both recognizable and easy to overlook), reflected the duality of the everyday setting, enabling producer Verity Lambert's input into the graphic design and sound treatments to work effectively on the cultural dissonance. Recorded 'as live' in cramped Studio D, the first 25-minute episode is slow-moving, with just 132 shots,[18] dependent on static dialogue exchange and camera fetishizing of props, the latter a visual hint that the ordinary should be regarded with suspicion. Sound has a vital job to do in communicating this doubling, in creating a *disquietening* that implicates our a priori knowledge of the sinister truth of objects that like a dream we have somehow forgotten. Although the early stories had 'only 1 or 2 minutes'[19] of incidental music, an amount dwarfed by the current series' reliance on it, there is an impressive 14-and-a-half minutes of musical effect in the launch episode. [20]

Lambert wanted the 'familiar yet different' thread to run through the signature tune and initially enquired after *Les Stuctures Sonores*, avant-garde composers Jacques Lasry and Bernard Baschet, who composed on custom-made glass and metal 'sound sculptures'. However, the job was handed to well-known composer Ron Grainer, who having seen a dummy of the title sequence, hurriedly penned a rough piano version, indicating timbre as 'wind bubble' and 'cloud'. Grainer handed it over to the Workshop to realize, intending to mix in a backing group later, but was so astounded with the results he asked for Delia Derbyshire to share co-composer credit, an idea vetoed by the BBC.[21] Derbyshire constructed the piece with the help of chief engineer Dick Mills, using electronic valve oscillators connected to keyboards to generate sounds, which were recorded and assembled onto tape machines by individually cutting the notes to the right length and arranging them in the order required. After initial processing, Derbyshire 'crash-synched' the three Phillips tape machines, occasionally having to unwind the rolls to correct misalignments, spilling them out all the way along the BBC corridors in Maida Vale.[22]

The resulting tune in E minor at 4/4 meter is experienced as an uncanny recognition, 'the combination of repeated base beat and pizzicato swoop' (Tulloch 1983: 18–19) not untypical of pop hooks at the time yet clearly radiophonic, dissonant and alien. The *tum-te-tum* bass repetition, the twang sound of which Derbyshire generated either on a custom electronic pickup device or a jack-bay blanking panel,[23] is already both futuristic and contemporary before it is accompanied by a wave-like swishing effect that rolls in and out of proximity, leaping up a minor sixth in the eighth bar as it is joined by the high swooping *woo-ee-oo* melody, which is theremin-like and reminiscent of sci-fi movies.[24] The theme is 'eminently hummable' (Niebur 2010: 100) and fulfils the role of signature tunes to 'establish an almost immediate familiarity' with the audience as well as identify programme differentiation (Tulloch 1983: 18–19). But Lambert felt the overall effect was too dissonant and reinforced the 'familiar yet different' dictum by insisting on a second master to break up the mechanical precision and regularity, deliberately introducing human error, and giving an impression of performance to what is 'pure' electronic collage.

The new master incorporated a hiss sound at the beginning, giving auditory weight to the first feathering of the altocumulus cloud shapes that appear in the title sequence.

Associate Producer Mervyn Pinfield approached another BBC specialist service, formed to research the potential of electronic graphic effects. The group had experimented with 'howlround' graphics, images created by positive feedback (that is, by optically feeding a camera's output back into itself by filming the monitor).[25] Bernard Lodge was given the job of integrating the abstract effect with the *Doctor Who* logo. The distorted graphics capture Lambert's brief, odd and abstract, but vaguely figurative, so much so that updates to the sequence clarify the random plumes into columns of a space – time vortex through which TARDIS and logo speed towards the viewer. To 1960s viewers, the effect would have been more profoundly strange than familiar, given the convention for still images and scrolling credits. The combination of sound and video, or sound *on* video since this is its impression, was fresh and startling, and prefigured both the unusual sound treatments and mystery to follow, ensuring they too would be experienced eerily.

The opening sequence is the first of several visual clichés of English life. Here a sole policeman on his night beat[26] checks the premises along a typical fogbound East London street. It is a difficult first scene, pulling the viewer into a darkness that immediately puts them on edge, straining their eyes to make out what is going on, asking them to rely for cues on familiar references to programmes like *Dixon of Dock Green* (1955–76). This standard fictional caricature of fogbound London is then undermined by the strangeness of the theme music.[27] While sound is often called upon to compensate for poor visuals (Donnelly 2007: 198) here the struggle for visibility is aided only by the theme music which has mysteriously run on past the title sequence. It only fades out with the introduction of the first sound effect, that of Brian Hodgson's TARDIS hum. In the intervening period, the encoding of suspense and mystery is pursued rigorously, even at the expense of realism, as the gates to 'I M Foreman Scrap Merchant' open by themselves, despite having apparently been checked by the policeman. In retrospect it is perhaps the most surprising event in the entire transmission, but one the viewer tolerates as part of an unfolding mystery, perhaps erroneously suspecting an unearthly cause, and in any case having been carried away by the travelling camera, unable to pause and question it.[28] Anthony Coburn's pilot script elides any exposition, leaving the suggestion that the gate may have creaked open (Coburn 1963: 2), but in the transmission it is difficult to avoid the conclusion that this is a conscious breaching of the fourth wall. The unexplained strategy is the first of many unresolved mysteries, the next of which is already upon us as, having dispensed with the need to explain the shift in point of view, the camera conveys the viewer through the dark junkyard, settling before the familiar sight of a police telephone box, strangely out of place, a fact accented by its unfamiliar hum.

Again, we are not given much opportunity to reflect on the electronic sound, for as the camera hones in on the 'Police Advice and Assistance' notice, the point of view blurs and fades, cutting to a school sign, the odd humming sound replaced by the familiar one of the class bell. In spite of its status as a comprehensive school, an education system not fully rolled out in England until 1965, 'Coal Hill' relocates the viewer in the everyday, and provides the rationale for the introduction of Ian Chesterton and Barbara Wright, science and history teachers, as the main focus for audience identification as well as instruments of the Reithian pursuit of quality educational programming. It is through the perspective of these teachers' aroused suspicions that Susan Foreman is constructed as an enigma, an apparently normal teenage girl who shows signs of brilliance while simultaneously failing. We first encounter her listening to The Arthur Nelson Group's 'Three Guitar Moods 2'[29] on a transistor radio, her dress redolent more of street fashion than school uniform, details that situate her detachment as conventionally framed by 1960s youth culture. But her modernity is given a futuristic and spacey twist when we observe Susan's strange dance-gestures, as if her studied concentration on the music stirred somatic memories of a very different life.

Whereas Susan's response to the diegetic music is ambiguous, the non-diegetic music she is associated with – which later recurs as a leitmotif for the mystery of the junkyard, and finally the Doctor himself – encourages a reading of her character as doubling along genre-specific lines. Norman Kay wrote the incidental music for *An Unearthly Child*, and would go on to compose for *The Keys of Marinus* (1964) and *The Sensorites* (1964), two other stories from the William Hartnell era. Incidental music was used to build mood rather than back up action, due to the difficulties of setting up a correspondence with the live action in the studio (Potter 2007: 163). The ominous tones used in establishing Susan may seem overblown, and a better fit with thrillers and even horror movies, but the rarity of radiophonic sounds (Donnelly 2007: 201) meant 1960s audiences were rewarded in their genre recognition and were one step ahead of the teachers' investigation of the mystery.

The ominous motif continues to commingle with everyday sounds as the teachers follow Susan 'home' to the junkyard, the sound of the car 'pulling up' one of the many audio-natural effects deployed to turn the crammed studio into a dynamic space. As they wait, the teachers provide us with a back-story on Susan. The 'as live' production restricted the narrative to a largely chronological storytelling with expensive edits, for actor-led flashbacks, used rarely. In *An Unearthly Child*, the flashbacks are told in real time from the point of view of the teachers who cannot be featured since they are physically elsewhere in the studio (Potter 2007: 164–5). Film inserts were also infrequent due to time constraints, thus the confines of the studio space typically meant a discursive style of 'tell-don't-show' storytelling. These were tough conditions for a programme promoting the spectacle of infinite time and space, yet the practicalities influenced the philosophy and aesthetic of the programme, and the practices continued up until the more action-orientated Jon Pertwee stories. It was up to the incidental music and effects to establish the time and space in the minds of the viewer.

The consistency of sound treatments enabled the establishing of characters, as well as the identity of the programme, confirming its genre, and expanding its limited spatial fields along *audio-imaginary* lines. The recurring aural motif of Susan as enigma and the electronic hum of TARDIS, also ensure that, by the time the junkyard set is revisited, the vague feeling of familiarity has reached a sensorial overload as eerie recognition. As we follow the teachers through Foreman's gates, it is Chesterton this time who has the torch. The ominous motif replaces the signature tune heralding, after fifteen-minutes of absence, the entrance of the Doctor. Rather than resolving the anxiety, his presence only confirms the mystery that has been constructed in his absence, a puzzle that the repetition of sound treatments continues to work on. The characterization of the Doctor as a puzzle – Doctor *Who?* – is one that clearly cannot afford to be hastily unravelled, and the two sounds which signify him, necessarily qualify his narrative role as enigmatic *Other*, an unknown in whose presence lies an absence. In the pilot episode, he is played by Hartnell as arrogant and aggressive, but after Newman's intervention and corrections, subsequently redrawn as a figure of oppositions, much more along the lines Lambert had envisaged him, full of brilliance and humanity one moment, then 'suspicious and capable of sudden malignance' the next,[30] a duality fully supported by the soundtrack.

Although the new series makes much more of the notion of TARDIS as a character, even suggesting a specific gender affiliation, here the character development is acoustic, marking TARDIS as both aural space and primary figure. 'It's alive,' Chesterton says, responding to its sound by touching it. Once the teachers force their way inside, a new pallet of Brian Hodgson's electronic effects is used to construct the 'impossible' interior in a more clearly scientific register. The interior hum deepens, a non-diegetic sound we now firmly associate with its analogue. But not all of the effects are either clearly diegetic or non-diegetic. Having been kidnapped by the Doctor, who is concerned the authorities will be on to him, the teachers make a run for it. This is accompanied by another sound alert, a sudden electronic bubbling rising in pitch. But whereas the former ominous motif clearly requires no analogue, it is ambiguous whether or not this sound has one, whether, that is, it is intended as a diegetic sound. Does it emanate from the console with its array of buttons and levers, all potential triggers for diegetic effects? Is the alarm one that sounds for the audience only, a signifier of the danger and prefiguring of the long dematerialization sequence about to begin? A third possibility – one that draws evidence from the Radiophonic Workshop's experience in radio drama where 'special sound' was a means of conveying interior states of mind – is that the sound is 'extra-diegetic', an aural diagram of the panic that the characters and viewers have been thrown into. Finally, if we are given to the notion of TARDIS as character – a retrospective reading the new series makes plausible – could the alarm represent TARDIS as thinking, trying to make moral sense out of the Doctor's hostile actions?

Brian Hodgson's impressive repertoire of radiophonic effects for TARDIS, in particular the dematerialization treatment, demonstrate its core importance to the programme, not simply as the ship that conveys its crew from *a* to *b*, but, iconically and philosophically, as *home* to the crew, the base to which they consistently return no matter how far and wide they travel. While its hum in this episode is encoded as science fiction and mysterious, by the time the crew are fighting for their lives against the Daleks, two stories along, it will bring connotations of stability and comfort[31]. On the other hand, this home is a relational one, a surrogate of the one left behind, the space of refuge and 'family-ness'. Home is characterized by (Derrida's) différance, particularly for the viewers who are both 'at home' and simultaneously transported through home-as-hiatus, a liminal doorway between *concrete* space and fantasy, acoustically unsteady, both *heimliche* and *unheimliche*.

Hodgson's dematerialization effect generates a sound architecture that similarly shifts and steadies, seeming to concretize before flowing away, always in a state of becoming that is never finally still. Hodgson 'wanted a sound that seemed to be travelling in two directions at once; coming and going at the same time' (Marshall n.d.). The sound was created by scraping a key across dismantled piano strings, recording it with tape echo, reversing it, then treating it to notes created on the 'wobbulator'. Although identified as a sound effect, like many radiophonic sounds, it produces an atmospheric integrity hard to hear as anything but music. Hodgson used this 'special sound' to create a 'more "musical" backdrop for each episode', adding a unique electronic element to combine with stock stores 'wrapping listeners in a cocoon of alien sounds and atmospheres' (Nieber 2007: 205). The BBC reclassified the effect as music in 1973, even crediting Hodgson as the author (Howe et al. 1994 in Donnelly 2007: 190).

The first dematerialization is visually rendered as a montage of extreme close-ups to foster the sense of movement and establish the take-off scenario in the minds of the viewer. On a monitor, a still graphic of a London overhead scene is treated to a series of reductions, giving the impression of TARDIS rising above the city. The central column of TARDIS rises and falls, flooded in light, while Chesterton and Wright sway and stumble, as if describing a slow motion ballet, extreme close-ups of the Doctor and his granddaughter depict a stoic tension as though tolerating the now familiar G-force, graphic cloud effects overlaid across the strain on their faces.[32] The sequence lasts two minutes but is a one-time-only event that future episodes reduce to a short burst of light and sound, the spectacle obviated by audience experience. The synchretic relationship between TARDIS sound and analogue having been forged, the latter could be dispensed with where necessary, for example when budgets were tight, since the ship's arrival and departure was 'seen' via the aural architecture.

As TARDIS comes to rest, the only sound, its insistent hum, seems to fill the space entirely, and then this too is lost as the viewer is thrown outside, no longer a participant, but forced into the detached role of observer: the police box now sitting at a tilt in a dark and barren alien landscape accompanied by the chilling audio-naturalism of wind noise. After the long sequence of visual and aural overload, this sound intensifies rather than dissipates the anxiety, creating an *anempathetic* effect (Chion 1994: 8). In the silence of electronic sound, the audience ejection is experienced as sudden sensory deprivation, making the impression of *das unheimliche* the dominant one. Again the fourth wall is breached, this time a figure cuts between us and the ship, carrying a spear rather than a torch, his shadow lengthening impossibly across the landscape towards TARDIS. When the end titles and signature start up, the eerie recognition threatens to become full-blown horror as if the music, having transported us here, is now leaving us to face an awakening of our repressed pasts. Next week, the titles inform us, THE CAVE OF SKULLS.

The entire sequence is perhaps the most impressive in the history of the programme, partly as a consequence of its limited budget. It is the culmination of 'an artful and intelligent marshalling of resources' (Potter 2007: 161–2). The pattern of cramped and discursive storytelling, that the practicalities of live recording in tiny Lime Grove studios demanded, is suddenly and startlingly replaced by the still and painterly vista of the landing site, filmed (at greater expense) at the larger Ealing Studios. The cramped storytelling surely finds its corollary in the family living room experience of viewers. Viewing experience in the early sixties invariably meant sharing one television set with the entire family gathered together in the living room (Bignell 2007: 45). The monochrome sets took a while to warm up and were prone to break down, although reception was generally good when there was a roof aerial, and a close transmitter, but the picture was not always sharp, partly as a result of signal interference and the 405-lines screen set up (377 of actual image) which had remained since development in 1934.[33]

This switching of spatial conditions is of course one of the programmes' 'bigger on the inside' science fiction tropes, one enabled by intelligent soundscaping that draws the viewer into an aural architecture, transporting and alienating him. The deployment of electronic sound finds a counterpoint in electronic silence, the 'result of context and preparation' (Chion 1994: 57), enervating and unsettling the audience, effecting a discomforting sensation of disorientation as to where the electronic silence emanates. As before, it is not unambiguously diegetic, but *acousmatic*,[34] potentially metaphysical, the result of having been spatially resituated.[35] It is an experience of the sublime, beyond rational calculation, inspiring of wonderment and the terror of Freud's uncanny *unheimliche*, a familiar displacing of subjectivity that may partially account for the mythology of younger viewers hiding behind the sofa, as if anchoring in the here and now while secretly sonically drifting.

The philosophy of sound integral to the Radiophonic Workshop's treatment of *Doctor Who* could not be more different than that of the new series. In the latter, the incidental music is excessive, loud and melodramatic, constructed to hook the audience and keep them in a highly competitive television environment (Butler 2013: 163–4). The emphasis is on supporting the more visual-focused storytelling, on character development through recurring themes and leitmotifs, on reinforcing 'the program's emotional content' and connecting 'with a large, mainstream audience' (Butler 2013: 175). Its deliberate move away from radiophonics, and their association with the classic programme, leaves critics, notably ex-Doctor Sylvester McCoy, unhappy that it 'sounds as if it has been recorded on a cheap synthesiser in a backroom somewhere' (McCoy 2005). The signature tune, while referencing Derbyshire's theme, has a big bold 'Korngold' movie sound to it (Butler 2013: 165) reflecting its 'makers' perception of (and, possibly, lack of confidence in) the viewing habits of their target audience' (Butler 2013: 175).

In watching *An Unearthly Child*, the time-space of 1960s England is constructed as a series of visual clichés that deny our subjective experiential attachment to them on account of their consensual flatness: the bobby on his beat; the fogbound and claustrophobic Totters Lane, an atmosphere that tiny 'Studio D' augments considerably; the comprehensive school that the Doctor's granddaughter attends; the teachers who represent the twin strands of tradition and modernity – history and science – that are such an early focus of the programme and which hark back to Reithian pedagogy; the modern figure of the teenager; the junkyard and the police telephone box. The London rendered here is the familiar one promoted by linguistic and visual cultural production, from *Sherlock Holmes* to *Dixon of Dock Green*. Yet it is precisely this lack of a creative and plural lens on London and on Englishness that promotes a crude, bleak neo-Edwardian materialization of the city as the unlikely habitus of the uncanny. The look of *An Unearthly Child* corroborates the mundane familiarity we already expected, an Englishness as flattened out as the background inlays onto which the BBC projected sets. It is the sound of *Doctor Who* that constructs and destabilizes, that finally recuperates the spatial, and recruits us to it, not en masse, but one by one, a subjective immersion that is differentially contingent, dematerializing and rematerializing. It is the radiophonic sound that finally opens our 'eyes' to a notional Englishness, to England as a becoming space, to identity as fluid, to ideas that the BBC, the capital and the country had just begun articulating.

Notes

1   To Dick Mills, who I had the pleasure of chatting with at the Official 50th Anniversary Celebration in London.

2   Voegelin argues that subsuming sound into the visual blights music criticism since we are no longer hearing 'sound but the realisation of the visual' (Voegelin 2011: xi–xii).

3   Although the adoption of portable devices is changing consumption habits, 'traditional TV remains vibrant and continues to thrive as viewers continue to engage with their sets by seeking out the entertainment and information that appeals to them'. Nielsen Cross-Platform Report, October 2013.

4   See Nielsen Cross-Platform Report, October 2013 for rising influence of portable platforms on programme consumption.

5   Hornecker, E. (2006), Space and Place: setting the stage for social interaction, http://www.informatics.sussex.ac.uk/research/groups/interact/publications/ Hornecker.pdf, (accessed March 2012).

6   Harrison, S. and Dourish, P. (1996), Re-place-ing space: the roles of place and space in collaborative systems. *Proc of CSCW'96*. 67–76.

7   See for example Merleau-Ponty 2002.

8   See for example Friedman 2005.

9   Sydney Newman responding to 'General Notes on Background and Approach, authored by Cecil Edwin "Bunny" Webber'. An Unearthly Series – The Origins of a TV Legend, The tenth in our series of features looking at events leading to the creation of a true TV legend, http://www.doctorwhonews.net/2013/05/ unearthly-series-10-040513171617.html (accessed May 2013).

10   For a critique of modernism in British music, see Riley (2010: 1–11).

11   Dick Mills in conversation, 2013: 'We didn't set out to be experimental or avant-garde. We had a job to do and we were too busy doing it. We only experimented within the framework of the job we were on.'

12   BBC press conference 22 May 1958 (quoted in Niebur 2010: 62).

13   Dick Mills said: 'It was all done with actual knob-twiddling then – there was no other way! We did it in lots of little pieces, then joined all the bits of tape together' (quoted in The Story of the BBC Radiophonic Orchestra Steve Marshall, Sound on Sound).

14   Dick Mills in conversation, 2013: 'There was a hierarchy at the BBC which placed composers at the top and engineers were seen as support staff who

got less credit. ... But in reality we were all involved. ... Delia and I worked together in Room 12. We worked together, but Delia was the creative one. I assisted her with all the technical bits. ... You could say I took the bullet on that' (See also Nieber 2010: 58).

15 Dick Mills in conversation, 2013: 'A wobbulator is a huge oscillator in a wooden box with a built in modulator and big circular dial. You could set the dial to whatever depths you wanted and that was your science fiction alarm, rather than having to cut up bits of tape.'

16 Dick Mills in conversation, 2013. See also *A History of the Doctor Who Theme,* Mark Ayres, http://markayres.rwsprojects.co.uk/DWTheme.htm accessed April 2013).

17 Dick Mills in conversation, 2013: 'The sound making equipment tended to be test equipment. The rest of it was tape and razor blades. We didn't have any specialist equipment for music production, not in the beginning.'

18 The number of shots changed little 'over the first nineteen years' reflecting the programme's 'essentially discursive studio-bound nature' (Potter 2007: 169).

19 Paterson, J. (n.d.), The Music and Sound of Doctor Who [http://www.mfiles. co.uk/doctor-who-music.htm accessed May 2013].

20 By 'musical effect' I include incidental and stock music as well as 'special sound', but not dialogue of sound effects where there are unambiguous analogues (like the sound effect for Chesterton's car). I have also included the theme music since, in this episode, the music of the opening (in particular) and closing theme is much more than a signature theme, overrunning the titles and bleeding into the scenes, thus contributing to the overall soundscape of the programme. Here are the scene lengths with musical effect: 1. The opening theme which runs over into the first scene, colludes with the breach of the fourth wall, and fades into the electric hum of TARDIS (1:54); 2. Stock sound of The Arthur Nelson Group which is juxtaposed against Susan's unearthly dance movements (0:46); 3. Ominous incidental music accompanying Susan's rapid reading of a book on the French Revolution (0:15); 4. Three 'flashbacks' exemplifying Susan's Otherness accompanied by incidental music (0:57); 5. Ominous music accompanies the teachers as they enter the scrap-yard fading to the electronic hum of TARDIS (2:00); 6. Interior TARDIS volume is intermittent during the dialogue exchange between the teachers and time-travellers, its hum switching between low and high focus for the viewer, with occasional tumultuous whooping and bell noises (5:04); 7. A burst of frenetic stock music, with comedic connotations, accompanies the scuffle as the Doctor begins the first radiophonic TARDIS dematerialization (2:18); 8. The audio-natural wind effect provides a counterpoint to the wall of TARDIS sound (0:12); 9. The theme music, prefigured by the use of title overlays in the TARDIS take off, plays over the scene of the landing site which then fades into the end titles (0:43).

21 This did not happen as the BBC considered the Workshop a unit of anonymous individuals. However, as Dick Mills suggests, the lack of accreditation was countered by the common knowledge of Derbyshire's involvement while the contribution of the engineers was rarely revisited (Dick Mills in conversation, 2013).

22   Dick Mills in conversation, 2013: 'In order to correct misalignments, it came to me that we'd have to check it physically. Maida Vales studios had very, very long corridors. It was a very old build, a converted skating rink. The signature tune was thirty seconds long. That's about 700 feet. So we'd roll out three spools of tape all the way down this corridor. That's how we'd find the "bum" note. It would really stand out as out of place.' Dick Mills in conversation, 2013. Also see: Marshall, Steve. *The Story of the BBC Radiophonic Orchestra*, Sound on Sound [http://www.soundonsound.com/sos/apr08/articles/radiophonic.htm accessed April 2013].

23   Dick Mills in conversation, 2013: 'For the bass line, Delia pre-recorded the plucked string and moved up and down the frequency scale.' For the different versions of this story, see The Story of the BBC Radiophonic Orchestra Steve Marshall, Sound on Sound.

24   Dick Mills in conversation, 2013: 'The main melody is made using a melodica. The sweep noise was Delia on the oscillator. She did the original sweeps and then cut them together.'

25   For a fuller discussion on where howlround started, see Letters Page, Prospero magazine, July 2011, Issue 5: 4.

26   It is 3 o'clock in the morning according to the script for the pilot episode (Archival script BBC 27 September 1963, BBC Drama).

27   As Tarkovsky says, 'Music has the capacity to change the whole emotional tone of a filmed sequence' (Tarkovsky 2000: 158).

28   It is also ironic given Cecil Edwin 'Bunny' Webber's reluctance to use everyday objects for the design of the Doctor's ship since the 'magic door' had become a well-used science fiction trope (see Weber, General Notes on Background and Approach, May 1965, BBC archives). This was superseded by writer Anthony Coburn's suggestion to use a police box ('Revision Time'. An Unearthly Series – The Origins of a TV Legend, The eleventh in our series of features looking at events leading to the creation of a true TV legend).

29   Although Susan refers to the music as by John Smith and The Common Men, it is actually performed by The Arthur Nelson Group. The track was written by Nelson and Raymond, released on the Conroy label and first broadcast on Z-Cars in 1962.

30   'General Notes on Background and Approach, authored by Cecil Edwin "Bunny" Webber'. An Unearthly Series – The Origins of a TV Legend, The tenth in our series of features looking at events leading to the creation of a true TV legend. [http://www.doctorwhonews.net/2013/05/unearthly-series-10-040513171617.html accessed May 2013].

31   'When Susan returns to the TARDIS to retrieve the crew's anti-radiation drugs … the sound of the TARDIS seems to embrace her like a blanket as she enters' (Niebur 2007: 213).

32   The grim determination etched on the pair's faces supports both the proposition that they are well-seasoned TARDIS travellers, and that they are not entirely happy ones.

33   652-lines was around the corner with the advent of BBC2 in 1964.

34 Acousmatic sound can be defined by the lack of visible sources of sound (see Shaeffer 1966) not something normally associated with natural wind sounds unless, as an audience member, you become conscious of the sound-as-effect. Such dissonance between sound and a common correlative must have been the experience of the audiences to silent films, this cinematic experience being one clearly comprised of the extraneous elements of projected film and musical accompaniment. Coming after a wall of incidental music and 'special sound' there is perhaps no sound which could be experienced without the immediate question as to its source. It is in this context that the wind sound becomes metaphysical, perhaps even existential.

35 As Voegelin says, 'In the quiet sounds of Silence the listener becomes audible to himself as a discrete member of an audience' (Voegelin 2011: xv). Listening is generative and inventive of noises from inside 'the body, where my subjectivity is at the centre of the sound production, audible to myself' (Voegelin 2011: 83).

References

Augé, M. (1995), *Non-Places: An Introduction to Supermodernity*, trans. John Howe, London: Verso.

Ayres, M., *A History of the Doctor Who Theme*. http://markayres.rwsprojects. co.uk/DWTheme.htm (accessed April 2013).

Bignell, J. (2007), 'The child as addressee, viewer and consumer in mid-1960s Doctor Who', in D. Butler (ed.), *Time and Relative Dissertations in Space: Critical Perspectives on Doctor Who*. Manchester: Manchester University Press.

Burlingame, J. (1996), *TV's Biggest Hits: The Story of Television Themes from Dragnet to Friends*, New York: Schirmer.

Butler, D. (2013), 'The Work of Music in the Age of Steel: Themes, Leitmotifs and Stock Music', in K. J. Donnelly and P. Hayward (eds), *New Doctor Who in Science Fiction Television: Tuned to the Future*. Abingdon: Routledge.

Chion, M. (1994), *Audio-Vision: Sound on Screen*, New York: Columbia University Press.

Coburn, A. (1963), No. 1 / Pilot 'An Unearthly Child', BBC Drama Dept archival Copy.

Crisell, A. (1997), *An Introductory History of British Broadcasting*, London: Routledge.

Deaville, J. (2011a), 'A Discipline Emerges: Reading Writing and Listening to Television', in J. Deaville (ed.), *Music in Television: Channels of Listening*. Abingdon: Routledge.

Deaville, J. (2011b), 'Introduction: The Problem of Music in Television' in J. Deaville (ed.), *Music in Television: Channels of Listening*. Abingdon: Routledge.

Deleuze, G. and F. Guattari (1987), *A Thousand Plateaus Capitalism and Schizophrenia*, Minneapolis: University of Minnesota Press.

Donnelly, K. J. (2005), *The Spectre of Sound: music in film and television*, London: British Film Institute.

Donnelly, K. J. (2007), 'Between prosaic functionalism and sublime Experimentation': Doctor Who and musical sound design', in D. Butler (ed.),

Time and Relative Dissertations in Space: Critical Perspectives on Doctor Who, Manchester: Manchester University Press.

Donnelly, K. J. and P. Hayward (eds) (2013), *Music in Science Fiction Television: Tuned to the Future*, London: Routledge.

Ellis, J. (1982), *Visible Fictions: Television, Cinema, Video*, London: Routledge.

Fiske, J. (1987), *Television Culture*, London: Methuen.

Fox, E. (2012), *Rainy Brain, Sunny Brain*, London: Random House.

Friedman, T. (2005), *The World is Flat: A brief history of the Twenty-First Century*, New York: Farrar Straus and Giroux.

Frith, S. (2007), *Taking Popular Music Seriously Selected Essays*, Burlington: Ashgate Publishing.

Fuller, G. (2010), Doctor Who's theme tunes: a complete history, *The Daily Telegraph*. http://www.telegraph.co.uk/culture/tvandradio/doctor-who/7615221/Doctor-Whos-theme-tunes-a-complete-history.html (accessed 20 April 2016).

Giles, J. and T. Middleton (eds) (1995), *Writing Englishness 1900–1950 An Introductory Sourcebook on National Identity*, London: Routledge.

Hayward, P. and J. Fitzgerald (2013), 'Rematerialization: Musical Engagements with the British TV Series Doctor Who in Music', in K. J. Donnelly and P. Hayward (eds), *Science Fiction Television: Tuned to the Future*, Abingdon: Routledge.

Harrison, S. and P. Dourish (1996), *Re-place-ing space: the roles of place and space in collaborative systems*. Proc of CSCW '96. ACM, 67–76.

Hendy, D. (2013), *Noise: a Human History of Sound and Listening*, London: Profile.

Hornecker, E. (n.d.), *Space and Place: setting the stage for social interaction*. http://www.informatics.sussex.ac.uk/research/groups/interact/publications/Hornecker.pdf (accessed March 2012).

Kassabian, A. (2001), *Hearing Film*, London: Routledge.

Koldau, L. M. (2012), The Soundtrack Album as Text and Medium to Re-Experience a Movie [Key note paper at the Korean International Film Conference, Seoul, 2 November 2012].

Lyotard, J. F. (1994), *The Postmodern Condition: A Report on Knowledge*, Manchester: Manchester University Press.

Marshall, S. (n.d.), The Story of the BBC Radiophonic Orchestra, Sound on Sound. http://www.soundonsound.com/sos/apr08/articles/radiophonic.htm (accessed April 2013).

McCoy, S. (2005), 'A new Who does it', *The Guardian*, Thursday 24 March. https://www.theguardian.com/media/2005/mar/24/broadcasting.g2.

Merleau-Ponty, M. (2002), *Phenomenology of Perception*, trans. C. Smith, London: Routledge [1945].

Metz, C. (1980), 'Aural Objects' in G. Mast, L. Braudy and M. Cohen (eds), *Film Theory and Criticism*, Oxford: Oxford University Press.

Neumeyer, D. and J. Buhler (2001), 'Analytical and Interpretative Approaches to Film Music (I)' in K. J. Donnelly (ed.), *Film Music: Critical Approaches*, 16–38, Edinburgh: Edinburgh University Press.

Newman, K. (2005), *Doctor Who. A Critical Reading of the Series*, London: BFI.

Niebur, L. (2007), 'The music of machines: "special sound" as music in Doctor Who' in D. Butler (ed.), *Time and Relative Dissertations in Space: Critical Perspectives on Doctor Who*, Manchester: Manchester University Press.

Niebur, L. (2010), *Special Sound: The Creation and Legacy of the BBC Radiophonic Workshop*, Oxford: Oxford University Press.

Nielsen Cross-Platform Report (October 2013), *The Cross-Platform Report: A look across screens*. http://www.nielsen.com/us/en/insights/reports/2013/the-cross-platform-report--a-look-across-screens.html.

Pasnau, R. (1999), What is Sound? *The Philosophical Quarterly*, 49(196) July.

Paterson, J. (2013), The Music and Sound of Doctor Who. http://www.mfiles.co.uk/doctor-who-music.htm (accessed May 2013).

Peel, J. (1986), *Files Magazine Spotlight on Doctor Who: Season One Part 1*, California: Psi Fi Movie Press.

Pless, D. (2012), 'The Decline and Fall of the British Empire', in C. Lewis and P. Smithka (eds), *Doctor Who and Philosophy: Bigger on the Inside*. Chicago: Open Court.

Potter, I. (2008), 'The Filipino army's advance on Reykjavik: world-building in Studio D and its legacy', in D. Butler (ed.), *Time and Relative Dissertations in Space: Critical Perspectives on Doctor Who*. Manchester: Manchester University Press.

Reynolds, S. (2008), 'Sorcerers of Sound', *The Guardian*, Saturday 20 September. https://www.theguardian.com/profile/simonreynolds?page=2.

Riley, M. (ed.) (2010), *British Music and Modernism, 1895–1960*, London: Ashgate.

Rodman, R. (2010), *Tuning In: American Narrative Television Music*, Oxford: Oxford University Press.

Shaeffer, P. (1966), 'Acousmatics', trans. D. W. Smith, in C. Cox and D. Warner (eds), *Audio Culture: Reading in Modern Music*, New York: Continuum (2004).

Smith, A. (1991), *National Identity*, Harmondsworth: Penguin.

Smith, J. (1996), 'Unheard Melodies? A Critique of Psychoanalytical Theories of Film Music' in D. Bordwell and N. Carroll (eds), *Post-Theory: Reconstructing Film Studies*, Madison: University of Wisconsin Press.

Stevens, E. C. (2010), 'The Popular Electronic Doctor Who and the BBC's Radiophonic Workshop' in M. Beattie, R. P. Garner and U. McCormack (eds), *Impossible Worlds, Impossible Things: Cultural Perspectives on Doctor Who, Torchwood and The Sarah Jane Adventures*, Cambridge: Cambridge Scholars.

Tagg, P. (1999), 'V music: Quick fixes, Semiotics and the Democratic Right to Know' [conference presentation, *Music and Manipulation*, Nalen, Stockholm, 18 September 1999]. http://www.tagg.org/articles/sth9909.html.

Tarkovsky, A. (2000), *Sculpting in Time: Reflections on the Cinema*, trans. K. H. Blair, Austin: University of Texas Press.

Toop, D. (2010), *Sinister Resonance: The Mediumship of the Listener*, New York: Continuum.

Toop, D. (2011), 'Special Sound: The Creation and Legacy of the BBC Radiophonic Workshop', *Times Higher Education*, 10 February 2011.

Tulloch, J. and M. Alvarado (1983), *Doctor Who: The Unfolding Text*, London: Macmillan.

Voegelin, S. (2011), *Listening to Noise and Silence: Towards a Philosophy of Sound Art*, New York: Continuum.

Various (2013), An Unearthly Series – The Origins of a TV Legend, doctorwhonews.net.

Various (2011), Letters Page, *Prospero Magazine*, Issue 5, July 4.

Weber, C. E. (1963), General Notes on Background and Approach, BBC Archives.

Discography

Arthur Nelson Group (1963) 'Three Guitar Moods 2', *Doctor Who: The 50th Anniversary Collection* (2013), Silva Screen Records [Album]

Ron Grainer and Delia Derbyshire at the Radiophonic Workshop (1963) 'Doctor Who Theme', *Doctor Who: The 50th Anniversary Collection* (2013), Silva Screen Records [Album]

CHAPTER SIX

Productive boredom and unproductive labour:

Cabaret Voltaire in the People's Republic of South Yorkshire

Jon Hackett

The focus of this chapter is twofold but in each case involves us returning to the 1970s. First, I propose to revisit some theoretical debates that were being conducted at that time from within British Marxism, in relation to certain concepts concerning labour and industry. Second, I wish to articulate these conceptions with the early work of Sheffield post-punk band Cabaret Voltaire, in terms both of the band and of the economic and political culture of their home city. Sheffield is synonymous in the popular imagination with the (de)industrialized North, notably for its steel and cutlery industries, something that Sheffield bands often draw on in their iconography and sometimes themes. Further, in the late seventies and early eighties, its reputation as the People's or Socialist Republic of South Yorkshire was a contemporary manifestation both of Sheffield's radical tradition going back centuries and more generally its reputation for bloody-minded independence. Therefore, I will argue that the link between certain debates within radical politics and popular music is far from accidental.

My overall thesis in this chapter is that during the time in question, there are a number of shared concerns between, on the one hand, cultural theory and, on the other, popular music practices. So much so, in fact, that in the case of certain musicians like Scritti Politti the separation between these two practices seems artificial. Further, returning to some of these debates and problematics allows us to dust down some concepts that were being worked out and elaborated at the time, specifically via debates in Marxism. Though these debates might appear to be rather of their time, I will argue first that they are helpful in understanding the developments in popular music production, distribution and consumption in the post-punk era, and second (and more tentatively) that they might in fact have interesting things to say to our current conjuncture.

Therefore, I will focus on three ideas in this chapter that were debates in Western Marxism in the 1970s: namely, the questions of productive and unproductive labour, of modes of production and moments of consumption, and of the potential or otherwise of machines. In the 1970s, translations of Marx's own texts such as the *Grundrisse* as well as those of twentieth-century Western Marxists such as Althusser and Gramsci, were very much part of contemporary debates on political, economic and, most pertinently for this chapter, cultural questions, including as we shall see for some post-punk musicians themselves. In seeking to make the link between concepts regarding economic practices, and a pop group, I am in fact in the midst of the base – superstructure problematic, which is one of the more rigid models that interpretation of these newly translated Marxist texts sought to complicate and render less reductive in the seventies. So the question as to whether and how much Cabaret Voltaire's work can be 'reduced' to its historical, economic and political context sees us return to the debates in Marxism contemporaneous to the group's early output.

Cabaret Voltaire

Cabaret Voltaire were one of the most visible groups in the Sheffield scene of the 1970s. The 'Cabs' were active from the mid-seventies, before punk broke. Though they are often seen as a post-punk band, the group themselves trace their activity back to 1973 and Roxy Music, with Brian Eno as the emblematic figure – a defiantly non-prog musician who claimed that musical training was not necessary to produce popular music (a very proto-punk idea) as well as championing the use of the synthesizer and tape machines (Reynolds 2005: 154).

Chris Watson, a telephone engineer by day, left the band for Tyne Tees Television in the early eighties but his early influence in constructing synthesizers via kits and using the tape recorders in his loft, where the band practised, was crucial. Of these loft sessions, Richard H. Kirk recalled: 'It was still just the idea of tackling boredom and of actually feeling that you were doing something, rather than just going out and getting pissed' (Fish 1984: 21). This is the productive boredom I allude to in my title, a familiar theme for punk bands like Buzzcocks or the Sex Pistols, as well as Cabaret

Voltaire. At this stage, Kirk's main instrument was the clarinet; Stephen Mallinder (known as Mal)'s bass and vocals, like Kirk's improvisations, were distorted and warped via various effects into a lo-fi dirge. This was combined with snippets from radio or TV recordings; the band likened their output to the Beats' cut-up techniques as well as Dadaist ready-mades (as their name would signal). The overall sound was the closest that British bands have come to Krautrock bands like Faust and Can – Kirk's clarinet adding a free-jazz squall here and there.

What struck early audiences was very much the electronic nature of the music: the centrality of Watson's synths to the sound as well as the use of electronic instruments for percussion – the band had no drummer. In this regard they were in tune with other Sheffield bands like the Human League, who used to go on stage with the spotlight on a drum machine, where the drummer would be – making a point of visibly pressing the play button to annoy keep-rock-live types (Reynolds 2005: 164). Cabaret Voltaire apparently went even further at Sheffield's post-punk venue The Limit, in response to the venue allegedly reneging on an agreed payment and promising the band some of the bar takings instead. The band looped some white noise and repaired to the bar; one audience member looking back was impressed nonetheless: 'They weren't even on the stage. It was mesmerising' (cited in Anderson 2009: 34).

Many have observed that for Cabaret Voltaire, punk provided a live-performance context and audience rather than a direct musical influence, perhaps like Suicide in the United States, who met with similarly hostile crowds not ready for synthesized music at punk concerts. However, the band interestingly note that when they were supporting Buzzcocks at the Lyceum in London, it was the latter band and not the Cabs that had an iron bar thrown at them (Reynolds 2009: 246); this was the gig at which Geoff Travis of Rough Trade was present, facilitating their signing with the label.

One of the crucial aspects for our purposes is the group's mode of production. Sheffield in the 1970s was a largely supportive environment in which to make music. Unemployment and housing benefit in the late seventies were much more viable a mid- to long-term option than they would be now. Sheffield abounded in rehearsal and studio spaces available for cheap rents, often in disused factories and warehouses. In addition, public transport was the flagship policy of Sheffield's Labour Council, and the brainchild of councillor David Blunkett and three of his colleagues. 'In 1977 the fare for a 2.5-mile journey was 7 pence, compared with 36 pence in West Yorkshire' (Price 2011: 152). Furthermore, an informal network of squats, parties and gigs emerged for young people – the future members of Cabaret Voltaire, The Human League, Heaven 17 and, according to some, Pulp, would be present on various occasions.

The band rehearsed initially in Chris Watson's loft. Later on the music department of Sheffield University allowed them to experiment with a VCS 3 synthesizer and a Revox tape machine – though the band were resistant to being seen as performance artists, which the university connection might imply. Richard H. Kirk's opinion was: 'The money must be available in England; it is just that the Arts Council grants go to the biggest wankers imaginable' (Fish 1984: 181). After this, cheap rent allowed them to set up their Western Works studios in an abandoned former office of the Sheffield Federation of Young Socialists. Western Works allowed the band to record other groups or offer them recording space; one band that admired the Cabs and took a trip to the studio was nearby Manchester's Joy Division. Nick Crossley has recently pointed out the importance of the band as 'support personnel for others' in the city (Crossley 2015: 186), given the relative dearth of such support in Sheffield, compared with Manchester's Factory Records, or Liverpool with Bill Drummond, Dave Balfe and others.

Before recording the series of singles and albums for Rough Trade that captured their early sound, on a non-contractual deal that allowed the band to record elsewhere too, label boss Geoff Travis lent the band enough for a four-track recording studio and mixing desk (Reynolds 2005: 168). The band's purchase of their own VCS 3 synthesizer was also courtesy of the deal. Essentially, the band could now control production, performance and recording; distribution was via a pioneering independent label rather than a major.

Unproductive labour

In order to locate the band's practices in terms of what were then current debates, it will be worth highlighting some of the theoretical engagements with labour and industry in the late 1970s, both from the radical Left and from the radical Right. What I hope to show is that from both sides there is a questioning of what constitutes 'productive' labour as opposed to 'unproductive' labour, and furthermore, what is at stake in the valorization of the former, whether from 'economist' Marxism or from Thatcherite monetarism. As regards the right-wing take on such questions, we can see emerging a set of discourses attacking the role of the state and nationalized industry, and valorizing entrepreneurs and the market that have remained dominant ever since.

We can see these debates against the post-war consensus on the welfare state. Austerity projects vaunt themselves as reducing public debt and deficit, as well as inflation, at all costs, but a recent political economist reminds us that this was for several decades not the orthodoxy: 'In the twentieth century, a totally different view of public debt emerged, based on the conviction that debt could serve as an instrument of policy aimed at raising public spending and redistributing wealth for the benefit of the least well-off members of society' (Piketty 2014: 132). This Keynesian alternative to free-market economics was in fact hegemonic in the West in the mid-century and would only begin to lose ground during the time in question here, the turn of the 1980s.

As one of the emerging opponents of the post-war consensus, we can take as one canonical exposition the Stockton Lecture of Keith Joseph, future education minister and a key intellectual force behind Thatcherism. Joseph's target in this polemic is what he sees as 'our socialist anti-enterprise climate: indifference, ignorance and distaste on the part of politicians, civil servants and communicators for the processes of wealth-creation and entrepreneurship' (1976: 9). What needed to be defended for Joseph were the 'wealth-creators', currently held back by the wasteful practices of the 'wealth-consuming sector' or 'state-cum-subsidized sector' (ibid., 14). Joseph's monetarist prescription was cuts to state spending, inflation and the money supply, in order to support the heroic but bureaucratically hampered entrepreneurs.

Behind Joseph's views are the right-wing economics of Hayek and the Chicago School, often seen as the architects of what these days is commonly described as neo-liberalism. It is an obvious point to make a link between the Thatcherite project and more recent politics of austerity that are dominant now. It is in fact remarkable in some ways how long it has taken austerity projects to catch up with the formulas and remedies prescribed by monetarists in earlier decades.

One of the intellectual inputs into Thatcherism and neo-liberalism, more generally, was the Chicago economist Milton Friedman. He articulated his controversial ideas about the role of the state in the following terms:

> The humanitarian and egalitarian sentiment which helped produce the steeply graduated individual income tax has also produced a host of other measures directed at promoting the 'welfare' of particular groups. The most important single set of measures is the bundle misleadingly labelled 'social security'. Others are public housing, minimum wage laws, farm price supports, medical care for particular groups, special aid programs, and so on. (Friedman 2002: 176)

For Friedman, in almost all cases, the market will deliver more effective services and will guarantee 'freedom' of (or perhaps from) government much more effectively than any 'socialist' state intervention. To take another example, Friedman evaluates whether state education can be justified on the grounds that education for all promotes 'a stable and democratic society':

> The actual administration of educational institutions by the government, the 'nationalization', as it were, of the bulk of the 'education industry' is much more difficult to justify on these, or, so far as I can see, any other grounds. The desirability of such nationalization has seldom been faced explicitly. (Friedman 2002: 89)

Obviously it has taken quite a few decades for the full force of this to be felt with academies, trust and faith schools, tuition fees and the abolition of maintenance allowances and grants, but we can evidently see such ideas as a continuity between the era in question and our own. Ultimately, the marketization of education and other aspects of the welfare state is an attempt to open up the 'unproductive' state sector to competition and the market, which are taken as a guarantor of efficiency and plurality. From this perspective the reputation of Sheffield's Council as the People's Republic of South Yorkshire represented a bastion of municipal socialism and subsidized public services, much of which would be scaled back in the coming decades.

As regards Marxism, there was already a long-standing analysis of the question of unproductive and productive labour, stemming from Marx's own engagement with Adam Smith and later economists. The most extended analysis of these concepts appears in the first volume of the *Theories of Surplus Value*, where a long chapter is devoted to the question (Marx 1969: 152–304). On the whole, Marx defends Adam Smith's conception of productive labour from later objections from within 'bourgeois' political economy.

Marx supports Smith's 'first' definition of productive labour: 'Only labour which produces capital is productive labour' (1969: 156). Furthermore, this standpoint also allows us to define unproductive labour: 'It is labour which is not exchanged with capital, but *directly* with revenue, that is, with wages or profit' (157, original emphasis). What Marx rejects in Smith is the latter's further specification of productive labour as productive of a 'vendible commodity', which abandons the first definition's emphasis on the *social form* of the labour in favour of the particular type of use value involved. The crucial distinction is whether or not the labour is paid for by *capital* invested in production designed to make a further profit (productive) or by *revenue* that does not re-enter the circuits of capital (unproductive). In Adam Smith's time, for instance, much revenue was spent on domestic servants or luxury goods by landed gentry (yielding no return), where a capitalist might valorize it instead in further value-creating production.

In Marx, then, the distinction between productive and unproductive labour does not hinge upon, say, the utility of particular objects, which some vulgarized readings (returning to the 'vendible commodity' of Smith's second definition) stress. Further, apparently 'unproductive' labour in health or education may nonetheless contribute to the profitability of labour power for the capitalist, by ensuring a healthy and sufficiently skilled labour force. In the 1970s some Marxists were keen to defend such 'unproductive' labour as directly social labour from more reductive 'economist' critiques of it as unproductive. Peter Howell, writing in *Revolutionary Communist*, for instance, criticizes Denis Healey's and Tony Benn's valorization of manufacturing and their anxieties over 'deindustrialization' in the mid-seventies for falling into this trap, pointing out their common concern with Keith Joseph, of all people (Howell 1975). By favouring industrial production over, say, service industries, those on the Left risked reproducing the same hierarchy of productive over unproductive labour as emerging Thatcherites, according to this argument. The value of the distinction for

Marxists in the 1970s was its pertinence in analysing the relation of labour to capital, for its analytic precision – and not as an implicit valorization of some labour over other kinds.

As for Cabaret Voltaire, their labour was arguably even more unproductive than the wasteful public sector. Their records were commodities available on the market – yet in Rough Trade they had a pioneering independent label that was run, *to all evidence,* not for profit but as an old-fashioned hippie-style collective. Though certainly not opposed in principle to making a profit, the label early on appeared to be inspired rather by Geoff Travis's and his colleagues' fondness for idiosyncratic music styles rather than by a long-term business plan (Taylor 2010); what profit there would be might allow other records to be released by the label. Cabaret Voltaire's performances were ephemeral purchases that left no material ('vendible') commodity after leaving the venue except for the ticket. However, their mode of production and perhaps their very sound engage with the big industry and artisanal histories of Sheffield in interesting ways as we shall see in the next section.

It is tempting, here, to make a link between post-punk musical practices and the educational environment through which some of its practitioners had passed. As with so many post-punk musicians, Richard H. Kirk had been to art college and as we have seen, Cabaret Voltaire had been lent equipment by the music department at Sheffield University. More widely, the DIY spirit that had informed punk and that carried over into earlier post-punk is in line with some of the more experimental art college practices of the 1960s and 1970s. The musician Eno characterized the mid-sixties' art college motto as 'process not product' (Frith and Horne 1989: 117). This was a pedagogy stressing ideas and experiment rather than polished, marketable products. One might speculate whether the relatively unstructured, anarchic processes of the art college might be contrasted with the more output-focused, technical proficiency of contemporary 'creative industries' approaches in terms of another market-driven transition from 'unproductive' to more 'productive' cultural labour.

Sound of the city

Sheffield's municipal infrastructure, in the absence of any effective *entrepreneurial* mechanism, became inevitably enmeshed in the reification of the city's sound and unconscious celebration of its popular cultural forms. The sonic landscape is constructed upon its urban topology capturing the sound waves and rhythmic eddies and so shapes their movement, reception, incubation and production within the *community's shared past.* (Mallinder 2011: 82, emphasis added)

The above argument in fact comes from Cabaret Voltaire's own bassist Stephen Mallinder's recent PhD thesis. (So Mallinder, like those working in higher education, continues to labour *unproductively*.) In 2002, for the sleeve notes for *Methodology*, a compilation of their early loft recordings, Richard H. Kirk looking back wrote: 'It was just an innocent reflection of the times, no different than the Beach Boys singing about surfing and the good times in California. But there was no surf to ride in Sheffield, just post war desolation, unemployment and ugly urban landscapes.' It is something of a commonplace to connect the prevalence of synths and drum machines to Sheffield's past (such as in the metronomic percussion and clashing sheet metal sounds in some of the Cabs' recordings) but the constant reiteration of these parallels by those involved in the scene lends such observations some credence.

The sleeve notes for the 2002 release *Methodology '74/'78*, which collects the group's demo recordings from before the Rough Trade contract was signed, include a quotation from Jon Savage, writing in the punk fanzine, *Search and Destroy*: 'CV's sound is bland in texture, remote, synthetic – sucking up the boredom of flickering channels on TV when there's nothing else to do – the random sounds and noises of a collapsing, grey environment on the verge of entropy, the effect this has on people's psyche ... and throwing it back in your face' (*Methodology*, 2002). Savage's quote reiterates this linking of Cabaret Voltaire's *sound* with the post-industrial Sheffield landscape – while articulating this with a simultaneous sense of fascination and boredom with the media. On the one hand, as with much industrial music, there is an obsession with control and propaganda, nurtured by an interest common to many industrial bands (notably Manchester's Throbbing Gristle) in William Burroughs and perhaps by weed paranoia, as well as reflecting the importance of media as a resource for sampling in tape loops; on the other hand, a sense of boredom associated with punk, of course, and with the severely reduced media ecology of the late 1970s, with its three terrestrial television channels and its early broadcast curfew.

We can situate observations like these within wider arguments made about the industrial genre as a whole. One writer describes the genre in these terms: 'The music in question mimics the jarring, pounding, repetitive sounds of the factory and heavy machinery. Those sounds intentionally correspond to inhuman qualities. The sonorities (like the lyrics) tend to be dissonant and brooding, dark and morbid, harsh and severe' (van der Laan 1997: 137). Or for Michael Goddard, writing on Laibach, we might point to 'Western Industrial Music's fetishisation of the aesthetics of the industrial revolution and mechanical technologies' (Goddard 2006: 46). Obviously with its association with steel and cutlery, Sheffield is the perfect milieu for such a music, given Cabaret Voltaire's recollection of the sounds of factory work as a semi-permanent backdrop to their tentative attic recordings in the 1970s. Philip Long has recently characterized this frequent observation among Sheffield musicians of the importance of the city's ambient noise for their own music production as 'listening to the city' (2014: 56).

Mode of production – or moment
of consumption?

One of the most interesting parallels between (some) cultural theory and popular music at this time is a shift from what one might characterize as an emphasis on production and distribution, to one focused rather on the moment of consumption. Inevitably this will mean being selective in both areas – but taken as a whole the shared concerns reveal interesting parallels between problematics being worked out both in sociology and emerging cultural studies on the one hand, and in the strategies of popular musicians on the other.

One of the artists who exemplifies these trends is Green Gartside of Scritti Politti, one of the musicians most explicitly engaged with cultural theory, most notoriously perhaps in the group's 1982 song, 'Jacques Derrida'. Like Richard H. Kirk of Cabaret Voltaire, Green had been a member of the Young Communist League, and his indie label St Pancras was named after the squat he and the band, as well as various ideological co-travellers, occupied at the time (Taylor 2010: 107–8). St Pancras records were distributed by Rough Trade, whose staff shared the band's socialist and squatter commitments. The sessions recorded by the band for John Peel's show, later released on the 2005 compilation, *Early*, give the best picture of the band's initial post-punk aesthetic – scratchy guitars, funky bass and collapsing song structures bringing to mind the contemporaneous work of Bristol's Pop Group. 'Hegemony', one of the tracks recorded for Scritti Politti's Peel Sessions, combines Gramsci's ideas in the lyrics with brittle, stop-starting punk funk, in emblematic fashion for the band at this time.

Green's vocals at this stage of his career have been compared with those of Robert Wyatt. One of the interesting relationships outlined by Neil Taylor in his fascinating history of Rough Trade, *Document and Eyewitness*, is the one between these two artists, both signed to Rough Trade Records at the turn of the decade, who struck up a friendship based around music and politics. Green recalls some political disagreements between the older 'Stalinist' commitments of Wyatt and his own more (what we might call) 'New Left' theoretical concerns (Taylor 2010: 150). In particular, he recalls lending Wyatt a copy of *Mode of Production and Social Formation* by Barry Hindess and Paul Hirst, which was not well received by Wyatt: 'The phone stopped ringing for a bit' (152). Green is very clear on the close intrication of politics and popular music in this particular milieu: 'There was a lot of that Gramscian talk around at that time, talking about culture and ideology in a more straightforward Marxist-y way. And finally there was the whole punk thing about control of production and distribution, getting up and doing it yourself. So these were all separate but seamlessly contiguous areas' (Reynolds 2009: 182). The Rough Trade producer and member of Red Crayola, Mayo Thompson, also specifically mentions discussions of Hindess and Hirst in the Rough Trade milieu (Taylor 2010: 126).

Interestingly, *Mode of Production and Social Formation* might be seen as part of the cultural shift aforementioned from more 'economist' concerns with mode of production and distribution, to a more 'culturalist' emphasis on social formations. Hindess and Hirst were seen as some of the foremost British Althusserians – before increasingly taking their distance from his theoretical ideas. In *Mode of Production and Social Formation*, the target of their critique (apart from their own autocritique of their earlier work, *Pre-Capitalist Modes of Production*), is Althusser and Balibar's conception in *Reading Capital* of the 'mode of production' as determinate 'in the last instance'.

Hirst and Hindess do acknowledge Althusser's role in moving Marxist analysis away from economist determinism: 'Marx and Engels, with varying success, and virtually every other Marxist thinker (Gramsci and Althusser being the most systematic in their opposed ways) have been in retreat from the consequences of economism' (Hindess and Hirst 1977: 5). The relative autonomy of politics and ideology from economics, in Althusser's conceptions, already avoids the 'vulgar' reduction of other spheres of production from the narrowly economic. Nonetheless, Althusser's commitment to economics 'in the last instance' leads him, for these authors, to an untenable prioritization of 'mode of production' over the *relations* of production, both between the owners of the means of production and direct producers, but also much more widely in terms of other sets of class relations. Hence their conclusion, 'Mode of production, in other words, is displaced as an object of analysis' (ibid., 55).

In the early post-punk era, interventions at the level of mode of production and distribution were certainly still sufficiently novel and promising to be ends in themselves. John Peel observes, recalling punk, 'I like the DIY idea where if you got the bass player to sell his motorbike and you knocked over a few phone boxes you could generate enough money to make a record. People did, and an amazing number of them were really good' (Reynolds 2009: 169). The DIY inspiration was key for many of the personnel of Rough Trade Records, many of whom squatted in the Trafalgar pub squat in Ladbroke Grove by night (when not at gigs) while working in the 202 Kensington Road shop by day (Taylor 2010). Some of the workers in the shop were themselves band members of The Raincoats, Swell Maps and other bands released by the record label. The Rough Trade shop itself was a major outlet for independent records (as well as, for instance, reggae imports); later it was a leading impetus behind the independent distributors, the Cartel.

Cabaret Voltaire themselves were at a further remove of independence from what was already an independent record label. Part of this was a felt distance from the London-centric, post-hippy collective at Rough Trade (Fish and Hallbery 1985: 44–9); another was the working-class Northern identity they shared with some other label sign-ups like The Fall (Taylor 2010: 101–2). This was in marked contrast to the scene in the London shop. More concretely, the band produced their own work and in fact secured investment from Rough Trade in order to do so. One amusing anecdote that underlines their independence is related by Richard H. Kirk; on a visit to Sheffield in which Geoff Travis was to be involved in the recording process, the band gave him a dummy fader in order to prevent him from having any real input. This was on Jon Savage's advice to Kirk: 'On no account let Geoff mix the sound' (Taylor 2010: 135).

Another typical punk method for subversion at the level of production stems from the situationists, who were such a noted influence on Malcolm McLaren and others. This is the strategy of *détournement*, whereby a cultural product is diverted from its intended meaning via reappropriation (Debord and Wolman 1956). In the case of Cabaret Voltaire, we might point to their use of technology in general to produce sheer noise and sound collages that, pre-sampling, were novel in the extreme. Chris Watson's experimentation with electronics is pivotal; so too is the band's treatment of Steven Mallinder's vocals with ring modulators, to produce a Dalek-like vocal sound. Richard H. Kirk also recalls redeeming a guitar, amplifier and drum machine combination, a sort of disco all-in-one: 'It had glitter all over it, like it was a piece of technology for cabaret.' What attracted Kirk to it was its potential for repurposing as a programmable drum machine: 'Most drum machines just had preset beats, like the foxtrot or disco. ... But with this you could actually mess around with the rhythm – drop out the snare or bass drum or hi-hat' (Reynolds 2009: 253). One might compare this with the analogous creative *détournement* by Chicago acid house musicians of the Roland TB303 synth, used ubiquitously by these music practitioners to make squelching sounds presumably never envisaged by the company's technicians.

At the risk of over-simplifying, the initial emphasis of post-punk (with the stress here on 'punk') on independent mode of production and distribution was for some not much longer lasting than punk had been itself. After 1982 or so, much of the concern for at least some post-punk (with the stress here on 'post') was with an entryist strategy instead – to make New Pop on major labels and subvert the industry from within. The mode of production would not be challenged so much as the moment of consumption; pop music fans would buy records in droves on major labels which had been created as acts of subversion by interlopers. This is analysed at some length in Part Two of Simon Reynolds's *Rip It Up and Start Again* (2005). Scritti Politti replaced the scratchy agit-pop of their early work with the pristine plastic funk of *Cupid and Psyche* (1985), for which Geoff Travis of Rough Trade himself had helped source producers, realizing that the production values required were beyond the resources of an indie (Taylor 2010: 220–1).

Cabaret Voltaire had also left Rough Trade, releasing *The Crackdown* (1983) on Some Bizarre/Virgin. Following the departure of Chris Watson to Tyne Tees Television (he remains an accomplished television sound recordist), the Cabs' music on this record is more polished in a 1980s way, with 'Just Fascination' charting in the lower reaches of the mainstream, not just the indie, charts. Comparisons might be made with Joy Division's transformation from post-punk guitar band to New Order's 'Blue Monday', also from 1983, though New Order's chart success was considerably greater than that of Cabaret Voltaire. Both bands remained more identifiably post-punk, however, than some of the other New Pop arrivistes such as, say, Scritti, Simple Minds or The Thompson Twins.

Simon Frith and Howard Horne in *Art into Pop* (1987) provide a classic framework in which to think through this shift between independence and entryism for post-punk musicians. Emblematic of this shift, for them, is Manchester's Factory Records, home to Joy Division/New Order, as well as the punk-funk band A Certain Ratio: '[Factory] reveals a difference between punk and post-punk versions of pop "subversion". ... For Factory the key to the politics of the pop process is the "moment of consumption" – the shock effect has to be built into the circulation of commodities itself' (Frith and Horne 1987: 137). One might allude here to the near-fetish status of certain Factory releases, notably the 'Blue Monday' 12-inch itself, which lost money for Factory due to its expensive production values rather than sales (since it is the biggest selling 12-inch single of all time). One should note that Factory, nonetheless, was an independent label unlike the majors that many other post-punk bands signed to. Frith and Horne also specifically mention some of the other Sheffield bands who had made the transition to entryist New Pop: ABC, the Human League and Heaven 17. For these Frith and Horne, such music 'depends for its critical promise on a theory of the market not the media' (ibid., 137).

My contention is that this shift from a valorization of independent or alternative modes of production to mainstream consumption and subversion from within was to an extent shared by cultural theory and popular music. As Frith and Horne argue, 'Subversion was now a matter of form not content; even political interest moved from the forces of production to the moment of consumption. All that could be challenged now was "meaning"' (ibid., 155). We are now much closer to the territory of Stuart Hall's encoding decoding model, Hindess and Hirst's wider social formations and John Fiske's cultural populism, than in the oppositional 'modes of production' or even ideology critique of earlier left theorizing. As throughout this chapter, I wish to argue that the link between the theory and the music is far from arbitrary: it was a shared terrain for both cultural practitioners and theorists in the era in question.

In fact, I am making an even stronger case than this for returning to the concept of mode of production as a useful way of exploring Cabaret Voltaire's work. What makes them distinctive as a band is not just the originality of their fusion of electronic noise, tape loops, processed vocals, visuals and videos. As I have stated throughout, their independent mode of production and negotiation of the early setup of the independent music scene, their appropriation of found technologies and of rehearsal and recording sites in Sheffield's university and former political meeting places, all make them notable at the level of production and distribution. I have already highlighted the almost conventional links made between heavy industry and the sound of Sheffield music; in the next section, I will argue that Cabaret Voltaire's artisanal mode of production is in common with even some present-day metalworkers labouring in Sheffield's largely deindustrialized east end.

Machines

Here it will be appropriate to say a bit more about machines at a conceptual level – and in terms of their use in Sheffield's past and present. One of the most famous sections of Marx's *Grundrisse*, translated into English in the 1970s, is often referred to as the 'fragment on machines'. This fragment occurs after an analysis of what Marx calls 'fixed' and 'circulating' capital. Fixed capital is essentially the means of production (factories, machines, etc.) – where circulating capital is taken up with raw materials and labour. In industrial production, the part taken by fixed capital becomes proportionately larger and larger: as machines become more and more costly, they are invested in more and more relative to the labour cost to operate them. This increases the efficiency of labour, pricing out production on a smaller scale (bankrupting artisanal workshops), where labour costs increase the value of the commodity beyond competitive rates. For Marx: 'Machinery appears, then, as the most adequate form of *fixed capital*, and fixed capital, in so far as capital's relations with itself are concerned, appears as *the most adequate form of capital* as such' (1973: 694). It is worth pointing out that Sheffield, with its preference for 'putting out' cutlery manufacture to artisan workshops well into the industrial era, held out much longer against the subsumption of labour to the capitalist mode of production than most other industrial centres in the country.

Now, the consequences of machinery for labour are twofold. On the one hand, for Marx, '*the most developed machinery thus forces the worker to work longer than the savage does, or than he himself did with the simplest crudest tools*' (1973: 709). On the other hand, and more promisingly for New Left Marxists reading the *Grundrisse* in the 1970s, the introduction of machinery has two positive consequences. First, it sows the seeds for the overcoming of capitalism and transition to more rational production (albeit in ways not always fully explained by Marx). Second, machine production ushers in and is dependent on the development of society's intellectual capacity: *science*.

Free time – which is both idle time and time for higher activity – has naturally transformed its possessor into a different subject, and he then enters into the direct production process as this different subject. This process is then both discipline, as regards the human being in the process of becoming; and, at the same time, practice [*Ausübung*], experimental science, materially creative and objectifying science, as regards the human being who has become, in whose head exists the accumulated knowledge of society. (Marx 1973: 712)

Science, or what Italian Marxism calls 'general intellect' (Virno 2007: 4), is a way in which the machines might work in ways inimical to the capitalist mode of production that brought them into being, one more way in which capital produces its own gravediggers. In the quote above the 'idle time and time for higher activity' seems once more to allude to 'unproductive' labour – here conceived as 'experimental science, materially creative and objectifying science'.

However, for Cabaret Voltaire, the machine has still other connotations, ones rather deriving from the city's artisanal and informal economies. In his recent work, the anthropologist Massimiliano Mollona discusses two working cultures in present-day Sheffield factories. One he identifies with the 'hot' labour of steel making; the other he identifies with the 'cold' labour of steel finishing. In the abandoned workshops of the east end, tool finishing and other metal working continues with machines that literally date back to the nineteenth century. Those involved in the 'hot' labour of casting the tools, unlike the proletarian finishers, are able to *détourne* some of the machines for their own purposes, for sideline projects to other Sheffield small enterprises, or jealously to guard their own apprenticeship system.

The table below outlines some of the oppositions Mollona draws between the 'artisanal' production of steel and its 'proletarian' finishing. Broadly speaking, we can see that Cabaret Voltaire's work seems to be aligned with the Sheffield tradition of *artisanal* production of the hot workers to the extent that it is based on a relatively independent production, seeing itself as part of a tradition (rock and artistic) and community-based via the importance of the 'scene'. In addition, machines are not, for the group, 'technological monsters' – but improvised devices, manufactured on an ad hoc or craft basis or appropriated from independent distributors as an organic part of their music making. We can also point to the fascinating parallels between Mollona's observations of the oscillating neon lights and regular, rhythmic machine noise of the hot workers' factory milieu and the Cabs' noted performance style. Though clearly describing very different activities, Mollona's scheme advances a phenomenology of manufacturing labour that applies both to steel making and to industrial music performance contexts.

'Hot' workers	'Cold' workers
Steel making	Steel finishing
Noise: regular, low, rhythmic deafness	Noise: irregular, electric, acute stress, high blood pressure
Dark, neon lights oscillating rhythmically, red light from ovens	Uniform light: sunlight and neon lamps high up on ceiling
Artisan	Proletarian
Apprenticeship	'Our labour is worth all the same'
Machine: symbolic extension of workers' bodies	Machines as 'technological monsters' in competition with them
Pre-capitalist ethos of work	Flexible labour
Cottage system rooted in the formal economy of the family and the neighbourhood	Same homogeneous 'class' of workers and following scientific principles of labour organization

Source: Mollona (2009).

From this perspective, Cabaret Voltaire's repurposing of tape machines, electronics, ring modulators and disco drum machines is not so much a practice of situationist *détournement* as a perennial practice of Sheffield artisanal labour. As with the hot workers in the east-end workshops analysed by Mollona, there is the pride of workers not directly (or at least not entirely) subsumed under an industrial mode of production, repurposing and reprogramming technology to suit their own independent material: sonic and visual productions.

One can hear this wilfully independent music practice on the band's 'Kneel to the Boss' from their 1980 Rough Trade LP, *The Voice of America*. The track is powered by what sounds like an elementary pre-programmed Casio drumbeat (or even reminiscent of a primitive Atari television game console), which offsets the deep and warm bass as well as some dub-influenced rim shots, echo and reverb. Processed through a ring-modulator or similar, Stephen Mallinder hisses the phrase 'Kneel to the Boss' with what is best characterized as reptilian disdain. Or on 'Expect Nothing' from 1979's *Mix-Up*, one can hear the similarly distorted vocal lines about selling yourself and expecting nothing against the backdrop of distorted guitar, apparently filtered through a wah wah pedal to leave a brittle mid-frequency dirge. This is accompanied by scraping, buzzing percussion and squalls of machinic feedback. Each of these records feature the band's repurposing of analogue technologies together with a surly if rather vague lyrical opposition to uniformity and control.

What many have noticed is that these lyrical concerns, as well as an interest in machines in general, typify Sheffield music from around this time. Though addressed differently by the two bands in question, we might point to the Human League's *Dignity of Labour* released in 1979 and, very differently, Heaven 17's (1981) *Penthouse and Pavement* LP, whose cover featured the breakaway Human League musicians dressed as yuppies in suits, skinny ties and pony tails, in a gesture that has been variously interpreted as satirical as well as using postmodern irony. The polished synth-pop sheen of the latter, however, is in stark contrast to the forbidding noise of Cabaret Voltaire's early Rough Trade recordings.

As a footnote to the above, we might also point out to an anecdote recalled by Paul Unwin, DJ in Sheffield post-punk nightclub The Limit. Next to the club was a chip shop at the back of which was a workshop in which 'little mesters' (Unwin uses the archaic term for self-employed Sheffield craftsmen) were melting down half crowns, no longer legal tender, for metal content. Surveillance of this operation led HM Customs to turn their attention to The Limit, which was then investigated for unpaid VAT (cited in Anderson 2009: 113–14). Here we have once more the juxtaposition of Sheffield post-punk and artisanal wheeler-dealing.

Residual artisanship

I do not want to argue that Cabaret Voltaire's work as a band was a politically radical practice *in itself* – and the Cabs would frequently assert that they were not a 'political band'. Simon Reynolds, I think, is fairly accurate when he states: 'Through the eighties and into the techno nineties, this kind of self-sufficient entrepreneurial collective would become widespread. In 1978, Cabaret Voltaire were developing the model for a kind of post-socialist micro-capitalism, an autonomy that represented – if not exactly resistance – then certainly grass-roots resilience in the face of top-down corporate culture' (Reynolds 2005: 168). In this respect, like David Blunkett in Sheffield Council at the turn of the decade, minor struggles such as in Blunkett's case public transport costs and council rates, and in the Cabs' case autonomous production and independent distribution, carved out a limited space outside neo-liberal valorization projects.

But I would also state that 'entrepreneurial' micro-capitalism is perhaps wrong, if it brings to mind Keith Joseph's value-extracting vanguard. 'Artisanal' is a word that preserves a sense of independent production within a largely capitalist sphere – what Raymond Williams would refer to no doubt as a 'residual' cultural formation. Williams reminds us that residual cultural elements can be and have to be co-opted by the dominant culture to some extent – but that some 'values which cannot be expressed or substantially verified in terms of the dominant culture, are nevertheless lived and practiced on the basis of the residue – cultural as well as social – of some previous social and cultural institution or formation' (Williams 1977: 122). This is the sense in which, I think, we can situate the practice of Cabaret Voltaire and the other Sheffield bands in the late seventies – engaged in questions of labour and machines in a deindustrializing city – while preserving values of community and class that changes in the economy and national politics were seeking to undermine.

Conclusion

To us now, of course, to rehearse these questions of production and distribution, in terms of obsolete formats and analogue technologies, not to mention what are to some obsolete theories, might seem largely of historical interest. While surely there is nothing wrong with reconstructing cultural histories, we might seem to have moved on, for better or worse, to an era in which some of the previous barriers to entry have been removed through cheaper production technologies and a radical new distribution network, namely the internet. Though it is undoubtedly true that these developments have facilitated the production and distribution of popular music fundamentally, I will conclude with some observations from a present-day musician, who has within the recent time of writing released a well-received new record. I do not claim that these comments are representative of contemporary musicians (how could we reasonably evaluate this claim?) but at the very least they might serve as a warning against 'presentism' and an uncritical internet evangelism.

Jack Latham, who records under the name Jam City, has just released his second album, *Dream a Garden*, on Night Slugs. His debut, *Classical Curves* (2011), was admired for its repurposing of house and more recent UK dance music; the new record sees him providing vocals, mixed low, over a more less minimal, more noise/ambient sound. In some ways, Latham and other bedroom producers, whether or not they are aware of the earlier band, seem to be the natural successors to Cabaret Voltaire's independent studio production (initially in Chris Watson's bedroom before securing their own studio) and concern with noise and technology. My interest here is in comments in his recent interview with Dan Hancox (2015) in *The Guardian*. According to the interviewer, the recent album came about due to Latham's own consideration of 'how music – or art more generally – can help provide some small resistance to the perils of late capitalism'. This in itself might pique one's interest; but what is more poignant still is Latham's discussion of the difficulties, in purely economic or financial terms, for his generation: 'being able to afford to study; and meeting people, and forming a band, or starting a club night'.

Production in itself has become cheaper and more viable – especially for electronic music. But the non-virtual infrastructure and social security were, I hope to have established, precisely the things in which many of the post-punk bands were facilitated by the more favourable economic and social climate for students and unemployed musicians decades ago. And as caution to those who feel that internet prosumption provides an instant remedy, there is the following:

> It's like the internet's all we have, and none of us really have any money, so of course that's the way that we organise and seek comfort from other people. But the doors to do that in real life, that historically have made other movements possible, just seem quite closed to our generation. (Hancox 2015)

My purpose here is certainly not to wallow in nostalgia (for what it is worth, post-punk was a little too early for the author to have taken notice of at the time). But what it surely does underline is that the questions of production, distribution and political economy of popular music, as well as of the social formations and culture that facilitate the flourishing of its practitioners, are not merely of potential interest to those around at the time. There may be utopian impulses in the obsolete modes of production of music's past that speak to us now – the 'moment of consumption' as well as online distribution removed from a geographical scene or readily available venues, for some contemporary musicians, are not adequate substitutes for the supporting networks provided by pre-austerity social formations, whatever the gains in ease and affordability of technology.

References

Anderson, N. (2009), *Take it to The Limit: The Story of a Sheffield Rock'n'Roll Legend*, Sheffield: ACM Retro.

Crossley, N. (2015), *Networks of Sound, Style and Subversion: The Punk and Post-Punk Worlds of Manchester, London, Liverpool and Sheffield, 1975–80*, Manchester: Manchester University Press.

Debord, G. and G. Wolman (2006), 'A User's Guide to Détournement', *Situationist International Anthology*. Available online: http://www.bopsecrets.org/SI/detourn.htm (accessed 26 July 2015).

Fish, M. and D. Hallbery (1985), *Cabaret Voltaire: The Art of the Sixth Sense*, Harrow: Serious Art Forms.

Friedman, M. (2002), *Capitalism and Freedom*, Chicago and London: University of Chicago Press.

Frith, S. and H. Horne (1987), *Art into Pop*, London and New York: Methuen.

Goddard, M. (2006), 'We are time: Laibach/nsk, retro-avant-gardism and machinic repetition', *Angelaki: Journal of the Theoretical Humanities*, 2(1): 45–53.

Hancox, D. (2015), 'Jam City – "Music is a place for freaks"', *The Guardian*, 28 May. Available online: http://www.theguardian.com/music/2015/may/28/jam-city-interview-dream-a-garden-music-place-freaks (accessed 19 July 2015).

Hindess, B. and P. Hirst (1977), *Mode of Production and Social Formation: An Auto-Critique of Pre-Capitalist Modes of Production*, London and Basingstoke: Macmillan.

Howell, P. (1975), 'Once Again on Productive and Unproductive Labour', *Revolutionary Communist*, 3(4): Available online: https://www.marxists.org/subject/economy/authors/howell/produnprod.htm (accessed 19 July 2015).

Joseph, K. (1976), *Monetarism is Not Enough: The Stockton Lecture 1976*, Chichester and London: Barry Rose.

Long, P. (2014), 'Popular music, psychogeography, place identity and tourism: The case of Sheffield', *Tourist Studies*, 14(1): 48–65.

Mallinder, S. (2011), 'Movement: Journey of the Beat', PhD thesis, Murdoch, WA, Australia: School of Media Communication and Culture, Murdoch University.

Marx, K. (1969), *Theories of Surplus Value*, Part 1, London: Lawrence and Wishart.

Marx, K. (1993), *Grundrisse*, Harmondsworth: Penguin.

Mollona, M. (2009), *Made in Sheffield: An Ethnography of Industrial Work and Politics*, Oxford: Berghahn.

Piketty, T. (2014), *Capital in the Twenty-First Century*, Cambridge, MA: Belknap Press.

Price, D. (2008), *Sheffield Troublemakers: Rebels and Radicals in Sheffield History*, Stroud: Phillimore and Co.

Reynolds, S. (2005), *Rip It Up and Start Again: Post-punk 1978–1984*, London: Faber.

Reynolds, S. (2009), *Totally Wired: Post-punk Interviews and Overviews*, London: Faber.

Taylor, N. (2010), *Document and Eyewitness: An Intimate History of Rough Trade*, London: Orion

van der Laan, J. M. (1997), 'Is it Live, or is it Memorex?', *Bulletin of Science, Technology & Society*, 27(2): 136–41

Virno, P. (2007), 'General Intellect', *Historical Materialism*, 15: 3–8.

Williams, R. (1977), *Marxism and Literature*, Oxford: Oxford University Press.

Discography

Cabaret Voltaire (1979) Expect Nothing [Single] on *Mix-Up*, Rough Trade [Album]

Cabaret Voltaire (1980) 'Just Fascination', Rough Trade [Single]

Cabaret Voltaire (1980) *The Voice of America*, Rough Trade [Album]

Cabaret Voltaire (2002) Methodology '74/'78 *The Attic Tapes*, The Grey Area, [Album]

Heaven 17 (1981) *Penthouse and Pavement*, Virgin [Album]

Human League (1979) 'The Dignity of Labour', Fast Records [Single]

Jam City (2012) *Classical Curves*, Night Slugs [Album]

Jam City (2015) *Dream a Garden*, Night Slugs [Album]

New Order (1983) 'Blue Monday', Factory [Single]

Scritti Politti (1979) *Work in Progress: 2nd Peel Session*, Rough Trade [Album]

Scritti Politti (1985) Cupid & Psyche, Virgin [Album]

Scritti Politti (2005) *Early*, Rough Trade [Album]

CHAPTER SEVEN

Flag of convenience? The Union Jack as a contested symbol of Englishness in popular music or a convenient marketing device?

Johnny Hopkins

I was interested in the visual impact of iconic post-war and patriotic images, and the irony (and audacious invitation of controversy) of adopting such symbols on clothing.

PETE TOWNSHEND INTERVIEW WITH AUTHOR, 13 JUNE 2013

Introduction

When the Beatles posed in front of a huge Stars and Stripes in January 1964 to promote their first trip to America for the Ed Sullivan show, English/British pop acts were still not taken seriously in the United States. Even though the band had just secured a US Cashbox No. 1 single, their manager Brian Epstein was nervous. Epstein told a US journalist that the trip was a 'test run. ... We really didn't know what to expect. Would Americans take to the boys? Certainly I didn't want a failure. So everything had to be right, planned. We had to look good' (Kane 2003: 20). The promotional shot can be seen as an attempt to grab attention and connect with the American media and public. It could also perhaps be seen as the band betraying a lack of confidence in their Englishness/Britishness as a way of marketing themselves in America. This is understandable, given that Britain was still scarred by the impact of the Second World War and post-war decolonization. As Paul Gilroy argued, the country was suffering from 'post-colonial melancholia', in which it remained 'paralyzed by the inability to really work through the loss of global prestige and the economic and political benefits that once attended it' (2000: 53).

When the Beatles returned triumphant to London from their US tour, George Harrison waved a Union Jack flag as they came off the plane. Times were changing when a pop star of Harrison's fame unselfconsciously claimed the Union Jack for the Beatles' own ends. Following the breakthrough of the Beatles, pop music increasingly became 'the cultural currency of Englishness' (Bracewell 1998: 82). Englishness became fashionable globally and carried a certain new cultural power. American producer Joe Boyd noted: 'In a way, the best groups, the most influential, the most powerful and the ones that did the best in America were the ones that were quite unafraid to be English' (Green 1988: 61–2). The unprecedented US success of the Beatles and near contemporaries like the Who was termed the 'British Invasion' – an interesting use of the language, given the frequent use of imperial symbols like the Union Jack and the country's need to rebuild its global-standing post-Empire. In America, the appeal of England and its iconography of key symbols – the Union Jack, the Queen, Big Ben, beefeaters, red London buses, red phone boxes etc. – was strong. Music, fashion, film and photography all helped to redefine and reinforce notions of Englishness and influenced those that consumed it.

There had been a significant shift in the national, cultural mood. Indeed, on 20 March 1966 the Who appeared on the cover of the *Observer Magazine* with a huge Union Jack, stolen from a hotel by Keith Moon, as a backdrop (Savage 2015: 67). Pete Townshend is out front, dressed provocatively in a jacket made from a cut-up Union Jack. Here, as Angela Carter (1996) noted, 'sacrosanct imagery is desecrated'. The photograph by Colin Jones is multifaceted. It appears to mirror and answer the Beatles' Stars and Stripes shot. It can also be read as the Who asserting their Englishness in response to the threat of Americanization, yet at the same time reinventing Englishness and cocking a snook at the English establishment. It was also at least an indicator of the changing power base in the music industry from one side of the Atlantic to the other. Jon Savage calls it 'a punky subversion of a national symbol and a serious statement about the rebranding of a fusty, static, class-ridden country as the international centre of a synaesthetic youth culture' (2011).

For at least a year previously the Who had been draping the Union Jack on their amplifiers, which Pete Townshend 'symbolically speared at the end of a show' with his guitar (Neil and Kent 2005: 46–7). They had also been using Union Jack jackets for publicity photos and stage wear since at least 1965, as evidenced by the cover of their debut album *My Generation* (1965) – a sure statement of intent to invert the militarist/colonial context of the Union Jack. These were subversive acts in the context of the time. As Carter (1996) said: 'Clothes are our weapons, our challenges, our visible insults.' The *Observer* photo became a defining image of the Who and proved popular abroad – for instance making the cover of Spain's *Actualidad* magazine (19 May 1966) and USA's *Go* magazine (28 April 1967) as well as the sleeve of the band's Japanese single 'Dogs' (1968). From the Who onwards, the Union Jack became part of the dressing up box of pop, as costume, visual device, prop and backdrop, as well as a way of communicating more serious messages. My aim in this chapter is to explore the intentions behind this performative usage of the Union Jack in popular music, its meaning, and what the impact has been, by looking at the mid-1960s and specifically the Who within their political, social and cultural contexts.

State of the nation

The mid-1960s were a transitional time when cracks started to appear in the structure of society. Old beliefs about religion and morality were being questioned. Stuart Hall talked of a de-centring, displacement, dislocation and fragmentation of the postmodern individual and society in the post-war period, and noted particularly that the 1960s were a 'great watershed of late-modernity' (1992: 290). The 1960s were also characterized by Britain's continued and rapid withdrawal from empire. The sense that the country's international status was on the wane contributed to a crop of 'what's wrong with Britain' books in the late 1950s and early 1960s. These included John Strachey's *End of Empire* (1959), Michael Shanks's *The Stagnant Society* (1961), Colin MacInnes's *England, Half-English (1961)*, Anthony Sampson's *Anatomy of Britain* (1962) and John Mander's *Great Britain or Little England* (1963). Tom Nairn and Perry Anderson in *New Left Review* also addressed this issue of Britain's postcolonial loss of confidence and declining influence on the international stage. In fact, Strachey was so alarmed by Britain's loss of global cultural and political prestige that he wrote: 'The morale, the spirit, the mental health even, of all of us ... are deeply involved in the question of the dissolution of our empire ... a sense of loss – almost amputation – when some colony or semi-colony ... becomes independent' (Faulkner and Ramamurthy 2006: 3). The playwright, John Osborne, shared this sense of national deprivation and in 1961 wrote a letter exclaiming: 'Damn you, England. You're rotting now, and quite soon you will disappear' (Osborne 1961). Add to this fractious atmosphere the growing mistrust of the political establishment following the Suez crisis (1956) and the Profumo Affair (1963), and one can see why British national identity was becoming caught between radical self-questioning and a compensatory strident nationalism. Webster concurs that the loss of empire 'messed with British English identities in a period of decolonisation' (Faulkner and Ramamurthy

2006: 190). Kobena Mercer has noted that 'identity only becomes an issue when it is in crisis, when something assumed to be fixed, coherent, stable is displaced by the experience of doubt and uncertainty' (Hall 1992: 275); and the milieu of 1960s British popular culture was characterized by a reconfiguring of British identity. One strand of this reconfiguration was the freedom to play with, subvert, reinterpret, reimagine and rebuild symbols of national identity.

Despite or perhaps because of the country's diminished status, attempts to project images of a strong England and a clearly defined Englishness were often reproduced and reinforced, including through the use of flags – as seen in Carnaby Street and associated symbols of Swinging London. The Who's use of flag iconography, in particular, reflected a general questioning of ideas of nation and allegiance during a tumultuous period that also saw the exponential growth and creative explosion of English/British popular music. Through this post-war era 'the nation state and its attendant identity and collective values remained a source to be tapped by musicians, consumers and purveyors of youth culture' (Gildart 2013: 9). The Who's Union Jack jackets and the Swinging London spectacle can be seen as part of a process of trying to understand the country's diminished status and then to reframe it in other (cultural) contexts. Here new meanings were embedded and new forms of national identity were created.

The flag and art

Historically the Union Jack, like many other national flags, has been tied to the politics of power, monarchy, empire and nation, and thus has been treated with near reverence. Even in the postcolonial era these associations linger – not just in far-right politics. The Union Jack, with its combination of three crosses, also signifies its Christian origins. National flags are icons that represent their country and help to produce what Stuart Hall calls a 'narrative of the nation' (1992: 293). They are visible at times of triumph and tragedy (e.g. military and sporting), in the spectacle of royal celebrations and the normality of everyday life. National flags are used to express a common union of interests through national signifiers: 'Symbolic devices like flags have long been employed to communicate meaning and to identify groups and territories' (Elgenius 2007: 26). Indeed, the Union Jack not only identifies both English and British people, but also more specifically members of the mod or Britpop subcultures among others.

During the height of the British Empire the Union Jack was often reproduced in cultural works. Historical painters routinely employed flags as symbolic visual devices in depictions of heroic battles or state portraits. 'Wider circulation by the burgeoning print market … introduced historical images to a broad demographic, making historical painting an intimate yet powerful means of addressing the nation' (Smith 2015: 85).[1] This would also have reinforced ideas of nationhood. Gilroy clarifies the impact of history painting: 'Artists yielded to jingoism and the popular imperatives of propaganda, they contributed to making the aims of imperialism vivid and alluring to new political constituencies as well as to the functionaries and foot soldiers who would administer imperial commerce and kill or die in the name of imperial sovereignty' (2015: 8). Wright noted that 'it is in the service of the nation that public images and interpretations of the past circulate' (1985: 24). Since the early twentieth century this has increasingly been through the media or mediated events. This is why popular music has become, at times, a useful vehicle for communicating ideas of this kind.

In the postcolonial era Faulkner and Ramamurthy note that 'visual forms were important forms for the fashioning of the late / post-colonial self' (2006: 9). While one might think of paintings and photographs, it can also apply to political posters, record sleeves, marketing material, adverts and badges that feature loaded national symbols like the Union Jack. Sixties pop culture took possession of the Union Jack as a generation of artists, including David Hockney, Derek Boshier and Peter Blake, emerging from the same art school system as Pete Townshend, examined and questioned ideas about national identity. This was reflected in the frequent use of the Union Jack in their artworks, particularly between 1960 and 1962.[2] In pop art the Union Jack was often placed next to commercial objects – such as milk or an England's Glory matchbox, transforming products into pieces of commercial art. Alternatively it would be placed near the American flag but in noticeably smaller scale. This visual symbolism was a device for engaging with issues around imperial decline, national identity and the allure of American pop culture, as well as with the more general political and cultural threats of Americanization.

Geoff Reeve, a student at the Royal College of Art, seems to have started a trend in 1960 by painting a fellow student's sunglasses with a Union Jack to celebrate the wedding of Princess Margaret. That same year he produced a textile design of multiple Union Jacks in various stages of completeness. This got him into trouble with his head of department, who was shocked as Reeve had reduced the flag, with all its royal and national associations, to a state of 'serial meaningless' (Mellor 1993: 120). But Reeve had clearly seen the flag's dynamic graphic possibilities. Another student, Peter Phillips, was reprimanded the same year for painting *Purple Flag,* in which the Union Jack was rendered in shades of purple with all of its decadent associations. In 1960 subverting the flag was still viewed as highly disrespectful. But by 1965 when Michael English (who was at Ealing Art School with Pete Townshend, and then later part of psychedelic design duo Haphash and the Coloured Coat) designed sunglasses with Union Jacks painted across the lens for the Gear boutique in Carnaby Street, they proved hugely popular. English's sunglasses entered a much more 'socially-relaxed environment' than Geoff Reeve's textile design due to the success of the Beatles and the related pop culture. These sunglasses had 'a multitude of connotations:

principally the tension between the patriotic sign and its decontextualized, transgressive identity, as one more "hard edge" colour abstract pattern' (Mellor 1993: 120). On a purely aesthetic level, the Union Jack has always been a striking, dynamic image because of its sharp angles of composition, with the diagonals, verticals and horizontal lines and the resulting triangles and lines of bold colour (red, white and blue). This is key to its enduring use and appeal. Between 1964 and 1967, its design aesthetic was fully congruent with the clear, 'hard edge' graphics of pop art and mod culture, as exemplified in the set design of the *Ready Steady Go!* (1963–6) television pop show.

The Who, pop music and the flag

The success of the Beatles and near contemporaries like the Who alerted politicians to the economic and PR value of popular music and other cultural industries like fashion, film and art. They tried to harness it, not least when Prime Minister Harold Wilson awarded the Beatles MBEs in 1965. Tellingly, in response to complaints about the award, *Melody Maker's* editor defended the band saying: 'The Beatles have waved the British flag all around the world. They have raised the standard of popular music. Immeasurably' (*Melody Maker* 19 June 1965). After decolonization and the breakthrough of the Beatles it became slightly easier for the flag to be reinvented and reused extensively in pop culture. 'It had changed, but not very much. In 1964 the Union Flag was still semi-sacred,' Townshend (2013) told this author. His knowledge of pop art through his art school training was certainly an influence on his use of the Union Jack. 'I saw the Jasper Johns' [American flag] paintings in the college library. I was also influenced by Peter Blake's collages in which he used similar imagery' (Townshend 2013). Townsend believes that 'there is an element of detournement in the Union Jack jackets. There was no political mischief [in the situationist sense] at work. ... My generation were rather in awe of those who'd fought for our freedom, and so "rebelled" by appearing to embrace their flags, emblems and standards, and any irony was very low level. It was implicit, but easy to fob off as childishness' (Townshend 2013). Interestingly, Townshend's father played in the RAF's dance orchestra – so this may have been an influence. On the other hand, Townshend had once been a member of the Young Communists and performed on CND (Campaign for Nuclear Disarmament) marches, both of which signal his rejection of British cultural-militarism.

After years of American dominance of the UK pop charts, asserting one's Englishness, in a non-nationalistic way, was important. As Townshend says: 'In those days – 1964–1967, American music was our competition. We wanted to signal that we were very different to bands like The Beach Boys' (Townsend 2013). Reflecting on ideas of empire he noted: 'We might be soft on the outside but we were full of power inside. The colonial, empire-related images all supported this idea. Our music was associated with Empire and Colonialism, but also with the inevitability of decline and equalisation. We felt we were keeping the British standard flying with art, music and anarchic behaviour I suppose' (Townsend 2013). The idea for the Union Jack jackets was a strong one but due to the controversial nature it was difficult to get them made. As Townshend told this author: 'It was hard to find a tailor willing to cut several up in order to make jackets. People were outraged. That may be why I allowed John Entwistle to start wearing them instead of me, he was a bigger chap' (2013). They tried a Savile Row tailor who refused to deface the flag, but managed to get one made using a designer who worked for the Carnaby Street shop, Lord John (Neil and Kent 2005: 47). Sometimes they used a more straightforward printed fabric – for instance Pete Townshend wears a jacket made from this in a set of shots that featured on the artwork of the Spanish, Belgian and Italian versions of their single *A Legal Matter* (1966) and the Norwegian release of *I'm A Boy* (1966). While not quite as iconoclastic as the cut-up flag jackets, they would still have helped get Townshend's points across.

Clearly the band was actively involved in choosing the clothing they wore for photos. But in the case of the artwork for *A Legal Matter*, the decision to use those particular photos would have been down to the record company as they were releasing the single without the band's permission due to a dispute following the Who leaving the label. The global usage of these Union Jack photos and the *Observer* shot suggest that the record label understood the cultural value of Englishness at this time, with its strong association with the global commercial phenomenon of Swinging London, as well as appreciating the visual dynamism of the design itself. The photographic evidence in magazines and on record sleeves shows that generally the Union Jack jackets were worn by either Entwistle or Townshend, but there is at least one occasion where Keith Moon did (see the back cover of *Record Mirror* – 3 September 1966). The Union Jack jackets appeared in group photos in conjunction with clothing decorated with other dynamic images – Bridget Riley op art, medals, the red, white and blue RAF roundel (target), and the newly designed British road signs. These fitted well with and helped to define the dynamic streamlined visual culture of the mod subculture. Referring to the Who's emphasis on image, Robin Richman of *Life* magazine (USA) noted that they were 'living out a chronicle of costume' (Richman 1968: 61). By covering the surface of their clothing with all these symbols in their pop art phase, they prefigure Umberto Eco's statement: 'I speak through my clothes' (1973).

While the idea for the jackets has been variously attributed to Townshend, bassist John Entwistle and manager Kit Lambert, what is clear is that the jackets were part of the marketing and PR for the band: 'At the time I just wanted the band to continue to look mod (which was generally quite a constrained look, all greys and blacks) but be colourful on stage and in PR photographs for teeny-bopper magazines like *Fabulous*' (Townshend 2013).

So there was a thought-out practical PR element to it as the jackets provided a strong dynamic colourful image that would stand out and get them attention. This was astute as it exploited new printing technology that produced full-colour music magazines like *Fabulous* and *Rave,* as well as the youth-orientated weekend newspaper supplements like the *Observer Magazine.* Not only did the jackets prove eye-catching in photos, but Townshend was also keen to talk about them in press interviews.

Defining their pop-art look to *Melody Maker* on 3 July 1965, he said: 'It is re-presenting something the public is familiar with, in a different form. Like clothes, Union Jacks are supposed to be flown. We have a jacket made of one. Keith Moon, our drummer, has a jersey with the RAF insignia on it. I have a white jacket, covered in medals' (Kureishi and Savage 1995: 239). He knew what he was doing and understood the disruptive benefits of detournement. Within the music industry representational devices are used to convey messages and to connect with target audiences: 'The visual marketing involves an attempt to articulate the authenticity and uniqueness of an artist and to communicate this through a concise image which operates as a metonym for an act's entire identity and music' (Negus 1992: 72).

Given that Union Jack jackets were seen by some English people as 'sacrosanct imagery ... desecrated' (Carter 1996), it is interesting that the Irish Republican Army (IRA) allegedly threatened to bomb the Who if they wore them at a Dublin gig in May 1966. A local tailor was found who could make a version using an Irish tricolour, and so trouble was averted (Davey 1999: 84; Neil and Kent 2005: 83). As the Dublin-based English mods in the support act The Next-In-Line frequently wore Union Jack T-shirts with no negative reaction (Neil and Kent 2005:83), it is of course possible that the band's PRs or the British music magazine *Disc* that reported the story may have exaggerated it. Alternatively, it may have been because the Who were, by then, successful stars they were deemed more legitimate and newsworthy targets.

On 3 June 1966 on *Popside*, a Swedish TV show, the band made their entrance by smashing through a large paper Union Jack screen (Neil and Kent 2005: 84) – an act that was as similarly iconoclastic as the cut-up Union Jack jackets, though it is not known whether it was the idea of the band, their management or the TV company. Either way, the use of the Union Jack in this way outside of England was judged to be worthwhile. The subversion of the Union Jack worked effectively on television as well as in magazines. The final key image from this time period is the Art Kane shot of the Who for *Life* magazine (USA), taken in New York on 6 April 1968 with the band 'sleeping' at the foot of Grant's Tomb draped in a large Union Jack. This iconic shot was later revived on the cover of the soundtrack album for the Who's 1979 documentary film *The Kids Are Alright.* It was also reprised for a *Melody Maker* cover shoot in 1995.

The Who were not the only musicians to acknowledge the Union Jack in some way. The Rolling Stones' *Get Off Of My Cloud* single, released in 1965 at the height of the Union Jack's ubiquity, has a dismissive line about performers' use of the flag. The line was allegedly directed at Screaming Lord Sutch, but equally it might have been aimed at the Who, a band that the Stones considered to be emerging rivals by this time. Sutch himself recorded a track *Union Jack Car* in 1969 for his album *Screaming Lord Sutch & Heavy Friends* (featuring Jimmy Page, John Bonham, Noel Redding, Jeff Beck and others). The cover features Sutch leaning against a Rolls Royce painted all over with a Union Jack. Even American musicians were photographed with the Union Jack, including Jimi Hendrix pictured with a flag. For a few years having a connection with Swinging London was perceived as useful PR and marketing.

Fashion, Swinging London, and the pop life of the Union Jack

The formal transition to independence for former colonies was marked by handover ceremonies in which, as noted by Ramamurthy, old 'flags were lowered and [new flags] raised' (Faulkner and Ramamurthy 2006: 65). As the British Empire was dismantled, the Union Jack lost some of its accumulated power and meaning and became available to be reinterpreted and reused in new contexts. Thus the flag was increasingly co-opted into popular culture: 'Once a national symbol acquires connotations that ... have nothing to do with state or nation, this autonomy can take its uses and meaning into other places altogether' (Jenkins 2007: 131). In the aftermath of the war, decolonization, the coronation (1953) and the end of National Service (1963), an influx of military uniforms, parkas, bunting and Union Jacks flooded onto the open market through the many newly opened army surplus stores, such as Laurence Corner in London which opened in 1953. These items also found their way into Swinging London shops such as I Was Lord Kitchener's Valet (opened in 1964) and Granny Takes A Trip (opened in 1965).[3] These shops catered to musicians and the fans that followed them, thus contributing to the look of 1960s pop groups and fan culture. Ashmore credits I Was Lord Kitchener's Valet with starting the trend for putting the Union Jack on products (2006: 70). Old Union Jacks featured in their windows and inside the Portobello Road shop where they sold more fashionable second-hand army surplus. These symbols of empire may have been adopted subversively, ironically or unquestioningly by the sixties generation. Richard Neville, editor of counterculture magazine, *oz*, said: 'I assumed it was sartorial satire – a projection of anti-war sentiment' (Gorman 2006: 71). In contrast, George Melly argued that the 'rash of Union Jacks' that appeared in Swinging London were in fact a mask that the post-war capital used to 'conceal its uncertainty' (1972: 61).

In the consumer-driven society of the 1960s people were able to create new consumer identities at a time when identities based on nation and class were being challenged and fragmented. Briggs notes that during a similar period of decolonization an 'expansion of consumer power was harnessed as a method of re-creating France' (2014: 21). This was mirrored over here in the consumer society of Swinging London and the growth of the popular music and film industries. By 1966 much of the world looked to London for ideas about music, fashion and film. The country had found a new role. Andrea Adam, part of the editorial team at American magazine, *Time* says: 'We were all totally riveted by London. ... London was special, it had a kind of mystique. ... At the time in New York everything English had a cachet. Nothing American did' (Green 1988: 86). So intrigued were *Time* by what was happening in London that they commissioned a cover story that became the infamous Swinging London issue. The ideas were crystallized in the cover. This was emblematic of Swinging London as it has been mythologized. It featured five Union Jacks: one as the main backdrop; one being held by Prime Minister Harold Wilson; the other three feature on the lenses of the sunglasses and the British Made badge worn by a rock singer in a The Who T-shirt. Just as with the *Vanity Fair* 'Cool Britannia' cover it captured a scene that was already in decline, and just as with *Vanity Fair* it hastened that decline and 'sealed its fate' (Breward 2006: 12). Breward also stresses the role of consumption in Swinging London and Harold Wilson's New Britain: 'Fashion innovation and pleasurable consumption were at its heart, but it also incorporated a set of relationships between the values of old Britain and new Britain, and between London and the rest of the world' (2006: 8).

In its themed issue, *Time* produced a map of the happening places of Swinging London that catered to the rock aristocracy and their switched-on fans. Breward notes: 'Here the old heart of Empire with its palaces, parks and ceremonial routes is overlaid with a new geography of shopping outlets, restaurants and discotheques' (2006: 16). This was the geography of the new pop-cultural empire. Just as the music and success of acts like the Who and the Beatles were used to revive the country's spirit and fortunes, the mod fashion and the shops and shopping areas that were developed to sell it 'should also be viewed as part of a broader mechanism for social and material renewal' (Breward 2006: 16). Union Jacks hung all along Carnaby Street, one of these key shopping areas. The flag was so ubiquitous that you could even 'carry away your purchases in Union Jack wrapping paper' (Aitken 1967: 28). At a higher end of the market, Paul Clark was designing Union Jack-covered products for Woollands of Knightsbridge. The novelist Duncan Fallowell said: 'It began here with Swinging London. All the energy that had sustained the British Empire was brought back home, and it was still thumping away and it had nothing to do, so it produced this extraordinary local, colourful explosion, this fountain of activities' (Green 1988: 442).

Not everyone was caught up in the triumphalist spectacle of Swinging London. David Widgery wrote several articles in the countercultural magazine *OZ* and *New Statesman* during 1967 criticizing the idea of

Swinging London, showing how it did not represent the lives of most people in London, let alone the country more generally: 'I was very angry about Swinging London. I said it was all a hoax and had nothing to do with reality' (Green 1988: 146). This phoniness is another parallel with 'Cool Britannia' in the 1990s. Townshend sees it as a media creation: 'The Swinging London idea was created I think by US news crews coming over and putting girls in mini-dresses into Mini-Mokes[4] to drive around looking sexy. Fashion magazines soon took over the look' (2013).

The American media certainly named and magnified the scene, but they took their lead from the success of English music, fashion and film and the way it was being represented in English music magazines like *Rave* and daily papers like the *Daily Telegraph*. Carnaby Street certainly aided tourism and became 'a London spectacle on a par with the Tower or the Changing of the Guard', bolstering England's image abroad (Melly 1972: 151). The flag's usage in Swinging London hot spots like Carnaby Street and on mod clothing and scooters can be read as an example of what Billig calls 'banal nationalism'. But as he further notes, 'Banal nationalism can be mobilized and turned into frenzied nationalism' (1995: 5). Here it is worth pointing out that towards the end of this intense period of flag use in popular culture and everyday life, the National Front formed in 1967. Clearly we cannot blame the Who for this; however, in terms of the ubiquity of the Union Jack in London during this period, the timing is interesting, demonstrating how the Union Jack is constantly reappropriated by disparate groups for their own strategic and opportunistic ends. The Union Jack's pervasiveness might also be seen as tying in with Gilroy's idea of the 'morbid celebration of Englishness' (1992) that even now characterizes many aspects of England – that yearning for a past that is gone.

The Who's subversive use of the flag and the Swinging London usage clearly illustrate very different intentions, though the nuances of this difference may have been lost on many fans and observers at the time. These two contradictory strands weave through the story of the Union Jack in popular music and can be seen clearly for instance during the so-called Britpop era – for example, the distorted Union Jack on sleeve of Oasis's Live Demonstration cassette (early 1993) and the traditional flag on the cover of *Select* magazine (April 1993).

Rebranding the nation

Britain, like other countries, has long marketed itself at home and abroad, not least through events like the Great Exhibition (1851) and the Festival of Britain (1951). The 1960s saw a marked increase in the government's use of culture to promote trade, tourism and investment (Tickner 2012). In so doing it helped to create a renewed sense of power and confidence, dispelling some of the anxieties of the 'what's wrong with Britain?' period a few years earlier.

In effect pop culture was harnessed to nation-branding, which in turn can be seen as 'an important way of building a sense of national identity and a tool for international relations and tourism', achieved through 'commercial techniques' (Volcic and Andrejevic 2016: 5). This commercial nationalism means 'the use of nationalism to sell ... and the use of commercial strategies by public sector entities to foster nationalism and national agendas' (Volcic and Andrejevic 2016: 2). Of course, this process became more aggressive and overt with the Blair government's harnessing of Britpop in the 1990s.

The preponderance of Union Jacks in pop culture, particularly in London, was intense between 1964 and 1968. It is easy to see this phenomenon as a passing fad, but what was its long-term impact? While, as Breward notes, the Union Jack became one of the 'clichéd signifiers of an era' (2006: 8), the images of the Who discussed above retain a disruptive impact. The visual and metonymic power of the *Observer* cover is attested to by its use, complete or in part, on book covers for Davey (1999) and Tickner (2012). One can also trace a direct line from the Who's subversive cut-up Union Jack jackets, through Jamie Reid's slashed and bulldog-clipped designs for the Sex Pistols' 'Anarchy In The UK' poster, flag and handkerchief, to Oasis's distorted Union Jack going down the plug-hole. The Jam even wore Union Jack jackets and posed in front of Big Ben, another distinctively English icon, just as the Who had done a decade or so before. Each in their own way was a comment on the state of the country at a particular time, and each also reflected the participant's relationship to the existing power structures such as the older generation, the government and the monarchy. Yet as Pete Townshend told the author: 'The reinvention and re-use of the flag in subsequent manifestations of pop music has happened on much safer ground' (2013).

Music and national identity

A sense of national identity is often communicated, at least in part, by music. This goes beyond national anthems or certain instruments. Music often has a role in the construction of national identity. Connell and Gibson, following Benedict Anderson, see the nation state as 'an "imagined community" ... with a sense of unity created through national institutions ... and through a variety of cultural means' (2003: 118). Anderson himself noted how, from its earliest days, print capitalism in the form of newspapers and books played a key role in the forming of national communities (1991: 9–46). In the twentieth century, radio, television and film developed this further. For example, in the 1960s a run of films about the imperial past, such as *Zulu* (1964), *Khartoum* (1966) and *Charge of the Light Brigade* (1968), were important parts of the infrastructure of national collective memory. In related fashion, *Guns at Batasi* (1964) addressed the more recent subject of the end of empire, focusing on a group of British soldiers caught between warring factions in a recently decolonized African state. While we might suspect that these films functioned as apologists for colonialism, they were in fact often critical of imperial ideas and British military leaders. It was in this critical spirit that the films' displays of Victorian military uniforms and Union Jacks were picked up and copied by musicians such as Jimi Hendrix, The Who and The Beatles. Hendrix's appropriation of military regalia inverted the objects' original meaning. Similarly, the Beatles' image for the cover of their *Sgt Pepper's Lonely Hearts Club Band* was a psychedelic take on Victorian military style.

However, despite the general perception that popular music runs counter to dominant political-economic ideologies, it can also be harnessed to state agendas. To an extent in the 1960s, but more obviously in the 1990s Britpop era, pop music wrapped in the Union Jack was used to boost trade and the country's image abroad while creating collective self-confidence and social cohesion at home. With far more sinister effect, far-right political groups have targeted music subcultures as way of recruiting young followers and promulgating reactionary identity politics: 'Music can act as a powerful badge of identity for adolescents, perhaps more than any other aspects of their lives. ... As such it represents a fundamental influence on their identities' (MacDonald, Hargreaves and Miell 2002: 17).

Conclusion

The Union Jack has been part of the visual language of popular music for more than fifty years. It has been used by many artists since the Who, including Sex Pistols, The Jam, The Stone Roses, Morrissey, David Bowie, Asian Dub Foundation, Oasis and Stormzy, as well as by fans, music publications like *NME, Melody Maker, Select* and *Mojo,* and newspapers such as *The Sun.* The Union Flag is constantly recontextualized and adapted: it is a visual text that is instantly recognizable and as such lends itself to constant reinterpretation, depending on the whim of a particular group of designers, artists, musicians or political group.

As a response to a post-war loss of empire and an ensuing identity crisis, Britain sought to rebuild national status partly through its creative, cultural and heritage industries, and through the constant reproduction of symbols associated with past national glories. Through the 1960s the Union Jack shifted from being a symbol of empire (political and military power) to a symbol of music, fashion and pop-cultural cool – a new (cultural) imperialism. Within the context of the music industry it was possible to reinterpret these traditional symbols to create new meaning or even ambiguity. This is what the Who did with the cut-up Union Jack jackets. The proliferation of Union Jacks in this period – in music, in fashion, in politics, in big business – appear to represent a range of responses to decolonization and increased US power, in which one of the key symbols of Britain's imperial past was put to new uses, including trying to assert, consciously or not, English/British dominance in other spheres. In music, fashion and art Englishness was being remade. In this way the end of empire was processed, interpreted and mediated through the use of the Union Jack. The success of the creative industries at this time and the way that Englishness/Britishness was so overtly communicated in their products is evidence, in some ways, of the idea of the British Empire continuing in other forms.

The Who's use of the flag was driven by the context of the 1960s, a questioning of national identity, as well as a concern for marketing and image. Townshend was fascinated by all this and was encouraged by Kit Lambert, one of his managers. As Angela Carter noted 'He was impelled to do it by the pressure of the times' (1996). Through the distribution of multinational record companies and newspaper and magazine publishers, these images were spread globally. The fact that Pete Townshend was so attuned to the issue of Englishness and national identity, while at the same time being fascinated by 'iconic post-war and patriotic images' (Townshend 2013) may be down to his grandfather being from Cork, Ireland. This links into Campbell's idea of 'in-betweenness' (2011), which he uses to examine issues of identity and relationship to England in regards to second-generation musicians such as John Lydon, Shane MacGowan and The Smiths.

Stuart Hall noted that 'all images are multi-vocal and are always capable of bearing more than one interpretation' (1999: 309). This is true of the Union Jack in pop music. Clearly the same image can mean different things to different people depending on context and their own knowledge and assumptions. Indeed, the same image can mean many things to the *same* person. The Union Jack is a case in point: a symbol of monarchy and nation when seen on a royal occasion; a symbol of military power when displayed on a soldier's uniform or tank; proof of allegiance to mod culture when stuck on a Vespa scooter; a symbol of fascism when worn by a member of the National Front or a skinhead band; a symbol of anarchy when worn by a punk; and an exploration of national identity and imagery when used by Pete Townshend in the mid-1960s. For some, the Who's Union Jack jackets were outrageous and disrespectful, for others they were dynamic pop art fashion, for magazines they were a colourful and timely way of filling space given the Union Jack's fashionable ubiquity in the highly marketable context of Swinging London. From looking at the height of Union Jack usage in 1964–8, it is clear that this can be seen as political, nationalistic, sensationalist, subversive, confrontational, economic, aesthetic, or just convenient marketing.

In summary, then, the proliferation of traditional flags in music, in the wake of the subversive uses by the Who, and particularly the ubiquity of Union Jacks in Swinging London, acted as a form of Billig's banal nationalism. Whatever the intention of the producer, an image can have many different meanings to those that consume it. For this reason it can be seen as a flag of convenience within the music industry. However the subtleties of the original message can get lost when it circulates among multiple audiences.

Indeed, when the Union Jack jackets and patches were reprised in the late 1970s during the mod revival, not only did they look tacky, they had also by now acquired other troubling political associations. Ian Walker marked out the different meanings and contexts: '1965: Pete Townshend destroys property on a stage draped with a giant Union Jack: this is flying the flag upside down. ... [But] The Union Jack, in 1979, is a fascist symbol. The red white and blue chic is the perfect accessory to the white power sticker the young lads wear on their parkas down at the Bridgehouse in the East End of a Friday night' (1980:18).

Thus it should be stressed that those who invoke Union Jack symbolism in pop music culture should do so carefully. The Union Jack is undoubtedly a dynamic visual device that can be used to create clarity – that is, this is an English/British product artist, this is a mod fan, etc. It can also create provocation and ambiguity, for example, with the Who's Union Jack jacket Townshend was interested in its 'invitation of controversy' (Townshend 2013). Just as the meaning of the Union Jack varies depending on the context or the person using or viewing it, the Englishness that it represents is also fluid. Behind the bright colours and the feel-good atmosphere created through the harnessing of pop culture, this is what we see played out in the ubiquity of the Union Jack during the mid-1960s. At this point the Union Jack was both a contested symbol of Englishness and convenient marketing device. Thus the Union Jack, particularly when cut-up and made into jackets, was the perfect metonym for the Who and their ideas at this point.

Notes

1   See, for example, Francis Hayman, 'Robert Clive and Mia Jafar after the Battle of Plassey 1757' (c.1760); Benjamin West, 'The Death of General James Wolfe' (1770), (Smith 2015: 89–90).

2   Examples include: George Fullard, 'The Patriot' (1960); Peter Phillips, 'Purple Flag' (1960); Peter Blake, 'Self-Portrait with Badges' (1961) and 'The Toy Shop' (1962); Derek Boshier, 'Man Playing Snooker and Thinking of Other Things' (1961), 'Pepsi-Culture' (1961), 'Drink A Pink of Milk' (1962), 'Re-think Re-Entry' (1962), 'England's Glory' (1962); David Hockney, 'My Bonnie Lies Over the Ocean' (1961–2).

3   I Was Lord Kitchener's Valet produced a poster entitled *This is Swinging London* (1966) that inevitably featured a Union Jack. The poet Christopher Logue created a poster poem for the Gear boutique on an anti-war theme which was backed by a version of a Union Jack.

4   Indeed, the American singer Cher was photographed in London in a Mini Moke painted with Union Jacks. Continuing the military theme that seemed to underscore the era, Mini Mokes looked like small army jeeps and real army vehicles were being repurposed by the new pop generation – Scott Walker of the Walker Brothers used to drive around London in a Second World War jeep.

---

140   MAD DOGS AND ENGLISHNESS

Bibliography

Aitken, J. (1967), *The Young Meteors*, London: Secker and Warburg.

Anderson, B. (1991), *Imagined Communities*, London: Verso.

Ashmore, S. (2006), '"I Think They're All Mad": Shopping in Swinging London', in C. Breward, D. Gilbert and J. Lister (eds), *Swinging Sixties*, London: V&A Publications.

Barnes, R. (1982), *The Who: Maximum R&B: A Visual History*, London: Eel Pie Publishing.

Billig, M. (1995), *Banal Nationalism*, London: Sage.

Booker, C. (1969), *The Neophiliacs: a study in the revolution in English life in the Fifties and Sixties*, London: Fontana.

Bracewell, M. (2002), *The Nineties: When Surface Was Depth*, London: Flamingo.

Breward, C. (2004), *Fashioning London: Clothing and the Modern Metropolis*, Oxford: Berg.

Breward, C., D. Gilbert and J. Lister, (eds) (2006), *Swinging Sixties*, London: V&A Publications.

Briggs, J. (2014), *Sounds French: Globalization, Cultural Communities and Pop 1958–80*, Oxford: Oxford University Press.

Campbell, S. (2011), *Irish Blood, English Heart: Second Generation Irish Musicians in England*, Cork: Cork University Press.

Carter, A. (1996), 'Notes for a Theory of Sixties Style' [1967], in H. Kureishi and J. Savage (eds), *The Faber Book of Pop*, London: Faber and Faber.

Collier, P. (1910), *England and the English: From an American Point of View*, London: Duckworth and Co.

Connell, J. and C. Gibson (2003), *Sound Tracks: Popular music, identity and place*, Abingdon: Routledge.

Eco, U. (1973), 'Social Life As A Sign System', in D. Robey (ed.), *Structuralism: The Wolfson Lectures, 1972*, London: Cape.

Eco, U. (1982), 'Critique of the Image' [1970], in V. Burgin (ed.), *Thinking Photography*, Basingstoke: Macmillan.

Elgenius, G. (2007), 'The origin of European national flags' in T. H. Eriksen and R. Jenkins (eds), *Flag, Nation and Symbolism in Europe and America*, Abingdon: Routledge.

Faulkner, S. and A. Ramamurthy, (eds) (2006), *Visual Culture and Decolonisation in Britain*, Aldershot: Ashgate.

Gildart, K. (2013), *Images of England through Popular Music: Youth, Class and Rock'n'Roll, 1955–1976*, New York: Palgrave Macmillan.

Gilroy, P. (1992), 'Ethnic Absolutism', in L. Grossberg, C. Nelson and P. Treichler (eds), *Cultural Studies,* London: Routledge.

Gilroy, P. (2002), *There Ain't No Black In The Union Jack*, London: Routledge.

Gilroy, P. (2000), 'Joined-Up Politics and Post-Colonial Melancholia', *Nka: Journal of Contemporary African Art*, 2000 (11–12): 48–55.

Gilroy, P. (2015), 'Foreword', in A. Smith, D. Blayney Brownand C. Jacobi (eds), *Artist And Empire: Facing Britain's Imperial Past*, London: Tate Publishing.

Gorman, P. (2006), *The Look: Adventures in Rock and Pop Fashion*, London: Adelita.

Green, J. (1988), *Days In The Life: Voices from the English Underground 1961–1971*, London: William Heinemann.

Hall, S. (1992), 'The Question of Cultural Identity', in S. Hall, D. Held and T. McGrew (eds), *Modernity and its Futures*, Cambridge: Polity Press/ Open University.

Hall, S. (1999), 'Looking and Subjectivity: Introduction', in J. Evans and S. Hall (eds), *Visual Culture: The Reader*, London: Sage.

Hebdige, D. (1979), *Subculture: The Meaning of Style*, London: Methuen.

Hesmondhalgh, D. (2001), 'Britpop and National Identity', in D. Morley and K. Robins (eds), *British Cultural Studies: Geography, Nationality, and Identity*, Oxford: Oxford University Press.

Hoffman, D. (1982), *With The Beatles: The historic photographs of Dezo Hoffman*, London: Omnibus.

Hughes, R. (1997), *American Visions: The Epic History of Art in America*, London: Harvill Press.

Jenkins, R. (2007), 'Inarticulate speech of the heart', in T. H. Eriksen and R. Jenkins (eds), *Flag, Nation and Symbolism in Europe and America*, Abingdon: Routledge.

Kane, L. (2003), *Ticket To Ride: Inside the Beatles' 1964 Tour that Changed the World*, Philadelphia: Running Press.

Kumar, K. (2003), *The Making of English National Identity*, Cambridge: Cambridge University Press.

Kureishi, H. and J. Savage (eds) (1995), *The Faber Book of Pop*, London: Faber and Faber.

Kynaston, D. (2007), *Austerity Britain 1945–51*, London: Bloomsbury.

MacDonald, R., D. Hargreaves and D. Miell (eds) (2002), *Musical Identities*, Oxford: Oxford University Press.

Mellor, D. (1993), *The Sixties Art Scene In London*, London: Barbican Art Gallery/ Phaidon Press.

Melly, G. (1972), *Revolt Into Style: The Pop Arts In Britain*, 2nd edn. Harmondsworth: Penguin.

Negus, K. (1992), *Producing Pop: Culture and Conflict in the Popular Music Industry*, London: Arnold.

Neil, A. and M. Kent (2005), *Anyway, Anyhow, Anywhere: The Complete Chronicle of the Who, 1958–1978*, New York: Sterling Publishing Co.

Neumann, I. (2007), 'Afterword', in T. H. Eriksen and R. Jenkins (eds), *Flag, Nation and Symbolism in Europe and America*, Abingdon: Routledge.

Osborne, J. (1961), letter in *Tribune*, 18 August 1961.

Richman, R. (1968), 'The New Rock', *Life*, June. 64(26).

Savage, J. (2011), 'Celebrating five decades of *The Observer Magazine*', *The Observer*, 31 July. Available from: https://www.theguardian.com/media/2011/jul/31/five-decades-of-the-observer-magazine [accessed 5 January 2017].

Savage, J. (2015), *1966: The Year The Decade Exploded*, London: Faber and Faber.

Smith, A., D. Blayney Brown and C. Jacobi (eds) (2015), *Artist And Empire: Facing Britain's Imperial Past*, London: Tate Publishing.

Tickner, L. (2012), '"Export Britain": Pop Art, Mass Culture and the Export Drive', in L. Tickner and P. Peters Corbett (eds), *British Art in the Cultural Field*, 197–221, Chichester: Association of Art Historians/Wiley-Blackwell.

Townshend, P. (2013), Interview with author, 13 June.

Volcic, Z. and M. Andrejevic (2016), *Commercial Nationalism: Selling the Nation and Nationalizing the Sell*, Basingstoke: Palgrave Macmillan.

Walker, I. (1980), 'All Mods con?', *The Leveller*, January 1980, No.34 UK, https://standupandspit.wordpress.com/2016/04/15/mods-1980/ [accessed 11 June 2016].

Webster, W. (2006), '"There'll always be an England": Representations of colonial wars and immigration, 1948–68', in S. Faulkner and A. Ramamurthy (eds), *Visual Culture and Decolonisation in Britain*, Aldershot: Ashgate.

Wheen, F. (1982), *The Sixties: A Fresh Look at the Decade of Change*, London: Century Publishing/Channel 4.

Wright, P. (1985), *On Living in An Old Country: The National Past in Contemporary Britain*, London: Verso.

Discography

The Rolling Stones (1965) Get Off My Cloud, Decca/London [Single]

Screaming Lord Sutch (1970) Union Jack Car, *Screaming Lord Sutch and Heavy Friends*, Contillion [Album]

The Sex Pistols (1976) Anarchy in the UK, EMI [Single]

The Who (1966) A Legal Matter, Brunswick [Single]

The Who (1966) I'm A Boy, Reaction [Single]

The Who (1968) Dogs, Track [Single]

PART THREE

Performing discrepancy

The poison in the human machine

Raphael Costambeys-Kempczynski

Introduction: God save the Queen, the fascist regime

On 15 December 1976 the International Monetary Fund agreed to lend the UK \$3.9 billion in order to stay the declining value of sterling. Never had such a large request been submitted to the IMF. The Labour Party's popularity was falling in the polls; only the Lib-Lab Pact of March 1977 would temporarily save James Callaghan's minority Labour government.[1] If Labour was suffering in Parliament, however, media interest was turning its attention to the Queen's silver jubilee.[2] This apparent discrepancy is summarized by Jon Savage in *England's Dreaming: The Sex Pistols and Punk Rock*:

> Out of the morass of mid-1970s pluralism emerged the old spectres thinly disguised with a fresh lick of paint. Here was the blind superiority that had characterised the English world-view after the Second World War; here was a concentrated dose of all the unappealing traits – snobbery, insularity, xenophobia – that rendered England's continued claim to be a world power meaningless. (1991: 352)

It would appear that the expressions of jingoism and nostalgia brought on by the jubilee celebrations were not shared by everyone. To begin with, as Savage indicates, the silver jubilee was an English moment (1991: 352).

Indeed, with the adverse impact of the Second World War on its imperial power, Great Britain had had to come to terms with the progressive dismantling of its empire; with Labour's minority government having to make deals with the Scottish National Party and Plaid Cymru, devolution was now high on the agenda; and following the terrible events of Bloody Sunday, the IRA campaign had spread to the mainland. Indeed, a shadow was being cast by 'the old spectres'. In his book *Seasons in the Sun: The Battle for Britain, 1974–1979*, Dominic Sandbrook writes of the late 1970s:

> It was an age that saw two Prime Ministers broken by the unions, inflation heading towards 30 per cent, sporting occasions regularly disfigured by barbaric hooliganism and hundreds of people murdered by terrorists not only in Northern Ireland but in the streets of London and the pubs of Birmingham. Even before Mrs Thatcher came to power, the gap between North and South was growing, while manufacturing industries on which Britain's prosperity had long depended were in deep decline. In the industrial working-class cities, unemployment was mounting; in Westminster, almost everybody, from Tony Benn on the left to Sir Keith Joseph on the right, recognized that Britain was facing an extremely painful transition. (2012: xx)

Of course, one has to be careful about general historical statements that reduce the complexities of a time to stereotype. The introduction to Alwyn W. Turner's book *Crisis? What Crisis?* begins with the sentence, 'The lights were going out all over Britain, and no one was quite sure if we'd see them lit again in our lifetime' (2008: ix), but he is also quick to bring some balance to this somewhat pervasive vision of the 1970s:

> In 2004 the New Economics Foundation constructed an analysis of national performance based not on the traditional criterion of gross domestic product, but on what it called the measure of domestic progress, incorporating such factors as crime, family stability, pollution and inequality of income. And it concluded that Britain was a happier country in 1976 than it had been in the thirty years since. (2008, ix)

Furthermore, if the IMF loan negotiated by Denis Healey is often remembered as an act that for the first time put domestic economic policy in the hands of international bankers, Turner reminds us that the government was quick to realize that they were not going to have to call on the totality of the funds in question (2008: 188).

The popular portrayal of the 1970s as a decade of crisis, however, is not simply a view that has been constructed over the decades since Margaret Thatcher's election in 1979. The Labour Party Manifesto of October 1974 begins with the sentence: 'Britain faces its most dangerous crisis since the war' (Craig 1975: 453). And with the IMF bailout negotiations in full swing, the Labour Party conference of 1976 saw James Callaghan recall these words to the party delegates during his first speech as party leader and prime minister:

> Let me remind those who wish us to stick to the Manifesto what its opening words were: 'Britain faces its most dangerous crisis since the war.'
>
> The Manifesto went on to describe the worst world recession since the 1930s, the five-fold increase in oil prices, an ever-narrowing industrial base and a level of economic performance which had been in steady decline, compared with our major competitors, for almost a generation. It is all there to read – 'the most dangerous crisis since the war'. (Callaghan 1976)

This sense of decline finds itself expressed in Margaret Drabble's oft-quoted novel *The Ice Age,* published in 1977, where the country is repeatedly described as slowly suffocating: 'England, sliding, sinking, shabby, dirty, lazy, inefficient, dangerous, in its death-throes, worn out, clapped out, occasionally lashing out' (1977: 97). And faced with a seemingly absent future, lashing out in the name of youth culture were the punks of the King's Road.

Writing towards the end of the Second World War, George Orwell distances the English people from revolutionary tendencies and fascist regimes suggesting, 'England is the only European country where internal politics are conducted in a more or less humane and decent manner' (2001: 322). The English people, he claims, 'are not good haters' (2001, 304). It would appear that not everyone would agree: in counterpoint to the hippie generation's Summer of Love ten years earlier, 1977 would be the punk generation's Summer of Hate.[3]

As if to remind the establishment of England's social frailties, the Sex Pistols decided to release their single 'God Save the Queen' on 27 May 1977 in the hope of reaching the top ten by jubilee week. The release, however, was fraught with difficulties. Workers at the CBS plant where the record was being pressed protested against the single's content, refusing to work on various occasions. Once released the promotion of the single was equally problematic – the Independent Broadcasting Authority deemed the single to be in direct contravention of Section 4 (10) (A) of the IBA Act, that is, 'against good taste or decency, likely to encourage or incite crime, or lead to disorder'. The commercial television stations and radios were thus instructed by the IBA not to broadcast the single and the BBC went as far as banning the record.

Regardless of these efforts, or perhaps because of the media attention provoked by them, within five days of its release the single sold one hundred and fifty thousand copies sending it to number eleven in the official UK Singles Chart. Although by the end of jubilee week 'God Save the Queen' had sold two hundred thousand copies, the single only peaked at number two and was kept off number one by Rod Stewart's double A-side 'I don't Want to Talk About It/The First Cut Is the Deepest'. Richard Branson believes that the British Phonographic Institute and the British Market Research Bureau conspired to keep the Sex Pistols off the top spot (Savage 1991: 364–5).

There seems to be some continued sensitivity about the silver jubilee. After thirty years the classified government files of 1977 were taken to the National Archives in Kew and released to the public. Of the six files covering the silver jubilee, however, only two have been released. The others have been withheld under Section 40 'Personal Information' and 'Information Provided in Confidence'. In the spirit of punk, the journalist Martha Kearney concludes in an episode of her BBC Radio 4 documentary, *UK Confidential*, that we may never know how the Queen felt about being 'gobbed at by Johnny Rotten' (BBC 2007).

The decency fallacy: Everybody's doing just what they are told to

Orwell sees decency as a moral quality inherent to the English people (2001) and in his book, *Englishness Identified: Manners and Characters, 1650–1850* (2000), Paul Langford identifies decency as one of the six fundamental characteristics that defines Englishness.[4] In effect, somewhere along the line we are all led to believe that it is 'as if' the English are decent, 'as if' the quality of decency is essential to the quiddity of Englishness. Decency then becomes the thing-in-itself of Englishness or the *Ding an sich* to use the Kantian term. Eva Schaper writes:

> Things-in-themselves can consistently be seen as heuristic fictions, as devices enabling us to account for a given situation in terms of a theory. Things-in-themselves as heuristic fictions permit us to derive and exhibit a complicated set of consequences if we proceed as if they were real. (1996: 236)

Decency is a code that functions as an exclusion procedure to protect us against the free behaviour of others. Decency is thus a political fiction that operates at the level of the social system; it is a second order code. True expressions of freedom are understood as violating this type of second order code and, in the case of decency, the system reacts by categorizing indecent behaviour as violent, obscene, criminal or, even as, to follow on from Orwell, un-English. Indecency then becomes a marker for such legitimate violence as freedom of expression, of individualism, giving space for the Clash to demand 'a riot of my own' ('White Riot', 1977). The BBC may choose to ban a record such as 'God Save the Queen' (1977) but though this form of censorship may be an attempt to restrain and thus sustain meaning, it is based on the mistaken idea that it is at all possible to stabilize our understanding of reality or, indeed, the processes that we employ to communicate that understanding.

It follows then that the defining contours of second order codes are continually shifting, expanding, resolved on being comprehensive, and with the diluting agent of time so the indecencies of the Sex Pistols may appear tame to us today (if not to government agencies).[5] If indecency is meant as a mark of individualism, indecency like autonomy is not to be equated with solipsism since, as it has been written elsewhere, constructs are communalized or absorbed into the centre and contained by means of heuristic fictions or operative fictions of collective knowledge. These include, among others, politics, which allows for the exercise of authority over freedom; philosophy which allows for the exercise of authority over ethics, morals and virtue; religion which allows for the exercise of authority over salvation; and science which allows for the exercise of authority over truth (Costambeys-Kempczynski, Moreau and Piat 2012: 3; Grant 2003: 115). And so it follows that all of these categories serve to help define our sense of decency.

If we agree that various societal rules necessarily exercise their authority over second order codes, then decency must necessarily be considered to be a heteronomy. What place then is left to staying true to oneself, of legislating one's self? That is, what place is left to that most ineffable yet crucial characteristic of popular music: authenticity? As Hugh Barker and Yuval Taylor state in their book *Faking It: The Quest for Authenticity in Popular Music*: 'Attitudes toward authenticity were from the start a deeply confused part of punk' (2007: 266). They continue:

> [Malcolm] McLaren was influenced by a variety of artistic and political movements including Dadaism and anarchism, and he was especially interested in situationists. This political movement had little direct influence on the punk musicians but fascinated the older generation of McLaren and his friends, especially those who regarded hippie idealism with suspicion. Situationism was essentially a strand of anarchism, which had commented on, and to some degree influenced, the Parisian uprising of 1968, at which McLaren would sometimes falsely claim to have been present. Echoing the ideas of situationist gurus Raoul Vaneigem and Guy Debord, which became widely known in the years after 1968, he saw punk as essentially a posture, a consciously assumed style and pose that created friction and revealed the simulations in bourgeois society. (2007: 266–7)

Punk, therefore, poses a number of paradoxes one of which, I will contend, establishes both decency and indecency as preconditions for authenticity. It is 'as-if' punk is indecent and this indecency is a characteristic of authenticity.

Decent society is thus perceived as inauthentic. Therefore, punk, in its attempt at reinjecting authenticity, is itself a code of decency.

Commodifying decency: You are in suspension

In English popular music terms, 1977 began at 6.15 pm on 1 December 1976. This was the historic moment when television presenter Bill Grundy infamously interviewed the Sex Pistols on his Thames Television *Today* programme. Grundy appeared to be drunk on screen and led a condescending and confrontational interview. Within a few minutes, punk, as a liberal socially complex phenomenon, was reduced to 'white boys' noise'. The punk phenomenon would still prove to be violent and political but it had already been subsumed by the establishment as bad boy rock in the same way as the Rolling Stones had been fifteen years previously. What had been an underground musical development was transformed into an over-the-top theatre of ridicule. The Sex Pistols had made it, but had destroyed themselves in the process. Before this event punk had been a musical movement; now it was a media phenomenon, no longer a preserve of the musical press but front-page news.

The ensuing scandal was aggravated by the following day's press coverage as typified by the front-page article written by Stuart Greig, Michael McCarthy and John Peacock, and published by the *Daily Mirror* under the now infamous headline, 'The Filth and the Fury'. Local authorities began cancelling concert dates leaving the Anarchy in the UK tour irreparably damaged. EMI was urged to do the 'decent' thing and take action, but this was the media condemning a scandal of their own making.

This media frenzy appears as an example of what Jürgen Habermas says about late capitalism and its propensity for crisis tendencies where policy becomes the management of these crises, a management which contains in itself the possibility of further crises, rather than the resolution of the fundamentals (1975). The fundamental issues in 1976 and 1977 were not punk or the Queen's silver jubilee but such great deniers of common public decency as the economic crisis and rising unemployment that would lead to the winter of discontent of 1978–9. On 10 January 1979, on returning from an international summit in Guadeloupe, Prime Minister Callaghan was asked by an *Evening Standard* reporter his view of the 'mounting chaos' in the country. Callaghan told reporters: 'I promise you that if you look at it from outside, and perhaps you're taking rather a parochial view at the moment, I don't think that other people in the world would share the view that there is mounting chaos' (Robinson 2012: 217). It would appear that Callaghan was not only blind to the fundamental socio-economic issues of the day but also the industrial crisis that placed the country on the brink of a state of emergency. During the press conference, Callaghan seemed to ask the reporters not to be jealous of the fact that he had gone swimming on this trip to the Caribbean. With undoubtedly fortuitous Habermassian irony, the following day *The Sun* famously ran the headline 'Crisis? What Crisis?'

It is worth noting that during the concluding remarks of his interview of the Sex Pistols, Bill Grundy turns towards Siouxsie Sioux, who is there as part of the group's entourage, and suggests, 'We'll meet afterwards, shall we?' The Sex Pistols guitarist Steve Jones reacts to this by calling Grundy, among other things, a 'dirty old man'.[6] As Jones's comments suggest, for him it is Grundy, the broadcasting institution, and his proposition directed at Siouxsie Sioux that are indecent.

Writing in the fanzine *Bondage* shortly after the interview, the singer of the punk band The Nipple Erectors and future member of The Pogues, Shane MacGowan, immediately identifies the vagueness of the notion of decency and projects it as a heuristic fiction:

> Since when did EMI or any of those old cunts put 'public duty' before their precious money or the security it gives them? What it really is is they feel that security is threatened just by what the Pistols represent. And how could anything that appears on ITV offend public decency? There isn't any public decency – people only know what's decent by being told by ITV and the rest of the media and EMI too. (1976: 2)

Punk's message may have been one of decency – or the reappropriation of decency – but the medium had to be consistently indecent to ensure the vibrancy of that message. Even this, however, would prove difficult to sustain as Lydon later admitted when talking about Public Image Limited, the band he would form after the demise of the Sex Pistols:

> I formed PiL because I got bored with the extremist point of view that I'd had with the Sex Pistols. ... I attempted to move toward a liberal point of view and see if that could slowly but surely change society into something more decent. (1993: 270)

In 1977, however, the Sex Pistols as 'the poison in the human machine' ('God Save the Queen') ensured that they would enflame the stereotypes of middle England they were reacting against, the population that the song 'Liar' claimed to be in 'suspension' (*Never Mind the Bollocks Here's The Sex Pistols*). One such candidate was Bernard Brooke-Partridge, chairman of the Arts Council who had banned the Sex Pistols from performing in London. Writing in *Rolling Stone* Charles M. Young recounts his exchange with Brooke-Partridge:

> 'I will do everything within the law to stop them from appearing here ever again,' he says. 'I loathe and detest everything they stand for and look like. They are obnoxious, obscene and disgusting.'

'Doesn't the question of who should decide what's disgusting in a free society enter in here?'

'I am the person who decides,' he says. 'The electorate put me here. My power is not in question. If the Sex Pistols want to change the system, they are free to stand for election from my district.'

'In the United States, the First Amendment to the Constitution says the government is not allowed to make such decisions.'

'We have our own way of doing things here. The Sex Pistols are scum trying to make a fast buck, which they are entitled to do under the law. I am entitled to try and stop them. We'll see who wins.' (1977: online)

On 5 November 1977, WPC Julie Dawn Story informed the branch manager of Virgin record store in Nottingham that the word 'Bollocks' on the cover of the Sex Pistols album, *Never Mind the Bollocks Here's The Sex Pistols,* was in breach of the Indecent Advertising Act of 1899. Pivotal to the subsequent court case held at Nottingham Magistrates' Court on 24 November 1977 was the witness account of Reverend James Kingsley, professor of English at Nottingham University and former Anglican priest. In Kingsley's account of the etymology of 'bollock' he argued:

The word has been used as a nickname for clergymen. Clergymen are known to talk a good deal of rubbish and so the word later developed the meaning of nonsense. ... They became known for talking a great deal of bollocks, just as old balls or baloney also come to mean testicles, so it has twin uses in the dictionary. (Quoted in 'The Bollocks Court Case' 1977: online)

Calling upon a sense of pride in the English language's Anglo-Saxon inheritance, this line of defence was enough for the magistrates to find in favour of the Sex Pistols although the senior magistrate stressed this was done so 'reluctantly' (Cloonan 1995: 352).

The battleground between the Sex Pistols-led English punk movement and the establishment was that of decency. The punk events of 1977 were driven by a need to reappropriate decency as the domain of the subject, to inject responsibility back into a notion too long left in suspension. The claim of English punk music in 1977 was about empowering the social actor through responsibility with subjectivity.

Commodifying fracture: I wanna be Anarchy

There should be no mistake, however. Punk's English dream of decency was itself a construction. If the Sex Pistols were the unadulterated voice of the working class, or the unemployed class, this could only sit uncomfortably with their fame and money. The direct attack on the social realities of 1977 would lead to added attention, better record sales, increased wealth and greater distance from the class struggle within which the music knew its genesis. Critics have therefore argued that a popular musician's view of contemporary reality is fuzzy, distorted by the pull between the utopian message of production and the capital gain of consumption. Ultimately what we need to bear in mind is that beyond the performance of punk bands of this period, whether on stage or in the media, many of the band members did not have working-class backgrounds or were on the road to middle-classdom from an early age. Of the Clash, Joe Strummer's father was a diplomat and Mick Jones attended the Strand School, a boys' grammar school in South London with a reputation for preparing future civil servants, before going on to study at art school. John Lydon, the mouthpiece of the dole queue, had never been unemployed himself. Lydon had an ambivalent relationship towards class. He appears to have a nostalgic attachment to the English working-class community of his youth and yet his Sex Pistols persona, Johnny Rotten, an imagined alternative identity born out of his extensive cultural capital, a product of an intellectual construct, firmly rejects this wistful vision of the past. Rotten stood against tradition and conformity and as Sean Albeiz summarized: 'Lydon's identity cannot be reduced to being working class, but neither can he escape class as it underwrote his anger and yearning to attack and offend the British establishment' (2003: 367).

To attack the generation of the Second World War it would be necessary to demonstrate the suffering experienced at the hands of post-Empire inertia characterized by the silver jubilee. Perhaps the most violent aspect of 'God Save the Queen' is not the attack on the 'mad parade' itself – the song was written about a year before the jubilee celebrations – but the song's mantra that there is 'no future', leaving Jon Savage to conclude: 'In a country submerged in nostalgia, this was a serious breach of etiquette' (1991: 355). With the seeming impossibility of prospect, all that was left was the immediacy of a present perceived as the apocalypse. The Sex Pistols sang 'I am an antichrist' in 'Anarchy in the UK', The Clash sang 'London's Burning', X-Ray Spex sang 'Oh! Bondage Up Yours', The Stranglers sang 'Something Better Change'.

According to Richard Middleton, elements of culture are *in fine* determined by economic factors such as class. He calls this phenomenon 'principles of articulation' and explains that such principles 'operate by combining existing elements into new patterns or by attaching new connotations to them' (Middleton 1990: 8). Therefore, while elements of culture are not linked to specific economic factors they are shaped by the articulation of sets of values attached to these factors. This allows Middleton to conclude on the theory of articulation:

> It preserves a relative autonomy for superstructural elements (musical structures, for example) but also insists that those combinatory patterns actually constructed do mediate deep, objective patterns in the socio-

economic formation, and that the mediation takes place in *struggle:* the classes fight to articulate together constituents of the cultural repertoire in particular ways so that they are organised in terms of principles or sets of values determined by the position and interests of the class in the prevailing mode of production. (1985: 7)

Heavily defined by its class system, English society in 1977 had a voice for its alienated, bored working-class youth. The vicious sound of these English punk bands reflected the destruction around them: the dissonant snarling singing voice, the raw guitar wall of sound, every beat of every bar accented and the percussive high pitch of continuous crashing symbols makes listening uncomfortable.

The mounting unrest of the labour forces brought on by the continuing pay restraint policy of the Callaghan government led to what Stuart Hall has identified as a Gramscian crisis of authority (1988: 23–4, 33–5). Hall argues that this crisis focused on youth culture and, as Neil Nehring points out, McLaren parodied the crisis by invoking anarchy (1991: 226). Middleton argues that teenage rebellion in the 1950s and 1960s, though set against the backdrop of growing liberal ideology, was articulated to safe musical patterns with little subversive content. Punk offered a more testing musical and message-driven assault at a time of more critical socio-economic unrest. Yet even here it appears difficult to escape Gramsci's concept of hegemony whereby the status quo is maintained by shifting the focus away from the reality of economic concerns and onto a theatre of rebellion. Perhaps one could have seen punk as a working-class culture distinct from the hegemonic culture of the bourgeoisie, but this is difficult with the likes of McLaren at its helm. One could also return to the notion of the legitimization of crises – the various moments of youth culture are self-regulating revolutions as the actors of one generation necessarily grow older and therefore normalize any sense of fracture. In the meantime, the social realities of economic failure persist.

It would appear misleading then to suggest that punk helped shape the politics of the time but, as John Street points out, we are entitled to conceive that the 'music establishes a context through which politics is viewed and judged' and that 'punk gives a structure to the feelings of change and decay' (2001: 247).

Punk offers us then another framework through which to read the politics of decency. We are, perhaps luckily, entitled to engage with the politics of decency of the English punk movement without having to identify the oratory genius of Johnny Rotten's humanism. It is not at the level of his rhetoric that the political principles of articulation are performed. Indeed, the punk groups of the late 1970s simply project themselves as the voice of the English underclass. This is the little man against the big man mentality seen as a defining characteristic of Englishness – as the sociologist Krishan Kumar puts it, the English have always 'championed the good sense, resourcefulness and courage of the ordinary "little chap"' (2003: 233). The argument resonates with George Orwell's belief that more than any other nation in Europe, the English have no respect for 'the modern cult of power-worship' (2001: 298). Indeed, with such direct implications in movements like Rock against Racism, punk groups like The Clash, Buzzcocks, X-Ray Spex and Sham 69 did more than symbolic resistance.

Commodifying authenticity: Do not pretend 'cos I do not care

Class differentiation was also identified along musical lines, notably in the polarization of punk and progressive rock. 'Prog rock' was the genre of popular music seen to be indulgently arty, intellectual, romantic and middle class by punk. It lacked authenticity whereas punk was purer, had more street credibility. Contrary to many of its predecessors, at the musical core of punk, from its conception to its performance, lies the action of protest. Instrumental solos, seen as superfluous to this and a sign of slickness, were to be condemned along with the banks of electronic keyboards so revelled in by the progressive rockers of the time. The lack of rhythmic variation made punk un-danceable beyond pogoing but added a sense of urgency. The simplicity of the riffs was the stance of individualism and allowed the anger of the voice to stand out. Protest song in the form of folk or hippie music had been plaintive, punk, however, was declamatory. The Clash and the Sex Pistols confronted their audiences often, provoking them into a violent reaction. The sense of confrontation is then worked on in the studio to reproduce this live feel. No sense of artificiality must come between the band and the audience, and though it may be difficult to make out the message because of the sneer, the snarl and the slur, the sincerity of that message must not be brought into question. Often criticized for being out of tune one need only listen to a song like 'Pretty Vacant' to hear how Rotten aggresses the listener with his political message sung out of key during the verse but then neatly falls into key for the rousing chorus inviting us to sing along, to answer his call to arms. In this way punk positioned itself against the music that had come before – breaking away from rock and roll, from hippie music and prog rock, and expressing a real disdain for disco. In their song entitled '1977' (1977), the Clash severed all links to Elvis, the Beatles and Rolling Stones. Some writers see punk as fundamentally changing the nature of popular music. Ian Chambers, for instance, believed that punk created a breach in the sequentiality of pop which would lead to 'a proliferation of margins rather than a predictable return to a renewed "mainstream" and subordinated "alternative"' (1985: 200). And yet punk reworked rock and roll in a pub rock guise and inherited the rhythms of reggae. These articulations went some way to guarantee the bands' commercial success, pointed at their mainstream bent: this was punk rock.

Perhaps the public uproar over punk reflected a real threat to public order, but cultural theory teaches us well. Hegemony, crises and violence, as we are allowed to witness them, are legitimate, or legitimized, because they allow for the stabilization of vagueness. Decency thus redefines itself by appropriating manifestations of crises and violence. Although much of the media attention focused on the public displays of violence that characterized punk – the imagery of bondage, the aggressive musical snarl, the lyrics of desolation and oppression, the public goading – there was also a commodification of this violence. After the Grundy incident, small retailers began to take notice of punk's apparent individualist ethos and started setting up independent record labels. Added to this were the 'one stops', firms that bought bulk records from the major labels and then sold them on to independent record shops but without the small order surcharge imposed by the major record labels. This, in effect, decentralized the chain of distribution. The network of small-scale production and distribution of records helped, in the words of Will Straw, 'create micro-economies of sort' (2001: 68). This was the Do-It-Yourself drive of punk, though one should eschew all temptation to call this the democratization of the English record industry. If anything, this was the transformation of the punk from consumer to producer, from the unengaged to the socially responsible subjective agent. Moreover, you no longer had to feel frustrated by lack of talent or musicianship. Indeed, all that was needed was drive and desire, as was suggested by the infamous image originally published in 1976 in the fanzine *Sideburns,* featuring three guitar chords and the instruction to 'now form a band' (reprinted in Savage 1991: 280).

It is important to note that accompanying the music of punk and helping its impact was the enormous quantity of fanzines, continuing the tradition of English pamphleteering made easier by new cheap photocopying techniques. These decentralized networks – the independent record labels, the fanzines – were deemed, in the words of Kevin Dunn to be forms of 'counter-hegemonic communication' (2008: 202), or what we might wish to call autonomous expressions of authenticity.

Commercial pressures would call into question the authenticity of punk. Technical pressures of trying to reproduce the emotions of a live concert would also eat at the heart of the authentic punk experience. And then there was the gimmick. Soon it was difficult to escape the coloured twelve-inch or the limited edition thus promoted as a work of art – a direct affront to the authenticity of punk and an example of the growing control of the music industry over the phenomenon. Post-punk would come to embrace the commodification of authenticity and leading the way would be John Lydon, post-Sex Pistols with his new band Public Image Limited, the name of which itself conjures up the notion of privately owned limited liability companies.

The Sex Pistols and The Clash had both originally signed to major record labels; the increased exposure promised larger audiences and wider communication of the message. Though the Sex Pistols were only signed to EMI for five months and to A&M Records for less than a week, they eventually ended up on Virgin run by Richard Branson, even though Branson was perceived to be a hippie by the punk contingent. The Clash had signed with CBS, one of the top three major labels, and were offered an advance of £100,000. The signing angered many actors on the scene including Geoff Travis, owner of Rough Trade, who specialized in independent record distribution and saw this as a real blow. At first the Clash seemed vindicated as the radio-unfriendly 'White Riot' entered the top forty in early April. Fears concerning the autonomy of punk acts signed to major labels came to the fore, however, when in June CBS released 'Remote Control', perhaps one of the weakest tracks on their debut album *The Clash*, without the group's approval.

Although 1977 was the year of the Sex Pistols, commercially 1977 belonged to their rivals the Clash. They profited well from the Sex Pistols' ban from the Anarchy in the UK tour and were the first band to release a major punk album as early as April – the tracks mixed blue collar interjections with associations to the plight of the Afro-Caribbean immigrant community, most notably with their version of the reggae tune 'Police and Thieves' driven by punk rhythms (*The Clash*, 1977). At the beginning of what would become known as the 'Summer of Hate', the 'White Riot Tour' would see the first real signs of punk mania.

As with many English bands, the straw that finally broke the anarchist camel's back was the Sex Pistols' attempt to break America. The positivistic attitude popularly projected onto Americans did not appear to be a comfortable bedfellow for nihilistic apocalypse. And so nihilistic apocalypse decided not to turn up, as Savage puts it: 'There was no murder, no vomiting, no mutilation: just four twenty to twenty-one year-olds' (1991: 445). On 7 January 1978, however, John Lydon at a concert at Randy's Rodeo in San Antonia decided that this was his moment of hubris and shouted: 'You cowboys are all a bunch of fucking faggots' (Savage 1991: 449). Needless to say the concert had to be interrupted for several minutes. Just ten days later the Sex Pistols were no more.

It would be all too easy to conclude with an image of the stereotypical Sex Pistols, leaving us with an ironic sense of the commodification of authenticity. 'Pretty Vacant' (1977) may allude to a sense of dull idiocy which the band themselves sometimes fell victim to, but Lydon escapes the preconceived notion of the title of the song. This was the voice of punk challenging the original generation of teenagers as they were turning into parents. The Sex Pistols were also the enemy within, willing to expose the record industry to show their authenticity, as they sung on the track 'E.M.I.' (1977). The Pistols, Lydon, explained were 'for real'.

Conclusion: The death of punk

If punk's message was destroy, then inevitably wrapped up in its own scream of existence was its dying breath. No sooner was 1977 declared the year of punk then the death of punk was on the cards. The release of 'God Save the Queen' and its accompanying publicity stunt on the Thames were accompanied by the Sex Pistols' sighs of regret and the prerequisite boredom. With continued pressure from the broadcasting authorities, by the end of June the band were firmly on the way to breaking up. This phenomenon was not specific to the Sex Pistols. As Savage writes: 'Within the lapse that occurs between media time and real time, many groups were having hits just at the moment when Punk was over' (1991: 384).

Parallel to punk, post-punk had been developing and exploded onto the scene thanks largely to the 1977 album *Trans-Europe Express* by German electronic group Kraftwerk. The zeitgeist detector David Bowie, already influenced by Kraftwerk's earlier work, had isolated himself in Berlin and Paris and would produce four albums that year: two of his own, *Low* and *Heroes*, which would bookend the year, and two for Iggy Pop, *The Idiot* and *Lust for Life*, which would mark the beginning of Pop's post-punk career. Although on the one hand the sterile tones of this post-industrial soundtrack marked a disengagement with society, on the other post-punk was also more informed by gender politics, moving away from the 'white boys' noise' label that had come to plague punk. The Slits were an all-girl punk band but Siouxsie Sioux would see her band Siouxsie and the Banshees become major players on the post-punk, new wave scene. Within the space of a year the proliferation of generic punk bands with the formulaic snarl had turned punk into a conservative mode of musical expression.

With its investment in the immediacy of the present, punk, the musical expression of the blank generation, could only have a very short life expectancy before it was subsumed, legitimized and commodified by the establishment. The subsequent wave of punk and post-punk bands would push the Clash to survey the new scene critically in '(White Man) In Hammersmith Palais' (1978). Social decency suffered from the political upheaval of 1977: public decency could no longer be stabilized by its hypocrisy, and musical decency in the form of punk was commodified by post-punk before even the first punk album by an English band had been released. Perhaps one could see the symbolic death of punk as the election of Margaret Thatcher in May 1979.

Notes

1   A shorter version of this chapter was first published as an article by *Popmatters* in 2008: http://www.popmatters.com/column/1977-the-year-decency-died-part-i/. I thank the editors for permission to publish this revised and extended version. The Labour Party won the 1974 general election with only a three-seat majority. A by-election defeat in March 1977 left the then prime minister James Callaghan and his Labour government in a fragile position and facing a motion of no-confidence. Callaghan negotiated an

agreement with the Liberal Party and its new leader David Steel whereby there would be cross-party examination on government policy in exchange for Liberal support in the face of any future motion of no-confidence against the Labour Party. This Lib-Lab Pact, as underlined by Jonathan Kirkupp's *The Lib-Lab Pact: A Parliamentary Agreement 1977–78*, 'was not a formal coalition; nor indeed was it a "confidence and supply" agreement. The Pact has been regarded as a "grey area" in terms of analysis of coalition forming, party systems or political parties' (2016: 1). The Lib-Lab Pact officially came into existence on 7 September 1978 and lasted until it was terminated by the Liberal Party in May 1979. Callaghan was then forced into holding a general election following a vote of no-confidence. This led to Margaret Thatcher's appointment as prime minister by Queen Elizabeth II at the head of a majority Conservative government.

2   The silver jubilee marked the twenty-fifth anniversary of Queen Elizabeth II's ascension to the thrones of the UK, Canada, Australia, New Zealand, the Union of South Africa, Pakistan and Ceylon. Commemorations were held across the UK on the official anniversary date of 6th February 1977 and continued throughout the month. Official Jubilee Days were organized in June to coincide with the Queen's Official Birthday (11 June) with celebrations including parades and neighbourhood parties where the streets were often decorated with small flags strung together known as bunting. In her book *Royal Jubilees*, Judith Millidge writes: 'In Britain, "jubilee fever", was lukewarm in the early months of the year, but when the main events began in June, public interest gradually increased. The queen walked up Snow Hill at the end of the Long Walk in Windsor Great Park on 6 June to light the first bonfire in a chain of beacons that would blaze across Britain. The next day crowds numbering nearly a million people watched the procession of the royal family from Buckingham Palace to St Paul's Cathedral for the official Service of Thanksgiving' (2012: 52).

3   See for instance Joe Bonomo's *Conversations with Greil Marcus*, University Press of Mississippi (2012) or Victoria May Clarke's *A Drink with Shane MacGowan*, Pan Books (2002).

4   The other five characteristics are energy, candour, taciturnity, reserve and eccentricity. Each chapter of Langfrod's book is dedicated to one of these six traits.

5   An example of this can be seen in the 2008 British television advertisement for Country Life Butter fronted by John Lydon where parodic references simultaneously lampoon and give homage to both punk and establishment imageries.

6   A full transcript of the interview published by *The Guardian* can be retrieved from: http://www.theguardian.com/theguardian/2007/sep/15/greatinterviews.

References

Albeiz, S. (2003), 'Knowing history!: John Lydon, cultural capital and the prog/punk dialectic', *Popular Music*, 22(3): 357–74.

Baker, H. and Y. Taylor (2007), *Faking It: The Quest for Authenticity in Popular Music*, New York: W. W. Norton and Company.

BBC Radio 4 (2007), UK Confidential, 28 December.

Bonomo, J. (2012), *Conversations with Greil Marcus*, Jackson: University Press of Mississippi.

Booker, C. (1980), *The Seventies: Portrait of a Decade*, London: Allen Lane.

Callaghan, J. (1976), Leader's speech, Blackpool 1976. Available online: http://www.britishpoliticalspeech.org/speech-archive.htm?speech=174 (accessed 6 June 2016).

Chambers, I. (1985), *Urban Rhythms, Pop Music and Popular Culture*, London: Macmillan.

Clarke, V. M. (2002), *A Drink with Shane MacGowan*, London: Pan Books.

Cloonan, M. (1995), '"I Fought the Law": Popular Music and British Obscenity Law', *Popular Music*, 14(3): 349–63.

Costambeys-Kempczynski, R., M. Moreau and E. Piat (2012), 'Performing the Invisible', *Culture, Society and Masculinities*, 4(1): 3–12.

Craig, F. W. S. (ed.) (1975), *British General Election Manifestos, 1900–74*, 2nd edn. London: Macmillan.

Drabble, M. (1977), *The Ice Age*, London: Weidenfeld and Nicolson.

Dunn, K. C. (2008), 'Never mind the bollocks: the punk rock politics of global communication', *Review of International Studies*, 34: 193–210.

Grant, C. B. (2003), *Rethinking Communicative Interaction: New Interdisciplinary Horizons*, Amsterdam: John Benjamins Publishing Company.

Greig, S., M. McCarthy and J. Peacock (1976), 'The Filth and the Fury', *Daily Mirror*, 2 December.

Habermas, J. (1975), *Legitimation Crisis*, Boston: Beacon Press.

Hall, S. (1988), *The Hard Road to Renewal: Thatcherism and the Crisis of the Left*, New York: Verso.

Kirkup, J. (2016), *The Lib-Lab Pact: A Parliamentary Agreement, 1977–78*, Basingstoke: Palgrave Macmillan.

Kumar, K. (2003), *The Making of English National Identity*, Cambridge: Cambridge University Press.

Langford, P. (2000), *Englishness Identified: Manners and Characters, 1650–1850*, Oxford: Oxford University Press.

Lydon, J. (1993), *Rotten: No Dogs, No Irish*, London: Hodder and Stoughton.

MacGowan, S. (1976), *Bondage*, 1: 2.

Middleton, R. (1985), 'Articulating Musical Meaning/Re-Constructing Musical History/Locating the "Popular"', *Popular Music, Continuity and Change*, 5: 5–43.

Middleton, R. (1990), *Studying Popular Music*, Milton Keynes: Open University Press.

Millidge, J. (2012), *Royal Jubilees*, Oxford: Shire Publications.

Nehring, N. (1991), 'Revolt into Style: Graham Greene meets the Sex Pistols', *PMLA*, 106(2): 222–37.

Orwell, G. (2001), *Orwell's England*, London: Penguin.

Robinson, N. (2012), *Live from Downing Street*, London: Bantam.

Sandbrook, D. (2012), *Seasons in the Sun: The Battle for Britain, 1974–1979*, London: Allen Lane.

Savage, J. (1991), *England's Dreaming: Sex Pistols and Punk Rock*, London: Faber and Faber.

Schaper, E. (1966), 'The Kantian Thing-in-Itself as a Philosophical Fiction', *The Philosophical Quarterly, History of Philosophy Number*, 16(64): 233–43.

Straw, W. (2001), 'Consumption', in S. Firth, W. Straw and J. Street (eds), *The Cambridge Companion to Pop and Rock*, 53–73, Cambridge: Cambridge University Press.

Street, J. (2001), 'Rock, pop and politics', in S. Firth, W. Straw and J. Street (eds), *The Cambridge Companion to Pop and Rock*, 243–55, Cambridge: Cambridge University Press.

Thames Television (1976), Today, 1 December

'The Bollocks Court Case', *The Summer of Hate*. Available online: http://www.angelfire.com/zine/sexpistols/courtcase.html (accessed 6 June 2016)

Turner, A. W. (2008), *Crisis? What Crisis? Britain in the 1970s*, London: Aurum.

Young, C. M. (1977), 'Rock is Sick and Living in London', *Rolling Stone*, 205, 20th October. Available online: http://www.rollingstone.com/music/news/a-report-on-the-sex-pistols-19771020 (accessed 6 June 2016).

Discography

David Bowie (1977) *Heroes*, RCA Victor [Album]

David Bowie (1977) *Low*, RCA Victor [Album]

The Clash (1977) 'Remote Control / London's Burning (Live)', CBS [Single]

The Clash (1977) *The Clash*, CBS [Album]

The Clash (1977) 'White Riot / 1977', CBS [Single]

The Clash (1978) '(White Man) In Hammersmith Palais / The Prisoner', CBS [Single]

Kraftwerk (1977) 'Trans Europe Express / Europe Endless', Capitol Records [Single]

Iggy Pop (1977) *The Idiot*, RCA Victor [Album]

Iggy Pop (1977) *Lust for Life*, RCA Victor [Album]

Sex Pistols (1976) 'Anarchy in the UK / I Wanna Be Me', EMI [Single]

Sex Pistols (1977) 'God Save the Queen / Did You No Wrong', Virgin [Single]

Sex Pistols (1977) *Never Mind the Bollocks Here's the Sex Pistols*, Virgin [Album]

Sex Pistols (1977) 'Pretty Vacant / No Fun', Virgin [Single]

The Stranglers (1977) 'Something Better Change / Straighten Out', United Artists [Single]

X-Ray Spex (1977) 'Oh Bondage Up Yours! / I Am a Cliché', Virgin [Single].

CHAPTER NINE

'Brand New You're Retro':
Tricky as Engpop dissident

Christian Lloyd and Shara Rambarran

What's mad about trying to push the boundaries? I think it's mad trying to sound like the Beatles again and again. Tricky quoted in *Touch* magazine, 1996.

[The Union Flag] means nothing to me at all. ... I find it quite gross actually. Quite fucking disgusting. Tricky quoted in *Fix* magazine, 1996.

Tricky's comments on two long-standing shibboleths of Britishness were made at a juncture in the national identity that makes his words even more transgressive with hindsight. Summer 1996 began a twelve-month period that saw the zenith of both Britpop and New Labour. The group Oasis's sold-out imperial-phase performances at Knebworth were followed by Tony Blair's first election victory, inaugurating a new cultural–political complex in the UK (or at least in London). This mediated alliance, operating under the alibi of 'Cool Britannia', embodied a postmodern, post-imperial ideology that sought to reassert Britain as a power within a world grown indifferent to it. To this end, several fields of British life (art, music, politics, fashion, media) staged a replay of an imaginary 1960s, the last time that Britain pretended to world dominance. In particular, the complex found musical expression in Britpop, a style whose assumption of a bleached, backwards-looking version of British identity occluded the heterogeneous society from which it came. (In fact 'Cool Britannia' should have been dubbed 'Cool Anglia' and 'Britpop' was rightly 'Engpop', given their London location and implicit disdain for the other national cultures of the union, so we will use these terms.) The emergence of a gun-toting, wedding dress-wearing, spliff-smoking mixed-race Englishman – Tricky who whispered in a Bristol accent over US hip hop samples was then as 'off message' as it was possible to be.

We want to examine Tricky's work as a dissident element in his initial context, to see how his music and its paratexts (promotional photos, cover art) register a kind of internal culture shock at the retrograde politics of national identity in the Engpop era. We will argue that Tricky symbolically attacked the centripetal ideology of Cool Anglia by dialogizing his own music in a proliferating strategy of collaborations, production techniques and images. While the Cool Anglia construct of Englishness mistakenly assumed that national culture was isolatable and coherent, as Tricky's music demonstrates, Englishness is always in process from uncertain, often fictional origins, and may even be entirely performative. Tricky's complex, centrifugal art means the national becomes the notional; 'God Save the Queen' is now 'overdubbed' with his 'notional anthems' for contemporary England as the union disperses.

Tricky's own biography is important because it suggests the reasons why his music has such a strong centrifugal aesthetic. Tricky, real name Adrian Thaws, was born in 1968 on a council estate in Knowle West, Bristol, to a Jamaican father and a mixed-race Ghanaian–English mother. His father left before he was born and his mother, Maxine Quaye, committed suicide when he was four. His early life was marked by criminality, including a brief spell in prison for passing counterfeit currency. By his own admission he was an alienated and violent young man (Tricky in *A Ruff Guide*, 2002). The lyrics to 'Early Bird' (2010) register what we term 'internal culture shock' in Tricky's work. Whereas culture shock is normally experienced when an individual's own cultural sense of what is 'natural' is confronted by that of a foreign culture, here the sense of shock and displacement is internal to the national culture. Tricky articulates a terrible sense of alienation from his own nation, on racial, cultural and historical grounds, and one intensified by the Cool Anglia complex whose 'singularity' was the antithesis of his 'mixed' approach.

Thaws began his recording life as a lyricist and vocalist with the Wild Bunch sound system, members of which mutated into the trip hop collective Massive Attack. He remains best known for his debut *Maxinquaye* (1995), which gained worldwide kudos and sold about 500,000 copies in total worldwide (compared to estimates of around 2,000,000 for Blur's Engpop landmark *Parklife*). Tricky has followed his debut with nine further albums, notably *Mixed Race* (2010) and some wildly unconventional live shows. *Maxinquaye* – the album we will focus on – was glibly categorized by critics as trip hop, but Tricky had also created diverse avant-garde electronica, blues, rock, torch songs, minimalist pieces and more. Uniquely (and obsessively), Tricky, the supposed star male solo artist, has relied on female singers, such as Martina Topley-Bird and Alison Goldfrapp, often vocalizing with women in unison to carry his music and to blend with (or dominate) his whispery vocals. He sometimes performs under very low stage lighting or with his back to the audience, so it is unclear even whose voice the audience are hearing. The consequent difficulty in branding Tricky, who appears as a kind of revenant even on his own albums and concerts, is a sign of both his complex, slippery identity as a performer and as a man. In consequence, his work and its contentious implications remain under-explored by commentators who find it hard to follow music that is constituted within a series of category mistakes.

To fully understand Tricky's initial situation in English culture, it is worth reviewing a paradigmatic example of the expressions of Englishness dominant in the music scene in 1995, particularly since New Labour were attempting, with some success, to co-opt these. Leaving aside arguments about which band(s) inaugurated Engpop, by 1995 the style's cultural coordinates were firmly established by the media and this created a tight feedback loop as less talented bands worked within stylistic expectations to be validated by the same media. A superior example of this style is the title track of Blur's 1995 album *Parklife*. 'Parklife' delivers a Mockney narrative about suburban skiving at *moderato* tempo. (Engpop *tempi* typically range from 90 to 120 bpm.) In the promo film, signifiers of Englishness arrive by conveyor belt: a Routemaster bus, pogoing, football in the street, a flask of tea, umbrellas, a Union flag, gasholders, an ice-cream van, the crossing at Abbey Road, double-glazing salesmen, etc. It could be reckoned that these signifiers go beyond homage to a point of self-parody (or self-reflexive parody), but what is less noted is that in 1995 this semiotic saturation created powerful moments of identification for an English audience who enjoyed the concomitant alienation of foreign listeners. (Just how enigmatic this song remains to American listeners even now is clear from online US fan forums where it is variously misinterpreted as a gay anthem, or a song encouraging Londoners to go jogging, specifically in Hyde Park.) What is more, the main vocal is delivered by Phil Daniels, a London-born actor most famous then for starring in the Who's 1979 film of *Quadrophenia*. This link to a 1970s replay of the high 1960s creates a micro-lineage for Engpop, validating the 1995 style by rooting it in past English cultural triumphs, albeit at a mediated remove. This considered musical and visual construction represents a foreclosed, centripetal aesthetic whose acknowledged anti-Americanism has hidden the less visible way it alienated those non-white Britons for whom 1960s England was a culture of prejudice and discrimination, and not a golden age. (This is presumably some of what lies behind Tricky's derisive comments on the endless rethreads of the Beatles and the Union flag.)

Tellingly, the musical lineage behind 'Parklife' stops short of reference to the African–American R&B/soul tradition (e.g. James Brown, Bo Diddley,

Motown) that the Who, Kinks and the Small Faces themselves revered via their cover versions. Only English musical precedents are referenced (and mentioned in interviews with Engpop bands) because to do otherwise would erode the implied national exceptionalism. Put another way, during the 1990s, Blur covered traditional English/East London/Music Hall songs like 'Daisy Bell' and 'Let's All Go Down the Strand' while Tricky was covering or sampling artists like Slick Rick, Sarah Vaughan, Eric B. & Rakim, Prince, ESG and Mary McCreary.

The fashion associated with Engpop bands (Fred Perry shirts, Doc Marten boots, drainpipe jeans, school blazers, mod suits) reinforces this tendency, as seemingly innocent signifiers of London street fashion have a shadow side in their reference to skinhead culture of the 1970s, an issue played with irresponsibly in Blur's 'British Image 1'. In this widely released promo shot by Paul Spencer, the band address the camera thuggishly, slouching behind Damon Albarn who is holding a huge dog on a leash. Whatever the intent of the image, it is the kind of thing that could easily be interpreted as trifling with signifiers of street racism, and was grudgingly withdrawn in favour of 'British Image 2', a picture of the band sporting cords, rowing club blazers and slicked down hair that was swiftly produced to deflect the controversy about '1'.[1] The band's initial failure to realize how the image might be misinterpreted by Britons who had suffered at the hands of skinhead culture suggest Engpop's narrow awareness of Britain's mixed national history; there was no recognition that reducing the painful lived experiences of British minorities to props from a dressing up box might be problematic. 'British Image 1' verifies Engpop as a dangerously nostalgic zone, a confused fantasy of returning somehow to a Britain pre-immigration, pre-EU, pre-US dominance, etc.: Cool Anglia turned tepid. 'Brand New You're Retro', as Tricky mockingly put it in one lyric.

In some ways it is then surprising that *Maxinquaye* found any substantial audience on its release in 1995. This complex album about a dead mother, utter alienation from English society, being mixed race and indulging in altered states was presented not by a carefully constructed star persona (as Damon Albarn made for his work with Blur), but a proliferating, metamorphic figure. In his promos Tricky appears as a thug; boxer; Native American chief; Pierrot; bride; 'Vietcong'; member of a Supremes-type girl group; occult figure; demon; tattooed gang member; glam rocker; transgendered morph with vocalist Martina Topley-Bird; white-suited gangster; and man in whiteface (See Tricky, *A Ruff Guide,* 2002). There is no attempt here to create a defining icon of his English identity, even though this would have been a useful selling point. The person we glimpse looks different every time, and defeats our expectations of visual contract with a defined star and his musical style. Rather, Tricky's enigmatic appearances in these images counter, for example, 'British Image 1' by implying that English identity and music cannot be solidified and authenticated by reference to a singular history or genealogy, but exists in a complicated network of traces, projections and performances. Rather than trying to narrow the possibilities as post-imperial genres like Engpop do, Tricky's explorations of his image and identity reflect a complex, uncertain family tree that is *synecdochal* of a complex and myth-ridden national genealogy, not atypical.

Maxinquaye shows a deep, offbeat musical intelligence at work: the play of Shakespeare's 'Sonnet 138' (about lying/laying) in the lyric to 'Suffocated Love' (Tricky used a Method Man sticker to attach Shakespeare's text to the studio wall while working); the distorted, uncredited sample of Michael Jackson's song 'Bad' in 'Brand New You're Retro'; the unpredictable lyrical rips from The Young Rascals to Maya Angelou. Musically, Tricky is related to almost everybody, and this openness is in sharp contrast to Britpop's branchless musical family tree.

But what did *Maxinquaye* suggest about being English? The cover image for the CD offers an inkling. The word 'Tricky' is roughly stencilled onto a closed door or box lid, suggesting impermanence and exclusion. The door (or lid) is painted red and has the remnants of gilding on it but is now dirty and worn. It is tempting to read this quartered image as referring to a decayed union flag, or Cross of St George, long past its gilded age, and used here to shadow the use of the flag by Engpop bands who never considered its negative connotations of empire and internal exclusion. But we are interpreting from a cryptic trace only. The sole certainty here is a principle of uncertainty about nationality for those on the margins who can have no easy relationship to narrow 'heritage-based' Englishness and to their own flag. *Maxinquaye's* music goes on to comprehensively challenge Britpop aesthetics and politics.

The low tempi and leaden atmosphere of Tricky's songs imply a life of solitary alienation compared to the communal uptempo singalongs of Britpop: lyrically this alienation is frequently linked to race and so internal culture shock; Tricky's unreconstructed Bristol accent and the variety of other modes of English on the album (from Goldfrapp, Martina, Kidd Rasta, etc.) diverge from the obligatory Mockney of Engpop reminding us of a Britain beyond its capital; the laddishness of Engpop is scorned in *Maxinquaye's* use of female vocalists who often dominate the male vocals; the sampled intersections with US, Indian and Jamaican music acknowledge that British culture cannot be understood in isolation because it is always already mediated by many other (former colonial) cultures. (Symbolically, many of the samples Tricky uses are so distorted as to be barely recognizable in origin.) In short, Tricky's 'ragged' oeuvre registers his antipathy both to the neat, consistent 'project' that constitutes the practice of the Engpop bands and to the foreshortened view of Englishness contained in Cool Anglia.

One highly praised track, perhaps the anthem of *Maxinquaye*, is the truncated punk version of Public Enemy's 'Black Steel in the Hour of Chaos', unexpectedly sung by a woman (Martina). Perhaps an unfamiliar Public Enemy tune to some, it is misleading to think that the popularity of the song was down to Tricky. Rather, he freshened the sounds (and style from hip hop to a fusion of electronica and metal),[2] and transformed the song into a new masterpiece – with the help of producer Mark Saunders and Martina Topley-Bird. The song is from Public Enemy's *It Takes a Nation of Millions to Hold us Back* (1988) and was part of the 'golden age of hip hop' era. This movement smartly represents what Public Enemy is about – being musically controversial and political in the United States. In a way, the group are cousins of punk in terms of resisting and challenging political forces by protesting non-violently in the form of political rap (although this was misunderstood by the media and some social groups who did not approve of the group and their music). Chuck D narrates the voice of an African–American man facing the consequences of being locked up by the government for refusing to be drafted into war. The song then describes tormented situations like lockdowns in prison, and issues such as oppression, racism and violence. The title 'Black Steel' has two connotations: it may be the gun that the narrator needs to escape from authority, or a general symbol of the control and strength needed by African–Americans to 'Fight the Power'.

In his 1995 version, Tricky adjusts the original's US context so that it represents his own English experience of racism growing up in the 'ghetto' part of Bristol. For him to be accepted for his race was challenging. In a mini-documentary in the extras to his *Ruff Guide* DVD (2002), Tricky argues that disadvantages in his early life prevented him from gaining inspiration from formal education, such that the only association he felt was in music, where he could share his difficulties in searching for acceptance or survival. With this in mind, it comes as no surprise that Tricky lists Public Enemy as one of his inspirations, and the cover version justifies this as it displays anger and frustration. In the music, the timbre of Tricky's version may at first shock listeners who are familiar with the Bristolian trip hop sound – this is far from a typical trip hop track. This experimental version fuses contemporary Indian music, punk, reggae, electronica, industrial metal and hip hop. Tricky produced the track with British producer Mark Saunders (whose credits include Depeche Mode, The Cure, Bomb the Bass and The Farm), who found it challenging to cooperate with Tricky's ideas. He admitted: 'It was a complete un-learning experience and it was also a total re-learning experience. Think of how to make a record, then forget everything you've learned and start completely backwards and upside down' (Buskin 2007). Tricky's musical philosophy plays with surrealist and bricolage techniques where a fusion of 'incompatible' elements (in terms of musical styles, sounds, and noise) somehow results in outstanding art.

Tricky's 'Black Steel' begins with a short, distorted guitar riff that is swiftly responded to by another guitar with a high-pitched note. These sounds suddenly reverse to allow further instruments to be introduced and for the texture of the piece to gradually build the music. The timbre of the guitar riff offers an industrial sound that is supported with a slow, passing mechanical breakbeat which prepares the way for the reversed guitar part to join the main rhythm part of the track – the sampled breakbeat from the song 'Rukkumani Rukkuman' (1992) composed by Indian film composer A. R. Rahman (notable for the 2008 soundtrack *Slumdog Millionaire*). This rhythmic section serves as the main setting of the music. It carries a contemporary Indian flavour that is discreetly layered with a secondary drum loop (the previously described mechanical breakbeat), and includes external and internal ornamentations of individual flashes of industrial guitar sounds to signify a frantic atmosphere. This layered sound is a classic Tricky category mistake, as it symbolically includes material from 'incompatible' genres.

All this is reinforced by what he chooses to do with the vocals. In Tricky's 'Black Steel', his co-singer, Martina, does not rap but instead uses her soft, mellow vocals to recite the lyrics with an improvised melody. Her vocals truly represent trip hop because as she is not a rapper, she instead applies *Sprechstimme* and a touch of reggae-ness. Her voice is single-tracked with an added touch of reverb. She emphasizes the powerful words that bring out the song's intentions (e.g. 'suckers', 'damn', 'authority' and so forth). Here, the instrumentation is minimal but gradually builds up for the chorus. At first the main breakbeat, which is joined by a short, ascended bass loop, supports Martina. The main guitar part quietly reintroduces its role, and an interrupted clean electric guitar sound aides Martina when she stresses in the lyric how the 'suckers' hold authority. The texture of the song gradually thickens when a synth produces a low drone sound and adds tension as Martina contemplates the line about escaping from jail. Martina's unexpected vocal suggests the power of hip hop to British minorities, and its absorption into their daily lives, where it is 'reaccented' for their circumstances.

The clean guitar part then returns as a call for all instruments to play in what appears to be the main (and only) 'chorus' section. The musical direction changes at this point: pre-recorded loops are semi-replaced by live instruments (guitar, bass, drums). This section, however, does not represent a typical catchy chorus. Instead, it focuses more on the instrumentation that splits the chorus into different parts. A live drum fill that rounds off Martina's 'crime' semi-replaces the pre-recorded loops, and fully integrates a live instrumental section. The section plays a four-bar riff in a dynamical and full-on distorted sound. Then the loud guitar riff disappears and is replaced by an internal synth hook. On top of that, Martina affirms the song's animating line about getting a 'letter from the government'. Her non-emotional and minimal vocal line is quite effective as it unusually works with the frantic music – and thus makes it easier for the listener to connect and sing with Martina, should they wish to.

The mood of the music then changes back to its original form (the pre-recorded loops) when Martina resumes her role and begins to sign the second verse, but is quickly interrupted when the live instruments return. Here, Martina changes lyrical direction by repeating the first verse. The full texture of the music changes when she sings 'cold sweatin' and is assisted with a distorted guitar riff, which is quickly overshadowed by the full return of the instruments with extra, added guitar frantic noises. After the line about not being a 'fugitive', the music suddenly pauses and a distant breakbeat enters, followed by a bass loop and drone. It is here when Tricky makes his brief, shadowy appearance with his trademark vocals – the British-accented, laidback tones on the line that contains the triple use of the word 'switch'. His vocal contribution reminds the listener of the 'real' artist of the song, but also implies that people do indeed either switch 'in', 'on' or 'off' on societal matters. His brief 'presence' vanishes when Martina returns. She now appears to struggle or surrender when she sings the word 'steel' – a key word of the song and, of course, its title. As we noted, in Public Enemy's version, the word 'steel' represents both strength and a gun. In Tricky's version, 'steel' is more suited to the concept of still trying to gain strength in order to resist something, such as authority. At this moment, Martina indeed appears to be weak, yet she returns in full form supported by frantic industrial music. Now her vocal is more expressive, because she generates belief in the song by displaying 'steel'. Gradually she leads the music to an end, with the texture thinning out and the instrumentation becoming minimal, and this musical turn gently returns to the main introduction that serves as the outro – the contemporary Indian style breakbeat and alarming guitar riff.

It is worth noting that Tricky's version is simply renamed 'Black Steel'. This shorter title reflects the cut verses from the original version, and so the way the reworked song focuses on Tricky's personal experiences. The musical bricolage fuses styles to represent his musical ethos and also his frustration with singularity of any type. It is interesting to point out that the song could be more suited to the British audience because of the various British sounds and styles used in the track: these might appeal to various audiences of different ethnicities, as the female vocal might to those who find the dominance of male voices wearing. This track was released in 1995, the year when Britpop dominated the nation. In that year, Britain witnessed many Britpop-related events such as a famous chart battle between two rival groups initiated by the groups themselves, the media and the music industry. This was the moment when the fan base of Britpop increasingly grew larger and people identified themselves as either a Blur or an Oasis follower. The male, white-dominated and racist culture of Britpop did not invite artists such as Tricky and others to participate and demonstrate their own forms of 'Englishness'.[3] As confirmed in the lyric in 'Black Steel', Tricky's (little, obnoxious and racist) Britain is a land that dismisses a 'brother' like him ('Black Steel' 1995). It is the classic example of internal culture shock on the album.

The final track on Maxinquaye, 'Feed Me', further mutates Tricky's dissidence and dissonance from the expressions of Englishness dominant in 1995. In this song, Tricky's art is at its most experimentalist: his musical expression roils around confusing, fragmented sounds and utterances, making no attempt at unity or consistency. The postmodern bricolage technique here rejects Engpop's modernism whose yearning for a lost, unified

Britain (itself a prelapsarian myth) engendered songs that accumulated signifiers of Britishness, both musically and lyrically, aiming to attain a wholeness in anthemic status without ever considering how alienating and partial national anthems (or any anthems) can be to others. To this end, almost all of the Engpop classics of the 1990s used 'closed' song forms that resolve themselves 'satisfactorily' in the manner of the classic pop of the 1960s, and they have memorable hooks and choruses to create identification with the song in audiences who merely wish to see reflection of their own comfortable identity. In contrast, it is impossible to imagine a singalong to any of Tricky's 'messy' open song forms on Maxinquaye, and his complex, confusing soundscapes never come to anything like resolution, being 'notional anthems' if anything.

'Feed Me' combines a vibraphone (that resembles the harp hook in the 'Golden Girl' scene in the James Bond 1964 film *Goldfinger*, which was famously used in a fellow trip hop song '6 Underground' by Sneaker Pimps in 1997) with sampled drums, bass, a crackle track and an external vocal from Martina with a low, internal vocal from Tricky. Occasional bursts of distorted guitar, sampled Indian instrumentation and reversed sounds also appear. The track is a disorienting listening experience because the rhythm track and vibraphone are in different time signatures and tempi, hinting that it is about the difficulty of juxtaposed difference more broadly. Lyrically, the song begins with Tricky presenting a challenge to the listener over backwards clicking sounds, perhaps a reference to the Beatles' innovative use of backwards tapes on *Revolver* (1966), which would aim the words squarely at the Beatles-aping Engpoppers. This lyric, however, also interpolates reggae group Inner Circle's famous hook 'watcha gonna do' in the 1987 song 'Bad Boys' (which is about troubled youth getting in - to trouble with the police). Consequently, the first few seconds of the song confirm that the listener is about to undergo a melancholic cultural (re) mixing experience, as demonstrated by the binaries of Engpop (The Beatles) and reggae music (Inner Circle), and its strained postcolonial relationship between Britain and the Caribbean (including elsewhere). Tricky's reference to 'Bad Boys' may also signify two other concepts: 1) how to deal with being rejected in Britain or 2) displaying a warning to those who contributed to 'destroying' the so-called unified Britain. As the music begins to progress, Tricky intimately raps words that are heard subliminally throughout the song. Tricky's chanting on dominant Englishness acts as a musical layer in the track, and, where appropriate, enhances specific sections of Martina's parts.

Notably 'Feed Me' samples 'Sound of Da Police' by KRS-One from his album *Return of the Boom Bap* (1993). The sample is of beats only and works as a kind of musical depth charge in 'Feed Me' because it makes a sly link to a song about police brutality whose submerged significance is apparent only to those who know KRS-One's original. To the average Engpop fan, the ghastly significance behind these beats went unnoticed. Listening to 'Feed Me' then becomes a kind of shibboleth about awareness of the divergent lived experience of different Britons. For those British listeners who were aware of political hip hop and themselves feared police discrimination, the implication of what Tricky and Martina insinuate about their nation is clear; for those for whom trip hop was as far as they were willing to deviate from the comforts of Engpop, the song must have been mystifying if they gave it any serious contemplation at all. As such, 'Feed Me' may be heard as British hip hop rather than as its softer subgenre 'trip hop', the latter being a classification that Tricky himself openly scorned. As with 'Black Steel', Tricky 'contaminates' Englishness with a radical American element whose meaning is reoriented in a clever bricolage technique which is the antithesis of Engpop's habitual strategies. America, as goes too often unremarked, was a British colony, and hip hop is, in one sense, a postcolonial form.

Lyrically, the song is a dialogue between Tricky and Martina, a double voicing that suggests the split subjectivity of postcolonial art and identity. Martina's first verse asserts a need to obliterate the status quo. If some listeners might hear the lyric here as a call for transcendence of circumstances via a love relationship, then in a postcolonial listening it might be aligned with W. B. Yeats's opening epigraph to the poem 'Responsibilities' (1914). Here Yeats articulates the need of the colonized to project an alternative vision of nation and self imaginatively before that vision can become a reality, lest the terms of thought become trapped simply in opposition to current oppression. Tricky and Martina's bricolage seems in sympathy with this. Indeed, as the track continues, Martina's vocal explicitly rejects simplistic national history as a basis for current identity and states her confusion about her love and hate for the country. In fact, even though the musical arrangement is in continuous loop form, composed of a bricolage of displaced noises and sounds and polyrhythms (along with Tricky's vocals), it is Martina's vocals that disrupt the structure of the song. Each vocal layer has no obvious melodic direction: all of the layers are technically manipulated and melodically surreal. Lyrically, by identifying bad historiography as an English, rather than a British 'disaster', 'Feed Me' remembers the internal colonization within the UK rather than eliding such competing pre-Union identities as Britpop did. The play of vocals and sociocultural observations confirms the assertion on the questioning of the relationship between race and nationality at the heart of older versions of Englishness. In a characteristically subtle piece of vocalizing, when Martina sings the word 'origin' in a Caribbean accent in the song she reasserts the multiple origins of Britons.

The lyrics of 'Feed Me' also contain echoes of other postcolonial musical movements. Towards the end of the track, Martina refers to Two-Tone: this was the Coventry sound (and significant independent label) that emerged during the dangerous rise of the National Front in the late 1970s, mixing Jamaican and British elements to counter such regressive visions of Britishness. Martina calls this vision to our attention at the height of

Engpop and its narrowed sense of nationhood. By referring to concrete as her 'religion', she alludes both to the Specials' song 'Concrete Jungle' (1979) and also to Bob Marley and the Wailers' classic of the same title (1973). Both of these songs might be taken as 'notional anthems' to sustain those who are marginal in British society; both songs weave elements from formerly colonial cultures into British popular culture. In the end, the complex, open construction of 'Feed Me' is such that it is left to the responsible listener to untangle this powerful song of Englishness, so removed from Engpop's frequent oversimplifications and encouragement of singalong passivity in its audience.

The Cool Anglia complex mistakenly assumed that English culture is isolatable and coherent, when, as Tricky's music and image so dynamically demonstrate, every culture is always in process from mixed, uncertain, often fictional origins. As John Storey writes: 'National identities are always a narrative of the nation becoming; as much about "routes" as they are about "roots"' (Storey 2010: 13). It can be argued that postcolonial identity and its cultural articulations do not erase the historical existence of imperial countries and their former colonies. Instead, it may even serve as an opportunity for imperial countries to continue in dominating other cultures, particularly in a nation such as England. Tricky's 'Feed Me' embodies the contradictions of his situation in England and forces the listener to work actively to construct an interpretation, rather than passively absorbing familiar ideologies. 'Feed Me' is thus one of Tricky's many 'notional anthems'. Unlike the National Anthem, which is usually sung thoughtlessly as a fixed, unifying national shibboleth, Tricky's songs offer no immediate or singular meaning. They force listeners to think hard about nationality and place, to take responsibility for making their own meanings in a postcolonial Britain rather than assuming the givens of our culture. Tricky constructs, deconstructs and reconstructs elements from an eclectic musical past, present and future, regardless of cultural origin, to create a hybrid art form. His songs are a personal, observational, informative, contradictory musical palette. Ultimately, Tricky's dynamic, irreducible dissidence imagines a new musical world in anticipation of a future era in English life that still struggles to come into being.

Notes

1 Both images can be viewed at http://paulspencer.co.uk/music.html and http://www.snapgalleries.com/news/blur-british-image-1-and-2/.

2 It should be noted that a metal version of the song was covered by the Brazilian band Sepultura featuring rapper Sabotage (2003).

3 For other thoughts on artists/groups who are considered as 'outsiders' in Britpop culture, see the works of Sheila Whiteley, J. Mark Percival and Nabeel Zuberi in *Britpop and the English Music Tradition* (Jon Stratton and Andy

Bennett (eds), 2010, Routledge), and Shara Rambarran in *Reggae From Yaad: Traditional and Emerging Themes in Jamaican Popular Music* (Donna P. Hope (ed.), 2015, Ian Randle Publishers).

References

Buskin, R. (2007), 'Classic Tracks: Tricky's "Black Steel"', *Sound on Sound*. Available online: http://www.soundonsound.com/techniques/classic-tracks-tricky-black-steel.
Spencer, P. (N.D.), 'Blur-*British Image 1*', *Paul Spencer*. Fotógrapho. Available online: http://paulspencer.co.uk/music.html.
Storey, J. (2010), 'Becoming British', in M. Higgins, C. Smith and J. Storey (eds), *The Cambridge Companion to Modern British Culture*, 12–25, Cambridge: Cambridge University Press.

Discography

The Beatles (1996) *Revolver*, UK: Parlophone Records [Album]
Blur (1994) *Parklife*, UK: Food Records [Album]
Inner Circle (1987) 'Bad Boys', US: Island Records [Single]
KRS-One (1993) *Return of the Boom Bap,* US: Jive Records [Album]
Public Enemy (1989) 'Black Steel in the Hour of Chaos', US: Def Jam Records [Single]
Sneaker Pimps (1996) '6 Underground', UK: Clean Up Records [Single]
Tricky (1995) *Maxinquaye*, UK: 4th & B'way Records [Album]
Tricky (2010) *Mixed Race*, UK: Domino Records [Album]
Tricky (2002) *A Ruff Guide*, UK: Universal [DVD]
The Who (1973) *Quadrophenia,* UK: Track Records [Album]

CHAPTER TEN

The (un)masked bard:

Burial's denied profile and the memory of English underground music

Gabriele Marino

Intro (*South London Boroughs*)

A train crosses South London, late at night, sharp and feline like a blade trimming a thick, dark velvet fabric. The vehicle is running fast, but the time inside seems to be flowing slow. As if it was covered in formaldehyde. The wagons are haunted by fuliginous, diaphanous figures – They go to and fro, broken blocks, broken buildings, while dancing to the rhythm of a trembling heartbeat. A collage of memories, distant and vivid, personal and shared, clearly identifies the culprit of such a resigned pain, putting them under a dim spotlight.

1. 'He is (not) Burial': The media quest for a name and a face

Burial's media vicissitudes may be articulated into different phases, according to the degree of explicit – and implicit – information he lets us grab out of his interviews, social media posts and music production.

1.1. Masked and anonymous (2004–7): 'The mysterious Burial'

According to the Internet Archive Wayback Machine (*archive.org/web*), the oldest online reference to a musician called Burial dates back to the end of 2004. Kode9 (journalist, cultural scholar, DJ, and music producer Steve Goodman) lists 'Burial – Broken Home' in his 5 December *top9* on his personal blog (*kode9.blogspot.com*), along with tracks by Plasticman, Digital Mystikz, Roll Deep, Macabre Unit and himself. Later on, probably in the following February (as far as we can infer from Archive's snapshots), 'Burial – Southern Comfort' appears in another Kode9-curated top selection, on the Hyperdub website (*hyperdub.com*), along with tracks by Virgo, Terror Danja and – again – Plasticman, Digital Mysticz and Kode9 himself. Among such established underground producers, Burial is completely unknown and the mentioned tracks are still unpublished.

On 16 May 2005, Kode9's Hyperdub, the once-online magazine about electronic music which turned into a record label in April 2004, releases its first non-single record: Burial's *South London Boroughs*, an EP including the eponymous track, a track called 'Nite Train', and the two aforementioned Kode9-favourited ones ('Broken Home' and 'Southern Comfort'). With HDB001 as catalogue number, this record is the third one in the history of the label, and the first not directly connected to Kode9 (the first two were singles by Kode9 and Daddi Gee, alias Stephen Samuel Gordon, who will later be known as the Space Ape), as well as the absolute debut of the unknown producer. In an interview published on 26 March 2006 on Blackdown/Martin Clark's blog (*blackdownsoundboy.blogspot.com*), Burial says he stepped into Hyperdub by chance, while searching for old UK garage and El-B's records in particular. He would email 'some budget first tunes' to Kode9, who would surprisingly put one in a mix for the historic web radio Groovetech; it is approximately 2003. After a one-year hiatus, Burial would send a whole CD of tracks to Kode9, which provided the basis for his official Hyperdub releases to come.

On 15 May 2006, Hyperdub releases its first long playing ever, the homonymous by 'the mysterious Burial', as claimed by the official presentation on the label's website. The album includes the already published tracks 'Southern Comfort' and 'Broken Home'. On 26 August the *Distant Lights* EP is released, including the title track, 'Pirates', and 'Gutted', which were already included in *Burial*. Critically acclaimed worldwide, the full length is nominated 'album of the year' by *The Wire* magazine (no. 275, January 2007; cf. also Walmsley 2009), sanctioning the cult status of the artist and making the hype around him and his music increase.

Burial's success among the insiders is strengthened by his second album, *Untrue*, published by Hyperdub on 5 November 2007. The album is anticipated by the single 'Archangel' (issued without cover or insert) and the EP *Ghost Hardware* (14 June 2007), which includes the title track (which will be featured on *Untrue* as well) and the otherwise unavailable tracks 'Shutta' and 'Exit Woundz'. *Untrue* is an underground success – its best UK album chart placement will be 58th – and lots of national and international magazines list it as one of the best albums of the year: it will score second on the podium for *The Wire* (no. 287, January 2008) and Metacritic recognize it as their second best reviewed album (with a medium score of 90/100). *Untrue* will be his last album to date. In the article by Mark Fisher/k-punk published on *The Wire* (no. 286, December 2007: 28–31), two pictures by Georgina Cook/Drumzofthesouth, the photographer of London's dubstep scene par excellence (as well as the author of the pictures featured on *Untrue*), show Burial's silhouette. This interview will be his last accounted one to date.

'The mysterious Burial' – we know nothing about him, but his music. We do not know his name, nor his face. His records do not feature any photographic portrait, nor any biographical note. He gives very few interviews – there will be ten or so, overall, all of them concentrated between December 2005 and December 2007 – and he does not perform nor appear in public (not even in an acousmatic form, for instance when DJ Mary Anne Hobbs premiers his tracks on her weekly show at BBC Radio 1). Burial's identity is a proper mystery.

1.2. Unmasked and uncovered (2008): 'my names will bevan'

On 11 February 2008, *The Independent* publishes an article about the Elliott School ('The real school of rock'), portraying it as a true pool of talents set in South London and revealing that 'another former student is William Bevan, a.k.a. Burial, a dubstar artist who enjoys a cult dancefloor following and who likes to retain a Banksy-like anonymity'. The parallel with the graffiti artist will be a constant element in Burial's media odyssey.

On 21 April, a post on Backspin Promotion blog announces the new DJ-Kicks volume to be mixed by Burial; the news appears also on the series' label website, !K7 (26 May), spreading the buzz to the extent that some alleged track-lists start circulating. On 30 June, a post – the very first one – appears on Burial's Myspace (*myspace.com/burialuk*, created on 7 March 2006); the artist says the track-lists are fake and that 'if i do djkicks it will be mostly old jungle tunes & new tunes'. The release of the record, originally scheduled for June (United Kingdom) and July (United States), will be continuously delayed for years, up to the announcement that 'the reality of a Burial DJ-Kicks doesn't seem to be any closer' (DJ-Kicks website, 11 July 2011); along with such statement, a Steven Ellison/Flying Lotus' Soundcloud track is being linked in the post, with the note that it would have been one of the songs to be featured on Burial's album.

On 22 July 2008 the BBC announces the Mercury Prize nominees; *Untrue* is among the shortlisted and the favourite of insiders such as the *NME*.

The news makes the buzz around Burial explode. In August Gordon Smart from *The Sun* starts a real manhunt, offering a reward to anyone capable of giving him useful information about Burial's identity. Smart argues that behind 'the unknown Burial' there may be a celebrity such as Richard D. James (Aphex Twin) or Norman Cook (Fatboy Slim); such theories were dismissed as ridiculous by the most specialized press. In coincidence with the campaign on *The Sun*, on 7 August the double website *iamburial.com* and *iamburial.spreadshirt.net* was created, selling 'T-shirts, hoodies and other stuff with slogans such as I Am Burial and I'm With Burial', as Smart will say in an article. The phrase 'I am Burial' echoes the 'I am not Burial' written on the carton box worn as a mask by Kode9 in a series of iconic portraits by Georgina Cook (January 2008) and soon becomes a proper internet meme, leading to a number of manipulations, replicas and parodies. In a few days, the *iamburial.com* website turns into a static homepage with the message 'No I'm not'; by November, it will go offline.

On 5 August the second – and last – post on Burial's Myspace appears; starting off with his first ever self-introduction: 'my names will bevan, i'm from south london'; Burial confirms the identity revealed by *The Independent*. At the same time, the musician changes his profile's avatar by uploading a photo, presumably an *ante litteram* selfie, in which his face is clearly shown. Until then, Burial's Myspace profile picture featured the figure from the *Untrue* cover; a drawing by Burial himself and, perhaps a self-portrait, as it may be inferred. In the message, Burial explains his anonymity strategy and why he changed his mind about it: 'For a while theres been some talk about who i am, but its not a big deal / i wanted to be unknown because i just want it to be all about the tunes. over the last year the unknown thing become an issue so im not into it any more. im a lowkey person and i just want to make some tunes, nothing else.' The very same post, on the very same URL address, was edited and dated 3 October, cutting off most of the text and confirming the first name only, in the final greetings: 'Big up everyone, take care, will (burial).' On 9 September the Mercury Prize winner is announced: Elbow.

1.3. Is Burial Burial? (2008-13): 'burialisfourtet'

On 31 October 2008, Clark/Blackdown publishes on his blog a picture shot in 2006 by photographers Tim & Barry for a feature about the dubstep scene commissioned to journalists Chantelle Fiddy and Hattie Collins by an unidentified fashion magazine. As the title of the post suggests, echoing a classic moment in the history of jazz music ('A great day in Harlem', in 1958, when more than fifty notable jazzmen were photographed in a group), it was 'A great day in Brixton'. In the photo, sandwiched between Blackdown himself and Mary Anne Hobbs, Bevan/Burial is clearly shown.

On 15 October 2009, 'Gorilla vs. Bear' reports that earlier that year Flying Lotus had uploaded on his Myspace profile a four hands track produced with Burial, soon deleted. The news starts a big buzz, but on 19 October *Fact Magazine* explains that 'Hyperdub write in to establish that this isn't a Burial/Lotus collaboration, rather, it's a remix that Flying Lotus made from Burial samples'. In fact, the track featured a large portion from the track *Ravemond's Young Problems* by Flying Lotus's friend and collaborator Dimitri Grimm/Dimlite, still unpublished at the time.

Hypotheses such as the ones proposed by *The Sun* have spread throughout the years, suggesting that Burial's real identity may have been, from time to time, Damon Albarn, Thom Yorke or Kode9 in the first place. Already in 2006 (in the aforementioned interview), Blackdown had asked Burial whether he was Basic Channel (Moritz Von Oswald and Mark Ernestus) or The Bug (Kevin Martin). But the number one suspect in the case has always been Kieran Hebden/Four Tet, who had attended Will Bevan's same Elliott School (as confirmed by the aforementioned *Independent* article) and had collaborated more than once with Burial.

In November 2009, MIT Press publishes *Sonic Warfare: Sound, Affect, and the Ecology of Fear*, an essay by Steve Goodman (Kode9) focusing on the cultural significance of the usage of frequencies and sounds as weapons, in politics and war; in the acknowledgements, we find a Will Bevan as well.

On 23 December 2011 'Burial is Four Tet' (*burialisfourtet.com*) is created; a tumblr recapitulating, tickling and mocking the conspiracy theories spread around the two musicians. Four Tet himself will post the link to the website on his Twitter profile (14 December 2012). On 19 June 2013 'Equalizer' reports that Four Tet would have confirmed to be Burial via Twitter; the website provides a screenshot of the post (the classic 'I am Burial') and quotes most of the 'clues' presented by 'Burial is Four Tet', along with a tweet by Dan Snaith/Caribou (who had collaborated with Burial), dating back to 15 May: 'How has it taken me this long to figure out four tet is not burial?'. The news of the confirmation spreads across the fandom. Insiders, and Snaith himself, speak ironically about that, and Four Tet has to deny the claim more than once via social media. In a few hours, the real nature of the news is revealed: the website is not new to satirical announcements at all (namely, the screenshot is fake) and Snaith's tweet was just a sarcastic joke (disproved by Snaith himself on the very next day, 16 May).[1]

1.4. Burial is Burial (2013–14): 'Hi this is will'

On 10 December 2013, the very same day when Burial's EP *Rival Dealer* leaked on reddit (one day before its scheduled official release), *Fact Magazine* interviews Flying Lotus; in the stream of questions and answers the musician incidentally makes it clear he met Burial, adding that he is 'probably the only guy who wears full black addidas [*sic*] track suits too'.

On 13 December, two days after the official release of the EP *Rival Dealer*, Burial texts Mary Anne Hobbs during her live weekly broadcast at BBC Radio 1, in order to explain the meaning of his work, which was immediately judged by the specialized press as his most autobiographical and outspoken to date, including a hint about the artist's sexuality (a sample from the motivational speech held by director Lana Wachowski at the 2012 Human Rights Campaign gala) or, at least, about the artist's attitude towards sexuality: 'I wanted the tunes to be anti-bullying tunes that could maybe help someone to believe in themselves, to not be afraid, and to not give up, and to know that someone out there cares and is looking out for them.'

On 16 January 2014 songwriter/producer James Blake announces via Facebook that he will be airing a special interview with Burial during his debut as radio host at BBC Radio 1 that night. It turns out to be a joke: a surreal, Twin Peaks-alluding cut and paste of voices from Burial's productions, 'revealing' that Burial and Four Tet would both come from an ancient, almost extinct tribe.

On 31 January the page *hyperdub.com/burial* appears on Hyperdub website (which displays the records catalogue only, in this latest incarnation). It features a selfie of Bevan/Burial and a paragraph in which he thanks his family, fans, and insiders for their support throughout the ten years since he started releasing his music: 'Hi this is will, I just want to say thank you to anyone out there who liked my burial tunes & supported me over the years.' Burial says he hopes to be able to finish his new tunes as soon as possible, since 'Dark Souls 2 [the follow-up to an immersive, cult videogame; editor's note] is on the horizon soon so I'm not sure if I will have many new tunes for a while because I need to play that game a lot'. The webpage immediately becomes a meme; on the very same day, producer Joshua Leary/Evian Christ makes a parody out of it on his website's homepage and a fan, Cameron Reed, launches on Twitter a series of selfies marked by the hashtag #burialing.

On 1 February blogger Antonio Fatini creates a whole new website on the URL *iamburial.com* (cf. *supra*), featuring a template that allows one to semi-automatically generate one's own profile in Burial's fashion, modelled upon Hyperdub's post; Fatini launches also the 'I am Burial' Facebook fanpage (*fb.com/youareburial*), the posts of which are marked by the hashtag #iamburial. By 6 February Fatini claims to have generated more than 1,500 profiles, across 100 different countries worldwide.

After having eventually showed up and 'taken the mic', Burial seems to have disappeared again, except for sporadically releasing new tunes (Lambeth 2014; Temple Sleeper 2015; Sweetz with Zomby 2016).

2. Dig the Burial: Trails of meaning inside and around his music

2.1. London and music: A manifesto

Burial speaks little, but his words are clear. He does not give many interviews and all of them actually say almost the very same things. They are few –

but they are generally long, sometimes fluvial. Their tone is colloquial, sincere, intimate, they look like open confessions, wherein he justifies what he does, and how he does it, and why. They are constantly crossed by two encumbering presences, two main isotopies – that is, semantic field – which seem to innervate the discourse back and forth, constituting his environment, his whole ecology – two totemic presences before which everything else seems to disappear: London and music. They overlap one onto the other, the second being the expression of the first, the first the natural setting for the second. It would be quite unfair to say that the critical cliché of Burial's music as the 'soundtrack to late-night inner-city life' (Warren 2007) is untrue; but, at the same time, it cannot be passed over in silence that music here is meant to be more than a background to the city, more than a soundtrack. Burial's work aims at being not only a music *for* London, but the music *of* London; not its accompanying, but its sonic transmutation, its 'musicification'. Burial aspires to make London *sound*: to turn the matter of which London is made into a different substance.

The very first Burial interview, in fact a monologue (Interview: Clark 2005), already contains *in nuce* the key elements of his poetics; it is a kind of unconscious, yet programmatic manifesto. Burial's description of his lonely wanderings across the bowels of the urban world, in a kind of hallucinated, oneiric state, are excerpts of lyrical urban prose, featured with a strong adolescent, diary-like feel. He depicts a dark scenery, a city doomed to alienation, loneliness, lack of meaning, the inland of which can be just wandered across, aimlessly.

Such a ghostly, deadly or, at least, larval, survival-oriented status does echo the hollow, claustrophobic atmosphere exuding from a landmark underground electronic album such as Kevin Martin/The Bug's *Tapping the Conversation* (1997). Definitely marking the shift from jazzcore to electronic music in his career, conceived as an ideal, alternative soundtrack to Francis Ford Coppola's *The Conversation* (1974; not by chance a film about obsession, hiding, and loneliness), that industrial dub take has been generally considered a mood-defining milestone for dubstep's aesthetics (Scaruffi 2009). On the contrary, whereas The Bug's *London Zoo* (2008) reflects the very same dark and moody London, it does so in a completely different fashion, stressing its vital, energetic, 'spiced' nature. Burial's London feels more like a morgue than a zoo. And just like in a morgue, you do not only find the cold of pain and grief, but also the warm presence of the people you have always loved and will love for good. In turn, Burial's relationship with London is dualistic and such dualism is sonically embodied by his music; set between the dusk and the dawn of the metropolis, it is constantly shifting, dithering over love and hate, light and darkness. It may be not a mere coincidence that Burial's logo is a kind of stylized, two-piece shuriken tao.

2.2. Music as the night drug: The rough sleeper

Only when the wanderer gets hypnotized by his own personal 'nighttime train music' (the 'UK d&b dubstep jungle rave garage party tunes'), if not everything makes sense, at least 'the sorrow just come out of it'. He can even surprisingly exclaim, mesmerized: 'I love this place'. This music is a *pharmakon* by definition – a potion, a drug, a hailing, saving device. Burial's London is a dead block of concrete that may be turned on only when it is innervated by it.

When Burial makes his getaway about music, his speech becomes a soliloquy, an interior monologue, filled with references, artists' names, records, tunes – and fragments of everyday life connected to them – in an obsessive name dropping ritual. They are always the very same names, ever recurring and repeated, as if they were formulas, or magic spells: El-B, Photek, Digital Mysticz, Skream. Burial makes it clear he is, first and foremost, a passionate listener; then – maybe – also a musician. His relationship with music is quasi-pathological, as much as the one with his city: 'The compilation [he had prepared for his night rides] had some amazing tunes on it, but I didn't listen to anything for weeks after' (Interview: Clark 2005); 'All I listened to for a year was [A Guy Called Gerald's] *Black Secret Technology* [1995]' (Interview: Goodman 2007).

Burial's human figure becomes tinier and tinier, it weakens, and eventually waters down in music – the one he listens to and the one he makes on his own. Emerging from the meaningless of reality, solid like Kubrick's black monolith, the tunes become detailed and hyperrealistic, capable of expanding themselves beyond measure, filling up everything, becoming a totalizing reduction of reality.

2.3. Loneliness, darkness and debris: Splinters of imagery

Burial's visual paraphernalia look coherent with his poetic statements. Only two records of his feature pictures besides logos and track-listings. The 2006 eponymous album displays two uncredited aerial views of suburban blocks, absorbed in a dark violet, smoggy atmosphere – that is all. *Untrue*, the 2007 album, shows the drawing (made by Burial himself) of a lonely hooded guy, eyes wide shut, frowning, thinking, maybe even sleeping (and dreaming?), seated in front of a cup of hot drink. On the back of the album, a backlight silhouette of blocks; inside, a pile of debris lying within a tunnel (these two shots are by Georgina Cook; cf. *supra*), with the superimposed inscription 'THANK YOU' – that is all.

Burial's paratexts are nothing more than small hints meant to confirm what we are already hearing in his music and reading in his rationed statements: this is a world of loneliness, darkness and debris. Deep dense distant atmospheres, in the background and all around; small, shaky, magnified, broken objects, and defeated figures, in the foreground. Burial's track titles serve as a clue as well; they are short (three words, at most), they are always descriptive, cinematographic, and they are often locative, spatial-referencing, geographical: 'Nite Train', 'Distant Light', 'Night Bus', 'Broken Home', 'Near Dark', 'Dog Shelter', 'Homeless', 'In McDonalds', 'South London Boroughs', 'UK', 'Street Halo', 'NYC', 'Lambeth'. Burial's dubstep is

> about when you come back from being out somewhere; in a minicab or a night bus, or with someone, or walking home across London late at night, dreamlike, and you've still got the music kind of echoing in you, in your bloodstream, but with real life trying to get in the way. I want it to be like a little sanctuary. It's like that 24-hour stand selling tea on a rainy night, glowing in the dark. (Interview: Hancox 2007)

It can be said, with Adam Harper (2009), that Burial's vivid soundscape tunes – his sound sketches – are the musical equivalent of an impressionist's visual works of art.

2.4. Masked without a mask: The hero with a thousand faces

Burial's 'display of un-display' (he clearly shows that he does not want to show himself) recalls the 'tradition of mystery' of the 'techno jerks without face': the techno utopians of the 'second generation' and of the classic rave era. 'I like the old records, where you didn't know who made them and it didn't matter. You got into the tunes more' (Interview: Goodman 2007); music stands as an emissary, a plenipotentiary delegate, an anything-but-empty *simulacrum*.

There are two main strategies to hide one's identity and force the audience and the media to concentrate on the music per se: using an implicit or explicit mask (or logos used as masks; cf. Mike Banks' Underground Resistance, James Stinson and Gerald Donald's Drexciya, Mortiz Von Oswald and Mark Ernestus' Basic Channel) or multiply the monikers (Marc Trauner aka Marc Acardipane, Mescalinum United, The Mover, Pilldriver, Marshall Masters, Resident E; Richard D. James aka Aphex Twin, AFX, Bradley Strider, Caustic Window, Polygon Window, Universal Indicator, GAK, Power-Pill, Q-Chastic etc.). Besides mystery, masks give a connotation of universality; having no face means you might have any face, *a thousand faces*, to paraphrase mythologist Joseph Campbell (1949).[2] The fact Burial never wore a proper mask does not mean he was not masked: he was hiding his face in every respect and – moreover – provided a perfect substitutive icon with the drawing displayed on the cover of *Untrue*: 'I've been drawing that same one since I was little. Just some moody kid with a cup of tea sitting at the 24 hour stand in the rain in the middle of the night when you are coming back from somewhere' (Interview: Goodman ibid). Another obsessive, hypnotic image of repetition reported by the musician.

Even when his name and face have been eventually revealed, mystery continued to accompany his figure. That happened because one's identity is not simply an identity document, it is not something made just of a name and a picture (which are just signifiers), but of relationships, connections, overlaps between actor and person. And Burial has never had something like that to offer to us. We know Burial's name and face, still we know nothing about him. And we desperately scrutinize any possible clue, in his music, in his words, in order to come up with a personal profile (in this respect, the threads at *reddit.com/r/burial* are quite impressive). Burial's is a denied identity – a shadow play wherein to project our imaginary about him and his music.

2.5. Maverick and mistaken: The rubbish superhero

Burial stands, humble and proud, as an outsider, a maverick; almost a hermit, completely set aside from the contemporary electronic music scene: 'I don't know any other producers. I don't know anyone who makes tunes. I'm just out there. I'm not part of the scene and I can't get up and DJ. I'm proud of this music but I'm not a fully paid-up member of the board. I'm none of those things' (Interview: Clark 2006). Burial gives us the image of a musical nerd, a musical *hikikomori*, autistically self-secluded within the four walls of his bedroom: 'Only about five people outside of my family know I make tunes, I think. I hope' (Interview: Hancox 2007).

At the same time, he is not nerdy at all as concerns the production of music; compared to the compositional and technical skills of his colleagues, who have achieved the status of 'sound scientists' proper (e.g. Sam Shackleton, Rob Ellis/Pinch, Paul Rose/Scuba), his music looks pretty craft-made; in the sense of naïve and amateurish, as Burial himself clearly explains in his interviews: 'I'm a bit like a rubbish super-hero' (ibid). His signature, organic, wonky, crackling sound is the outcome of a literally hand-made compositional process, of him employing a non-professional music editor, with no sequencers: the infamous Sound Forge. Fans and other musicians all seemed really upset to learn how Burial actually worked, since it is generally agreed that with such a tool it is almost impossible to produce 'good beats'.

Obviously, Burial's sound is not only a matter of technical limitation, but also an aesthetic statement: 'I was thinking of the kind of shit I want to hear that isn't studioboy weak fucking clumpy drum fake tunes' (Interview: Clark 2005). The aim of Burial's music is to convey the feelings which had produced it in the first place, being the medium and the message of his discourse:

it's always been difficult for me to make tunes. I'd just sit or walk waiting for night to fall hoping I'd make something i liked. ... I still made most of the tunes in the dead of the night, and when you do that you have to let the tune kind of hypnotize you otherwise you'll just fall asleep or

play Playstation. The tunes just lulled. … The moodiness made the tunes.'
(Interview: Goodman 2007)

Burial's uniqueness lies in this diverse type of production skills; not technical,
but emotional. Yes: these takes on music are nothing but a series of cliché,
and definitely 'he is a romantic about music' (Interview: Hancox 2007 ibid).

This kind of 'epic of the lack of means', this 'triumph of the mistakes'
recalls the tradition of the early lo-fi and Do-It-Yourself ethics and poetics
of indie music, the golden age of pioneers and creativity in electronic
popular music, the recycled trash-technology of dub and hip hop of the late
seventies, the serendipity of DJ Pierre's Phuture *Acid tracks* (1987).

2.6. Before and beyond dubstep: The heretic traditionalist

Burial's relationship with tradition, an exquisitely English tradition, explains
his role and his importance as an innovator of the genre:

> Whereas Pinch [with his album *Underwater Dancehall*] looks at the future
> of dubstep, Burial submerges himself in the very past of the genre, going
> back to its primary roots: UK Garage and 2 step. *Untrue* holds entire years
> of history of the UK sound. … Burial carries to its extremes the work on
> voices developed within the English continuum, from hardcore to 2 step,
> passing through jungle and its affiliations.' (Galli 2007; my trans)

His secular devotion to those sounds has been translated into his music,
which pays tribute to his obsessive listening. Burial digs the sources of
dubstep and, at the same time: 'Fifteen years ago, we would have called
it trip hop' (Christgau 2013). When Burial and Massive Attack released a
collaborative work (*Four Walls/Paradise Circus*, 2011), the English tradition
of urban music seemed to have come to a full circle – he had become a
reference for the ones who had influenced him in the first place.

Burial managed to carry dubstep from being a subcultural genre, rooted
in dancehall, pirate radios and the club scene, to the zeitgeist, melancholic,
highly emotional – 'hypersoul', according to the icastic definition of
Kode9 – soundscape designed for the earlobes of the indie, arty listeners
worldwide. He is being a paradoxical innovator, a chiasm: he made the
genre leap forward, by bringing it back to its pre-genre roots. By reviving its
origins, Burial deeply changed the nature of dubstep as a codified genre; by
pointing to its tradition, he has renewed it, injecting new meanings. Whereas
we can talk of retrofuturism, including afrofuturism (Zuberi 2007), we
have to admit the possibility of an avant-pastism. Whereas we can identify
the invention of tradition (Hobsbawm and Ranger 1983), we can detect,
symmetrically, the recovery of invention. Burial used tradition to make
innovation – he reimagined a possible past, a possible passed time 'which
could have been'.

2.7. Faraway so close: The myth

All these features make Burial an icon, a mythical figure in every respect – not only in common sense terminology, but also in a specific structuralist one. According to anthropologist Claude Lévi-Strauss (1958), myth is something that is created in order to provide the chaotic world with meaning; it works by *bricolage*, by arranging the existing things together, employing the available means. One of its main outcomes is the capability of reconciling the opposites. This is exactly what Burial did. And as in every myth proper, cases of uncontrolled mythogenesis and mythography have been reported: apparition and autosuggestion (*the Flying Lotus-Burial collaboration*); apocrypha (*the DJ-Kicks affaire*); persecution (*'The Sun' affaire*); Urban legend; Imitation.

Burial became a kind of 'boogie man' to be chased, and this led to funny anecdotes such as the following: 'I've had times when I've had mates sitting next to me and they've put my tunes on without knowing. I would just sit there whispering to myself, "Please don't put that on – Or at least, don't say anything bad about it". … I've had someone say to me, "Yeah, Burial's a girl. I know someone who met her"' (Interview: Hancox 2007).

Burial's signature sound has been replicated obviously by others. Zomby's 'Natalia's Song' (2011), a plain plagiarism of the homonymous Reark's tune he was contributing to, is actually a stylistic plagiarism of Burial's 'hypersoul', in the first place. Zomby stated: 'I wrote it to give to Burial, really. It wasn't intended to be a single' (Parks 2011). Even Burial's antipode and 'nemesis' Sonny Moore aka Skrillex, the chief figure of 'the American way' to dubstep, the drop-based and metal-affected brostep (cf. the groundbreaking 2010 EP *Scary Monsters and Nice Sprites*), has been influenced by its style, as the eponymous tune from the 2013 EP *Leaving* testifies. Amateur music producers and fans tried to 'dictionarize' Burial's style, by analysing and re-creating his sounds palette, featured by memorable analogical glitches such as the ignition of a lighter or the shaking of a keychain; on 19 May 2012, someone uploaded on the Mediafire file sharing platform an accurate ten second lasting 32-file sound effect handbook, to make it possible to copycat Burial – to 'burialize' one's own beats.

2.8. Soundscape, memory and the continuum: How does Burial sound like?

Burial's interviews are obsessively focused on his obsession with tunes and music; he has always been open, outspoken about it, his speech in-depth and detailed in focus. He has thoroughly described, metaphorized and interpreted his own music. Audience and journalists have always been in agreement with him and each other, depicting his music with a repertoire of expressions which soon became crystallized: 'Burial "mourns the death of rave", his music is (to paraphrase a handful of commentators) a "plaintive echo from a bygone era of collective energy", "a melancholy, ghostly memory of the faded promise of rave, drenched in weathering and mired in urban decay"' (Harper 2009).

A 'degree zero' of the discourse about Burial, therefore, seems to have been set. But: How did Burial get to this largely agreed reading of his work, this largely agreed attitude towards his figure? How did he manage to construct a new musical form within the womb of dubstep?

Adam Harper maintains that Burial is other than the 'vulgata reading' of Burial; he is not only the 'pall-bearer of rave culture' (albeit this death-centred isotopy – I take the liberty to add – is obviously conveyed by his moniker, and has been so since his original, disturbing Myspace exergue: 'rest in peace Danny'), but a lot of other things at the same time. He is the impressionistic painter of Zone 2-London;[3] a storyteller, a poet, an architect. And also 'the Percussionist, the Audiophile, the Engineer, the Polyphonist, the Gamer, the Film-Watcher, the Music Fan, the Listener/Perceiver, the Orchestrator, the Gothic, the Socialist Realist, the Dancer, the Poststructuralist, the Bricoleur, the Romantic, the Diarist, the Raver, the Independent, the Victorian and the Myth' (Harper ibid). Harper claims that, among the twenty-first-century composers, in the 'post-experimental electronic musical style', a category which perfectly fits his music, Burial is an innovator, precisely within two specific areas: 'The complex electronic alteration of rhythm and pitch in vocal samples to create new, cyborg melodies [which] is referred to as "vocal science"'; and the harmonic and rhythmic cadence, namely 'a configuration that creates a sense of repose or resolution [finality or pause]' (Wikipedia).

In other words, Burial's discourse about music through music is much more musical than we may infer at a first listen. Burial's music works in a subtle fashion, outlining a double journey, both physical and metaphorical: it is a journey through London, a journey through music – a journey through London's music. Like a gifted homeless, a special rough sleeper, just like the Fisher King, Burial is doomed to wandering across the ruins of London's music continuum,[4] chased by painful illuminations.

An obsessive listener, Burial is an obsessive music producer as well. Obsession lies in the field of repetition, and repetition – at its peak of hypnotic power – is significant for the microscopic swerves it may be featured with. Say, Burial's tunes are more or less all the same, all of them exploring all the possible micro-variations of just one formula: the skeletal and dust-covered shaky jungle and 2-step cadences; the wooden timbre of the rimshot on the snare; the modified voice cuts; the dirty yet vaporous ambience – a place filled with the empty spaces of dub only. Burial's music has definitely changed, has evolved throughout time, but just like a plant which blossoms from a seed does, it has always been there, *in nuce*, encapsulated within a few key elements: The (anti)structural usage of the voices (at least, since *South London Boroughs*, 2005); a concrete music, field recording-like noise (a kind of background which has become more and more important and prominent, being no more a merely neutral sound canvas; since *Distant*

Lights, 2006); the 'discovering' of house and techno (since *Unite*, 2007; in fact, maybe the only Burial tune employing a sequencer). Burial's signature sound is a kind of after-bomb soul music, a resilient soul, a 'found' soul – found in the midst of debris: A desolated soundscape set by some skeleton rhythms, some dark dust, some ghostly voices – a blurry musical Polaroid from the past.

Space is a key aspect of Burial's music. And it is via this modulation of space that two different existential dimensions, which Burial is between, seem to have been set, outlining a semiotics of proper light. The sounds he displays are far-off, but still pretending an emotive closeness – a spatial rendition of the recurring 'distant light' (i.e. the spirit-ideology of underground music) he wants to keep alive. All the acknowledged genres, styles, and formal elements (all of them identifying a lost utopian dimension, 'there and then') are re-enacted, re-played as if they were dematerialized, as what remains when nothing is left of them but the idea ('here and now', the heterotopian dimension).[5] Burial's micro-shifts are not discoveries then, but memories. They are not just traces from the past, but fossils – it is a 'metaphysics of crackle' (Fisher 2013).

2.9. Those were NOT the days: Hauntology to the square

With his most recent works (*Kindred*, February 2012; the diptych *Truant/ Rough Sleeper*, December 2012; and *Rival Dealer*, December 2013), Burial carries his style to the extremes. He leads the riddim-resounding rhythms of dubstep to a more song-oriented set up (the most striking example is definitely 'Hiders', from the latest EP) and, at the same time, towards complexly layered textures weaving electroacoustic soundscapes (sometimes, they can even be beatless or 'Gorecki-like'; Reynolds 2012: 514), made of found sounds, cut and packed in the form of suites. Features such as these made Burial easily comparable to Aphex Twin or Boards of Canada's isolationism, or to the once-avant subgenre called illbient (Christgau 2013).

'Ashtray Wasp', the closing track from *Kindred*, displays a housey flavour, conveyed through a shining – a *slightly* shining – keyboard moving underskin. Burial's signature snare is absent, being replaced by a more 4/4 dancey rhythm. The voices are still Burial's hypersoul trademarks, Todd Edwards' modelled (Zingales 2008), now resounding even Clams Casino (who, interviewed by myself, unbelievably said he did not know Burial at all; Marino 2011) and footwork's high-pitched, cut-up confetti. Burial's hustle and bustle on the sonic matter here is so advanced and fine grained to be on the verge of classical-contemporary music; as testified by the disclaimer which clarifies that 'the skips and cut outs on the track "Ashtray Wasp" are intentional'. When Kode9 premiered *Truant/Rough Sleeper* at Club to Club music festival (Hiroshima Mon Amour club, Turin, Italy, 9 November 2012), it sounded like he was live processing the tunes. But Burial himself was playing the game, willingly deconstructing the musical matter with rips, needle sticks, jumps ('Etched Headplate' is the title of the sixth track of *Untrue*), and silences. He builds up a kind of 'slacked radio' switch, he continuously disappoints the listener's expectations, forcing them to continuously reset their attempts to 'go in time', since the stop and gos he implements are far different from the techno and house routines. This is an electronic music that has been mutated into a street-captured folk music: an ethnography of the remembrances, of the memory, an update of the ancient 'field recordings' – a new blues for this epoch. If it is still dubstep, this is a disturbed, hypnagogic, post-ecstatic dubstep, situated 'out there' – the club is surely somewhere else.

Dubstep has been icastically described as a double ghost: 'the ghost of jungle', for 'your brain supplies the missing hyperspeed breakbeats' (Goodman/Kode9, in Reynolds 2012: 515), and 'rave's afterlife, or even a form of mourning without letting go' (ibid). Burial's, thus, is already a post-dubstep music, something incorporating dubstep itself in the process of abstraction as the ultimate step of the UK dance and bass music tradition – the lymph for dubstep in the first place. If Burial can be set within the aesthetics of hauntology (Ulrich and Fogel 2012),[6] as one of its most prominent exponents, indeed (Harper 2009; Fisher 2013), we can do so since his hauntology is a 'to the square' one. A lo-fi hauntology, a phenomenological, non-ontological one, the re-presentification, the rendition of what you listened to *yesterday*, heard as through today's iPod shuffled noise-crammed ears – heard as from a crackling pirate radio, or a broken cassette. We do not listen to the contemporary revival of an old music, but to an old music being revived by the act of listening to it today, with all the beautiful *stigma* of the time that passed upon it.

> I'm not old enough to have been to a proper old rave in a warehouse or a field, ... but I used to hear these stories about legendary club nights, about driving off into the darkness to raves on the outskirts of London. But it's got this sadness now, because most club culture got commercialised in the 1990s; oftentimes it got taken off ravers and sold back to them. But it's still out there; there's a signal, or a light. It's like there's someone still holding a lighter in a warehouse somewhere. (Interview: Hancox 2007)

This mnemonic-oneiric journey within the (hi)story of English electronic music is largely an imaginative trip: it is a meditation, a speculation upon the genre and its macro-context – an 'audio essay about the London hardcore continuum' (Reynolds 2012: 515). At the same time, depicting a post-urban, Ballardian ambience (Sellars 2008; Reynolds 2012: 514), being a 'post-geographical sound ..., deterritorializing and border-crossing, ... it could equally be about any city anyway' (Reynolds 2012: 515). Burial's 'dubstep' is, just like every great work of music, both specific and universal in its identification mechanism: it is a specific place, with precise coordinates, but also a state of the mind everyone can feel, everywhere.

Tickling the forgotten pleasure of remembering, doubting and investigating, Burial presents himself as the borderline conscience of English underground electronic music: a secluded bard for these days of future past.

Outro (*Truant/Rough Sleeper*)

'I fell in love with you.' *It comes from my guts, I feel this abandon with no more struggle, no more tears, for I know it is not on you, not on this city. I am the culprit: I love you, but it* 'Doesn't really mean I want you.' *We move slightly blurry, wrapped within an upward pathos, moving amidst techno-house hints, trip hop skeletons, dark ambient dust, dub bubbles, up to an Arabic fusion sax playing down in an alley. It lasts just for a second. All these faded memories are resounding like the* tinnit *after a rave does. I am there again. The struggle is over, I am resigned, I have accepted myself for what I am, maybe, as a smile eventually appears shy on my face: a pulse, a ringing, a porcelain bell, blessed with simplicity, and tender grace, brings to light that pale, tepid hope. I feel at home, now. For just a second. Then, the wandering starts again.*

Notes

1 At this point, I cannot skip the anecdote. On 19 June 2013, I was about to take a flight from Turin (Italy) to London to participate in the conference about 'Englishness and popular music'. I was a PhD student in semiotics at the time, I was working on my thesis about the system of musical genres, and dubstep was particularly interesting in this respect for its multilayered history and intricate branches. Burial was a very interesting theoretical subject of enquiry indeed. Thus, the topic of my talk was Burial. Just before getting on the airplane, my then-fiancé – now my wife – texted me: 'Gabri, Four Tet just confirmed he is Burial.' I can say I panicked for a second, since my whole interpretation of Burial and his music was built upon one single belief: he was not the spin-off project of some other musician, but a kind of ephemeral revelation of the incredible strength of the imaginary connected to contemporary electronic music. I knew I was right. And I was. The conference was particularly important to me for a number of reasons: it was my first one ever, it was about a complex subject, and it gave me the chance to meet scholars with different backgrounds, dealing with a number of diverse subjects. Moreover, it definitely became clear to me that the perception of international music that my Italian peers and I had was quite distorted. I thought Burial was a 'dubstar' and, more in general, a popular music star in London, as much as in Italy. Well, it turned out that he was more a niche phenomenon, and cult act, than a proper 'star', since most of the participants, both among the speakers (some of them even talked about Tricky or the grime scene) and in the audience, had never heard of him.

2   It is quite interesting that, as noted by famed rock journalist Robert Christgau (2013), despite the scrupulous anonymity of its public moves in the beginning, on the one hand, and his peculiar work upon voices (and lyrics; Bradley 2013), on the other (they are 'chopped and screwed', pitched up, slowed down, gender ambiguous etc.), no one ever suggested Burial might have been a woman.

3   London's public transport system is divided into six main zones. The inner district is zone 1. Zone 2 represents the edge of inner London.

4   Since 1999 circa, journalist and cultural critic Simon Reynolds theorized that most of the traditions in the history of electronic popular music in the UK were interrelated; he named such phylogeny the 'hardcore continuum' (cf. Reynolds 2012).

5   The terms 'utopian' and 'heterotopian' are employed here in a semiotic, non-Foucauldian way.

6   Music journalists Ian Penman (1995) and Mark Fisher/k-punk (2005) were the first ones to apply the Derridian notion of hauntology (Fr. *hantologie*; a pun between *ontologie* [ontology] and *hanter* [to haunt]) to popular music. According to Derrida, hauntology is a phantasmal ontology, a palpable absence, a presence from the past which keeps haunting present times. The literature upon this topic in popular culture is incredibly rich, since it has been a growing trend throughout the 2010s. In order to get both a wider context and some key case studies (including Burial), please cf. Harper (2011) and Fisher (2014).

References

Bradley, L. (2013), Decoding Dubstep: A Rhetorical Investigation of Dubstep's Development from the Late 1990s to the Early 2010s, Honors theses, Paper 163, Florida State University, goo.gl/rygLaR.

Campbell, J. (1949), *The Hero with a Thousand Faces*, New York: Pantheon.

Christgau, R. (2013), Burial, goo.gl/4IQ4P.

Fisher, M. (2005), Unhomesickness, 'k-punk.abstractdynamics.org', 11 March, goo.gl/Ttju4G.

Fisher, M. (2013), The Metaphysics of Crackle: Afrofuturism and Hauntology, *Dancecult*, 5(2): 42–55, goo.gl/A74Sqo.

Fisher, M. (2014), *Ghosts of My Life: Writings on Depression, Hauntology and Lost Futures*, Winchester: Zero Books.

Galli, L. (2007), Review of Burial, *Untrue*, 'Blow Up' no. 115, December, 71.

Harper, A. (2009), The Premature Burial: Burial the Pallbearer vs Burial the Innovator, 'rougesfoam.blogspot.com', goo.gl/J0Rj4.

Harper, A. (2011), *Infinite Music. Imagining the Next Millennium of Human Music-Making*, Winchester: Zero Books.

Hobsbawm, E. and T. O. Ranger (1983), *The Invention of Tradition*, Cambridge: Cambridge University Press.

Lévi-Strauss, C. (1958), *Anthropologie structurale*, Paris: Plon.

Marino, G. (2011), *Clams Casino: Cloud rap? Trip hop soul?* [Gabriele Marino interviews Mike Volpe aka Clams Casino], 'Sentireascoltare', goo.gl/r6U5RW.

Parks, A. (2011), *The Self-Titled Interview: Zomby* [Andrew Parks interviews Zomby], 'self-titledmag.com', goo.gl/PD5ufi.

Penman, I. (1995), Black Secret Tricknology, *The Wire*, No. 133, March, 36–40, goo.gl/ktLhNw.

Reynolds, S. (2012), *Energy Flash: a Journey through Rave Music and Dance Culture. A Generation Ecstasy Extended Remix for the Twenty-First Century*, Berkeley CA: Soft Skull.

Scaruffi, P. (2009), Kevin Martin, Techno Animal, God, Ice, Bug, 'scaruffi.com', goo.gl/jPJ22E.

Sellars, S. (2008), A Ballardian Burial, 'ballardian.com', goo.gl/0PjbS.

Ulrich, P. and B. Fogel (2012), L'hantologie. Trouver dans notre présent les traces du passé pour mieux comprendre notre futur, 'Playlist Society', V2.10, Juin, goo.gl/V7Wf8I.

Walmsley, D. (2009), 'Dubstep', in *The Wire Primers: A Guide to Modern Music*, Rob Young (ed.), London: Verso, 87–93.

Warren, E. (2007), Burial, untrue, *The Guardian*, goo.gl/OVCT60.

Zingales, C. (2008), Burial, 'Blow Up', no. 116, January, 28–33.

Zuberi, N. (2007), Is This the Future? Black Music and Technology Discourse, *Science Fiction Studies*, 34(2): 283–300, 'Afrofuturism', July, goo.gl/BVOxI.

Burial's interviews

Clark (2005): *Blackdown soundboy end of year review: Burial. 2005 according to Burial*, 'blackdownsoundboy.blogspot.com', 21 December 2005 [Martin Clark aka Blackdown publishes a writing by Burial], goo.gl/sSs4F.

Clark (2006): *Soundboy Burial*, 'blackdownsoundboy.blogspot.com', 21 March 2006 [Martin Clark aka Blackdown interviews Burial], goo.gl/Y9pcj.

Galli (2006): Dubstep virus: *Burial e Kode9*, in 'Blow Up', no. 101, October 2006 [Luca Galli interviews Burial].

Hancox (2007): *'Only five people know I make music'*, www.guardian.co.uk, 26 October 2007 [Dan Hancox interviews Burial], goo.gl/1X61E.

Goodman (2007): *Burial – Untrue – November 2007*, 'hyperdubrecords.blogspot.com', 10 October 2007 [Steve Goodman aka Kode9 interviews Burial], goo.gl/pq5Mn.

Long (2007): *Burial*, 'factmag.com', 1 July 2012 [Nigel Long aka Kek-w's interview with Burial from 2007], goo.gl/PjY0G; original page via webarchive, 14 October 2007 goo.gl/Zryld.

Hennings (2007): *Burial interview by Emmy Hennings* [Emmy Hennins' interview with Burial], 'cyclicdefrost.com', 24 November 2007, goo.gl/w49F0.

Fisher (2012): *Burial: Unedited Transcript*, 'thewire.co.uk', December 2012 [Complete transcript of Mark Fisher's interview with Burial for *The Wire* #286, December 2007], goo.gl/oxWVL.

Park (2012): *Untrue: Burial*, 'clashmusic.com', 16 February 2012 [online re-issue of Adam Park's print-published interview with Burial from 2007], goo.gl/PgHkp.

Official webpages

burial.bandcamp.com
Burial's Myspace myspace.com/burialuk.
Burial's post on Hyperdub's website hyperdub.net/burial.

Discography

Burial (2005) *South London Boroughs*, Hyperdub [EP]
Burial (2006) *Burial*, Hyperdub [Album]
Burial (2007) *Ghost Hardware*, Hyperdub [EP]
Burial (2007) *Untrue*, Hyperdub [Album]
Burial (2009) 'Moth/Wolf Cub', with Four Tet, Text Records [Single]
Burial (2011) 'Ego/Mirror', with Four Tet and Thom Yorke, Text Records [Single]
Burial (2011) *Street Halo*, Hyperdub [EP]
Burial (2011) 'Four Walls/Paradise Circus', with Massive Attack, Inhale Gold/The Vinyl Factory [Single]
Burial (2012) *Kindred*, Hyperdub [EP]
Burial (2012) 'Nova', with Four Tet, Text Records [Single]
Burial (2012) 'Truant/Rough Sleeper', Hyperdub [Single]
Burial (2013) *Rival Dealer*, Hyperdub [EP]
Burial (2015) 'Temple Sleeper', Keysound [Single]
Burial (2016) Young Death/Nightmarket, Hyperdub [Single]
Burial (2017) Subtemple, Hyperdub [Single]

Note: All the online resources were last accessed on 13 November 2016; URLs have been shortened via Google's URL shortener (*goo.gl*). Images of Burial to accompany this text can be found at goo.gl/82OuQu

CHAPTER ELEVEN

Albion Voice:

The Englishness of Bishi

Simon Keegan-Phipps and Trish Winter

The spirit is ether no bottle can hold
The world I have wandered in search of a home
The burnt summer fields, the villages green,
The mills and the spires of old England's dream
Bewildering world with no end or start
I am Indian in skin but English of heart.
Bewildering world despair and rejoice
Indian skin, Albion voice.

The opening lyrics of the title song of Bishi's *Albion Voice* (2012) leave the listener in little doubt as to the album's explicit focus on themes of Englishness and belonging in a world that has 'no end or start'. In this chapter we examine Bishi's creative rearticulations of English identity, made in a particular time – the early twenty-first century – and from the particular perspective of a second-generation Londoner of Bengali heritage. We analyse the precise character of this articulation of English identity, considering how the significance of *Albion Voice* might be understood through the lens of cosmopolitanism.

Bishi

Bishi emerged from London's club and music scene in the early 2000s when, as an 18-year-old DJ, she became 'the face' of London club *Kash Point* (Liverani 2010). She has since released two albums, *Nights at the Circus* (2007) and *Albion Voice* (2012). Her profile has extended across cultural fields such as the club scene, fashion, film, art and performance as well as music. Reviews and published descriptions of Bishi's work usually make reference to her second-generation English biography. A press kit, for example, describes her as Londoner born to Bengali parents, and with polycultural musical interests within and beyond those of the England of her birth and the India of her parents:

> Singer, multi instrumentalist & DJ, Bishi was born in Earls Court to a Bengali musical family; her mother is an EMI signed artist to this day. She has studied Sitar at The Ravi Shankar School for Music and has a passion for English & East European folk, progressive pop & electronica. (Sonicbids 2008)

Likening herself to the 'half-caste hybrid' protagonist of Angela Carter's novel *Nights at the Circus,* after which her first album is named, she is quoted as saying, 'I have based the album on being an outsider. The space between two cultures can be confusing, but it can also be very energetic' (Liverani 2010). In explicitly framing her work as coming from what she terms 'the space between two cultures', Bishi echoes the concept of a 'third space' (Bhabha 1994). A key element of her musical and visual image has been its overt play with visual and audible iconographies of nation and nationhood. Although Englishness and Britishness are sometimes conflated or juxtaposed here, references to Englishness intensify around her second album *Albion Voice*, released in 2012 on St George's Day, and described as 'an ode to an ever changing England' (BFI 2013).

In an interview Bishi describes the motivation for *Albion Voice* as a response to Michael Bracewell's book *England is Mine: Pop Life in Albion from Wilde to Goldie* (1997). 'In this cultural analysis of all things British, I realised there were very few women and hardly any Asians included in the book. I thought I'd add something to this debate with a lot of love' (BFI 2013). Her claiming of an 'Albion voice' is thus framed as an intervention into a vision of English popular music culture from which English Asian and female voices are largely absent. Reviews of Bishi's work often highlight its recasting of Englishness, one blogger describing the single 'Albion Voice', as 'a brilliantly articulate reframing of Englishness within a global cultural remit' (Gray 2012). The singer refers to her own work as 'orchestral, folk-inspired, postcolonial pop' (Choudhury 2015). Self-described, then, in terms of a postcolonial identity that emerges from a space between cultures and, at the same time, asserting its place within the frame of Englishness, Bishi's work explicitly configures and comments on imaginations of Englishness in the early twenty-first century. Before beginning our examination of the specificities of Bishi's construction of Englishness, it will be useful to sketch a brief outline of the particulars of her context, identifying the key cultural fields in relation to which this work circulates and is framed.

First, there is the London club and fashion scene. Bishi's biographies usually start by marking her association with the club scene of the early 2000s, from which she emerged as an 18-year-old DJ and 'the face' of the club *Kash Point*. Described variously as 'an outlet for music experimentation, genre contamination, for fashion and individual art-expressions' (Liverani 2010), and as 'a polysexual mish mash of invention and experimentation' (Wikibin 2008), *Kash Point*'s ethos celebrated ideas of hybridity, difference and individual expression and had close links with the fashion world. Many of the people associated with the club featured in international fashion magazines such as *i-D, Dazed and Confused,* and *International Vogue,* including Bishi (Liverani 2010). Bishi continues to DJ,[1] and her markedly individual personal style also aligns her with this cultural field, as does her ongoing creative partnership with some of its inhabitants, such as Matthew Hardern and Matthew Glammore. Secondly, her live-performance work has often taken place in the spaces of, and been commissioned by, key national cultural institutions within the capital city: such as the British Film Institute; the Southbank Centre (the Yoko Ono-curated Meltdown Festival 2003; Alchemy Festival 2015); and the Barbican Art Gallery (2008), often placing her within contexts celebrating institutionally sanctioned imaginations of national identity. Thirdly, Bishi's work inhabits the realm of publicly subsidized and independent arts across fine art, film and music: including commissioned sound installations,[2] fine art and AV installations, and film soundtracks.[3] Finally, it should be noted that Bishi's two albums have been released on her own label, Gryphon Records, rather than being produced or distributed by a major record label; this very much frames her as an independent artist.

Albion Voice itself reaches across these different cultural fields. The album is described as forming the nucleus of 'a wider conceptual work: AV performance, online broadcast, gallery installation and the creation of a body of artefacts' (The Nest Collective 2016). The audio visual live work has been performed as, for example, part of Sonic Cinema at the British Film Institute (2015), at the Southbank Centre (2015) and in art galleries such as KOKO (2014), often combined with DJ sets, as well as being featured in film (*London: The Modern Babylon* 2012). Art works connected to the *Albion Voice* project, such as photographs, appear in galleries such as the exhibition embassyHACK (2016) at the Government Art Collection.

Cosmopolitanism

A significant feature of Bishi's work is the extent to which the multiple hybridities (explored in more detail in subsequent sections) are presented as resulting from a creative backdrop unhindered by distinct cultural boundaries – as articulated by the 'Albion Voice' lyrics ('Bewildering world, with no end or start') quoted at the beginning of this chapter. Academic work on cosmopolitanism has proliferated over the last two decades across academic disciplines including philosophy, political science, anthropology and social sciences, to the extent of 'cosmopolitanism studies' being proposed as an interdisciplinary or post-disciplinary field in its own right (Delanty 2012). We do not have space here to outline this substantial field, or the many and often contested meanings of cosmopolitanism, but we will draw out some key features and debates that help us to understand the place of Bishi's work in articulating shifting conceptions of English identities.[4] In its broadest sense, and going back to its roots in ancient Greek thought, cosmopolitanism implies an openness to social and cultural difference, 'the extension of moral and political horizons of people, societies, organizations and institutions' (Delanty 2012: 22). This has sometimes taken the form of a universalistic vision with implications for the nation-state; a vision of, as Cheah and Robbins put it, 'thinking and feeling beyond the nation' (1998). In common usage, cosmopolitanism is sometimes thought of as an attribute or disposition, and people or places might be spoken of as more or less 'cosmopolitan'. As Binnie et al. observe: 'Cosmopolites reject the confines of bounded communities and their own cultural backgrounds. Instead they are seen to embrace a global outlook.' A cosmopolitan disposition thus involves particular skills in 'navigating and negotiating difference' (2006: 7).

Tendencies towards a celebration of cosmopolitanism have been much criticized on the basis that they can underplay the relations of power that underpin the process, the ways that cosmopolitanism is, for example, implicitly gendered (Nava 2002), classed (Werbner 1999), or can be construed as a disposition of a mobile global elite, and as a concept with a distinctively Western genealogy. In scholarship of recent years there has also been an emphasis on cosmopolitanism as 'rooted' (see, for example, Appiah (1997) on cosmopolitan patriotism), and a recognition of the different forms of cultural displacement and movement experienced by people such as transnational migrants, refugees or asylum seekers – what Clifford influentially termed 'discrepant cosmopolitanism', wherein 'cultures of displacement and transplantation are inseparable from specific, often violent, histories of economic, political, and cultural interaction' (1997: 36). There has also been an analytical focus on how cosmopolitanisms are lived in particular places and times as can be seen, for example, in ethnomusicological literature.

Where cosmopolitanism is invoked as a cultural or social feature in ethnomusicology, the term is very often a concept of largely assumed meaning, generally signalling the worldwide inclination towards musical hybridity. This literature commonly frames such tendencies in a way that provides cultural and individual detail, drawing the discussion away from the relatively bleak portrayal of a capital-driven, automated system of globalization. Turino's (2000) seminal ethnography of Zimbabwean popular musicians through the twentieth century explores in detail the interconnections of cosmopolitanism, nationalism and colonialism; Stokes draws from the work the satisfyingly paradoxical conclusion that '[it] takes a musical cosmopolitanism ... to develop a musical nationalism, to successfully assert its authenticity in a sea of competing nationalisms and authenticities' (2007: 6). Stokes also suggests, more generally, that the discursive 'shift [from "globalization" to "cosmopolitanism"] restores human agencies and creativities to the scene of analysis, and allows us to think of music as a process in the making of "worlds", rather than a passive reaction to global "systems"' (ibid). This restoration of human agency can more recently be seen exemplified in Feld's close ethnographic account of the outlooks and approaches of his collaborators in *Jazz Cosmopolitanism in Acraa* (2012). Through this ethnography Feld's work aims to 'disaggregate ... multiple and proliferating vernacular cosmopolitanisms from elite multiculturalisms' (ibid., 7), thus continuing the presiding impulses of his discipline to explore and reveal the lived musical experiences of disadvantaged or 'grass-roots' musicians in their field. In these literary contexts, the concept is most commonly represented as one element in dialogue with some locally-facing expression of cultural specificity – what Regev (2007) has termed 'cultural uniqueness'. For example, in Bilby's (1999) exploration of Surinamese popular music, cosmopolitanism is shown to exist alongside processes of indigenization; Magaldi (2009) posits cosmopolitanism as an aesthetic force combined with – but nonetheless distinct from – the self-exoticism at the heart of early-1900s Brazilian music. While these and similar ethnographies of musical cosmopolitanism routinely cite as a focus the 'discrepant cosmopolitanism' identified by Clifford (1997: 36), such a narrative is predominantly explored in terms of the experiences and perspectives of non-Western actors within postcolonial contexts.

As we will demonstrate through close musical and textual analysis of her album *Albion Voice* and its attending discursive and visual artefacts, Bishi's work represents a 'rooted' (Cohen 1992; Werbner 2008) yet significantly self-aware and explicit combination of 'worldly' and local sensibilities such as those often unearthed within the musical ethnographies mentioned above. Moreover, the precise nature of the local identity at hand – a post-imperial and inherently multicultural Englishness – represents a particular form of cultural uniqueness distinct from those commonly explored in music-oriented literature on cosmopolitanism.

Ancient Englishness

Notably, in light of the album's reception as a celebration of a contemporary multiculturalism, Bishi's work draws on images of a premodern, if not always pre-industrial, England, invoking an 'indigenous', implicitly white, Englishness. The album starts with Bishi speaking Middle English, as she recites the opening sixteen lines of the prologue to Chaucer's fourteenth-century text *The Canterbury Tales*, over a background soundscape that incorporates the sounds of horses, birdsong and church bells. This is followed by the sounds of a selection of medieval European instruments: hurdy gurdy; wooden recorder; lute; Jews harp;[5] and later, a militaristic snare drum. English literary quotation appears again in the form of lyrics drawn from John Milton's 1667 poem *Paradise Lost*, in the song 'Di Ti Maria'. As with the pastoral soundtrack to the opening of the 'Prologue', the musical setting of Milton's poetry similarly reinforces a sense of antiquity: the monodic section in the third quarter of 'Di Ti Maria', in which Milton's words are foregrounded ('The more I see pleasures about me / So much more I feel torment within'), is reminiscent of an early English polyphonic madrigal or catch, with antiphonic imitation, repetition of a small amount of two lines as a stanza (in an ABAB AAAB structure), a diatonic melody (in the form AABA), and fleeting modulations between the home minor and relative major. The latter section of the track 'Di Ti Maria' includes booming bass notes that are – it eventually transpires – emitting from the 32-foot bourdon pipes of a church organ. Such a sound invokes associations not only with a historical England, but with the surviving cultural institutions of that place.

As signalled by its lyrical references to 'The burnt summer fields, the villages green / The mills and the spires of old England's dream', 'Albion Voice' also calls up the imagination of England as a timeless rural idyll, an image that has often come to stand for England itself (Williams 1973) and which has been central to the English folk arts (Winter and Keegan-Phipps 2013). This is referenced in the video accompanying 'Albion Voice', where Bishi appears in rural scenes including a churchyard, a meadow and, at one point, perched in a tree. Associations with the English folk music scene also run more widely through Bishi's image. She was, for example, one of the featured artists on a concert tour showcasing female English folk singers, *Daughters of Albion* (2008), where she performed alongside well-established icons of the genre such as June Tabor and Norma Waterson. These evocations of an ancient England are both highlighted and, as we will see later, disrupted by Bishi's treatment of them.

Rearticulations of imperial Englishness

Other references to historical Englishness within *Albion Voice* speak of a more recent past, and draw the listener's focus to the British Empire as an original contributing force behind contemporary multiculturalism in England. For example, the Victorian era is evoked in the closing track of the album, 'Ship of Fools', which takes the form of a rollicking, folk-style waltz. As with the 'prologue', an atmospheric, natural soundscape is invoked, but this time that soundscape is maritime, with a background of seagull cries and softly breaking waves. Here, instruments include the English folk staples of accordion and concertina, but also an instrument referred to in the CD booklet as 'Mr Tickle (the cabinet pipe organ from Worthing)'. The organ is clearly audible throughout the track, but its impact is also as a symbolic reference not so much to the British seaside town of Worthing in particular, but to the Victorian and early-twentieth-century British vernacular seaside experience – with its fairgrounds, piers and barrel/pipe organs – in general.

Direct references to Empire are explicitly made in the iconography surrounding *Albion Voice*. One of the most striking aspects of Bishi's performances of Englishness can be found in the photographic and video images that accompany the album on CD sleeve, online publicity materials and reviews, and video footage. Here, Bishi appears in a number of historical roles including those of two iconic British queens, Britannia and Queen Elizabeth II. Adopting the trappings of Britannia the warrior queen, in the seated pose with armour, shield and trident that featured on British coins until 2008, Bishi inhabits an image that has stood as a female personification of the nation and, historically, the empire.[6] She speaks – or rather sings – from this perspective; in the video of the album's title track, the still, posed image of Bishi-as-Britannia is suddenly animated as she voices the line 'Mysterious children of faraway lands'. The Royal Bengal tiger, national animal of India, sits in place of the English lion at her feet. In this way, she rewrites the racialized and othered 'mysterious child' of empire as the symbol of nation itself. In a similar move, the photograph of Bishi entitled 'Indian Queen' places her in the position of the monarch, and refigures this national imagery using elements of Indian symbolism. The iconography of the portrait is most redolent of Dorothy Wilding's studio portraits of Queen Elizabeth II that were used as the source for the queen's image on stamps, coins and banknotes as well as for the official portrait hung in British Embassies across the world (Royal Collection Trust 2016). This is not just any image of the queen, but signals some of the most official, standardized and globally distributed images. Bishi's 'Indian Queen' appears in a formal white gown with blue sash, her dark hair arranged after the style adopted by Elizabeth II, together with sparkling crown, necklace, earrings and medal, but with the significant addition of Indian bridal jewellery. The appropriation and refiguring of this national imagery goes further, as the photographic image is also reproduced on commemorative china complete with royal heraldry and again incorporating the Bengal Tiger.

Unsurprisingly, given Bishi's heritage, a Bengali perspective on imperial history is also evoked in the album. The song 'Gram Chara' is one of the *Rabindra Sangeet* repertory – that is, a composition by the celebrated

Bengali polymath Rabindranath Tagore (1861–1941). Sometimes referred to as the 'bard of Bengal', Tagore has been hailed as a key historical figure in the development of Bengali – and specifically Bangladeshi – cultural works, and subsequently a recurring figure in the (re)negotiations of Bangladeshi identity over the last century (Alam 2015). The presence of a Tagore song is not, however, simply symbolic of high-status Bengali repertory: Tagore is a significant figure for personifying early 'East-meets-West' cultural encounters. He is well known for his travels from Bangladesh to Britain, where he was schooled, and his journeys across Europe and Asia. His music is widely accepted to have been consciously influenced by Anglo-European musical culture and aesthetics. Tagore's songs are also significant because they are considered a 'traditional' canon, while being straightforwardly attributable to an educated, elite artisan. In other words, they come from a culture where the differentiation of 'folk/pop/art' are diffuse and complicated, in what is perhaps an interesting parallel with Bishi's own genre-crossing activities.

Cosmopolitan Englishness

The instrumentation and compositional techniques employed throughout the album, including those discussed above, combine to form meaningful and contrasting musical soundscapes and symbologies indicative of a wide-ranging, cosmopolitan aesthetic. Among numerous others, the Bengali 'component' of Bishi's multicultural Englishness plays a central role in the album's aesthetic palette. The Indian Englishness performed through the imagery of the singer's visual artwork and costume is echoed in the manifestations of distinctively Indian musical sounds that can be heard throughout the album. The sitar – that most recognizably Indian of instruments for Western audiences – appears in a number of places on the album, but is foregrounded most conspicuously in the title track and, most visibly, in the video of that track. The sitar is one of a number of features (including octave and unison glissando strings) that are instrumental in evoking raga-like melodies and modalities throughout the album, and such evocations are often structural, signalling new sections in a number of tracks ('Albion Voice'; 'Rade La Muri Rade'; 'The Last of England'). The thoroughly Euro-American aesthetics of 'The Last of England', for example – driven by a gentle diatonic ostinato figure on piano – are suddenly disrupted when the last moments of a (now familiar) vocal phrase are altered to include a flattened (rather than natural) supertonic, creating a subtle, fleeting, and markedly 'exotic' semitone dissonance with an inner vocal part.[7]

The significance of the pitches liberally evoked by the final third of the track (pitches of the *mayamalavagowla* raga in Carnatic music, or *bhairav* in the Hindustani tradition) lies in the fact that it is (in Western terms) akin to a double harmonic mode (that is, it contains the pitches of a major scale, but with flattened second and sixth degrees), and carries strong associations with a number of non-Western music cultures (also including, for example, Klezmer). Thus, the musical structure of the work offers to Western listeners a decidedly – but generically – Eastern soundscape. The 'exotic other' is also audible in the presence of the duduk – an Armenian woodwind instrument – in this track. This instrument, with its soft, distinctive tone, has been a touchstone of the 'world music' genre since its regular appearances on, for example, Peter Gabriel's early Real World Records albums, and its semiotic impact here is as an icon of a generically non-Western soundscape.

Aside from the linguistic and repertorical signification of Bishi's Bengali descent, alternative 'others' also make an appearance in the voices she adopts through the album. Specifically, Bishi evokes Eastern Europe through her performance of the traditional Bulgarian love song 'Rade Le Muri Rade' (in its original language), while Biblical Greek is placed alongside Milton's poetry in 'Di Ti Maria'. Her vocal performances on the album also invoke 'others' that are held up in contradistinction to conventionally white English voices. Ornamentation characteristic of Indian classical vocal performance can be heard in Bishi's singing throughout the album; the Bulgarian theme is introduced early on, with a multitracked vocal accompaniment to Chaucer's lines that is a cappella, employing open fifths, homophonic movement and glottal articulations that imitate closely the sounds of the Bulgarian State Television Female Vocal Choir, who found fame in the West through the success of the popular 1975 album *Le Mystère des Voix Bulgares* (The Mystery Of The Bulgarian Voices).

The album brings together such musical others with elements more associated with a Western art music canon; most notably it features no fewer than three string quartets, two of which (the Kronos Quartet and the Ligeti Quartet) also demonstrate cosmopolitan tendencies in that they are international in their scope, and make a feature of musical 'openness', regularly working with artists outside the classical music world and often presenting new music at the avant-garde end of the classical repertory.

The statement of a cosmopolitan Englishness is made visual by one of the striking costumes to be worn by Bishi in the videos and live performances of the album: a corseted gown made from a patchwork of three flags. The Union Jack predominates, accompanied by the English cross of St George, and the saffron and green of the Indian flag. We might compare this with an earlier appearance of the flag in a multicultural popular musical context; the T-shirt worn by another Asian English artist, Sonya Aurora Madan of Echobelly in the 1990s. Madan's customized T-shirt scrawled 'my home too' under a Union Jack entitled 'England'. This was presented later in interview as an angry political statement: 'This T-shirt is a reaction to the BNP [British National Party]. I wanted to make it clear that I won't be put into a victim role. Nobody's going to kick me out of the country' (unpublished Music magazine poster, 1990s).

In comparison, Bishi's claiming of an Englishness where the British, English and Indian flags combine in a glamorous ball gown reads more as a harmonious celebration of a meeting place for those symbols of nation. The endorsement of a harmonious postcolonial relationship between the UK and the Indian Subcontinent is also the underpinning value of the Southbank Alchemy Festival, at which Bishi was a performer in 2015: 'The Festival celebrates the rich cultural relationship between the UK and the Indian Subcontinent, and explores the creative influences generated by our shared history' (Southbank Centre 2015a).

The disruptive voices and images of Bishi

While it might be reasonable to assume that the *Albion Voice* referred to in Bishi's title is primarily a reference to her expression of a complexly English subjectivity, it is important to consider the specific nature of Bishi's vocal contributions on the album, since they are analogous to the complexity of the English identity she asserts. Significantly, her many voices, along with the imagery that accompanies her on the album artwork and in the staging of her performances, articulate a number of cross-cutting disruptions to key loci of discourse around English identity.

Most apparent is the disruption of an Englishness narrative built around conventional constructions of ethno-nationhood. The particular role of Bishi's voice in this process is marked. For instance, the multiple – and disparate – languages in which Bishi sings on the album: 'English, Bengali, Bulgarian and Biblical Greek' (Southbank Centre 2015b), are indicative of the wide cultural reach Bishi claims for her Englishness. Given that the dual aspect of Bishi's vocal performance – and identity as an artist – is so explicitly underpinned by the juxtaposition of Englishness with the Bengali 'other' of her family's nativity in the refrain 'I am Indian in skin, but English of heart', it is notable that the Bengali language itself appears on just one track on the album – the Tagore song 'Gram Chara'. Bishi's intimacy with this language and genre is nonetheless emphasized by the way in which the song is performed – as a duet with her mother.

Elsewhere, Bishi's adoption of multiple voices is made more direct and instantaneous: much of the album involves exploration of choral performance, although this is most commonly in the form of a synthetic choir, constructed via the sampling and multitracking of Bishi's voice to create dense textures and harmonies. The Bulgarian reference in the 'Prologue' is just one example of this: Laurie Anderson-style electronic manipulations of her multitracked voice also appear in the tracks 'Di Ti Maria' and 'Do Not Stand at My Grave and Weep'. In the latter of these instances, Bishi's multiplied voice takes on an instrumental accompaniment role, reciting vocables and closed-mouth humming beneath a lead vocal line, but only after the multitracking technique has been foregrounded in a lead-in of more than thirty seconds. Such a dialogue between solo and multiplied versions of Bishi's voice is mirrored by the integral role that solo and multiplied images of Bishi play in her performance and wider profile. For example, as already discussed, the *Albion Voice* album is accompanied by photographic artwork comprising posed portraits of Bishi playing different historical roles. The audio-visual stage show of *Albion Voice* features several extravagant changes of costume, and kaleidoscopic multiple identical images of Bishi are projected behind and across her body as she performs live. Through these musical and creative devices, then, Bishi moves – audibly and visually – in and out of multiple personae, which has the effect of reinforcing her centrality as author of the work (emphasized by playful evocation of the 'diva' figure), while simultaneously disrupting the singularity of her subjective position.

Her multilingual and multivocal characteristics notwithstanding, Bishi spends the majority of the album singing in the English language, with an unmistakably English accent. The particular variety of English accent is significant for this discussion: unlike the English voices commonly associated with British popular music, Bishi's is not a regional or working-class accent, but one characterized by Received Pronunciation (RP).[8] Her vowels are rounded and elongated; her consonants are precisely articulated; overall, her diction is clear, verging on theatrically self-conscious. Bishi's voice is essentially the voice of the affluent and educated classes of middle England, and far from the vernaculars more widely heard (and associated with national identities such as Britpop) within popular music. And we argue here that there is a deep level of significance to Bishi's performance of the 'Queen's English'. This is mirrored in the visual imagery of the 'Indian Queen' in the CD's artwork, described earlier.

Accents are widely understood as powerful symbols of class and political status, but pronunciation is held by linguists to be particularly significant in British society. Cruttenden suggests that the British demonstrate an 'extreme sensitivity' to the pronunciation of the English language, 'not paralleled in ... other parts of the English speaking world' (1994: 76). In the case of English RP, Upton acknowledges that 'a commonly-held view persists that RP is a very narrow [upper-]class-based and region-based variety of English pronunciation' (2008: 238). Specifically, RP's strong associations with aristocracy and the bourgeois, 'public-schooled' (read 'privately educated') ruling classes of the Southeast have meant that the accent's presence in creative performances is usually indexically linked to 'establishment'-oriented or elite-sponsored activities (see e.g. Hughes, Trudgill and Watt 2013: 11). Regardless of a performer's natural speaking voice, the conscious use of Received Pronunciation is considered best practice for the performance of most high-status English-language choral repertory in Britain, such as that found in churches and 'high-art' concert venues.

Bishi's RP here, then, represents disruptions of multiple narratives. On the one hand, it plays a very personal and humanizing role in the momentary suspension of generic boundaries; that is to say, her voice contrasts starkly with the popular cultural memes of the album, the singer-songwriter, the guitar-strut (although in the case of Bishi's shows, it is very strikingly a sitar that is being played from a stood position, with a shoulder strap), and so forth. Similarly, her fluency with Chaucer and Milton speaks of a particular kind of elite cultural capital. In these ways, Bishi's voice combines with her performance modes and contexts to articulate – literally – a liminal space between the resilient vernacular/elite dualisms enshrined in the resilient taxonomic principles of staged performance in England.

Beyond this, however, there is a more subtle – but arguably more significant – disruption of hierarchies of class and race. Taken together with the photographic works discussed above, this recalls the creative subversion of the white-elite conflation that can be found in the art work of Yinka Shonibare, and claimed by Bishi as one of the inspirations for *Albion Voice*. For example, in the photographic exhibition *Diary of a Victorian Dandy* the British-Nigerian artist is pictured as a Victorian aristocrat in a series of nineteenth-century stately-home settings (Yinka Shonibare MBE 2010).

Finally, the prominence of Bishi's RP is significant in the context of her exploration and articulation of a strongly individualized Englishness. Literature concerned with the mediated voice in popular culture generally holds to the assumption that an identifiably regional (and, implicitly, working class) accent bestows upon the performer a claim of authenticity, denoting legitimate authority to speak on real-world experiences, knowledge and values (e.g. Beal 2009: 2). Coupland discusses how:

> Vernacularity of speech generally implies localness and embedding in a social milieu, sometimes with the implication that the milieu in question is where a speaker was first socialized. But vernaculars are also taken to be 'nonstandard' ways of speaking (Wolfram and Schilling-Estes 1998), echoing early use of the term vernacular to distinguish a local, everyday, 'on-the-ground' language from a superposed, high-prestige 'standard'. ... As a result, vernacular ways of speaking have readily taken on value-laden connotations of authentic cultural being and belonging, at least for some sociolinguists. (2009: 284)

By contrast, then, Bishi's RP represents a thoroughly standardized English voice, which not only disrupts common perceptions of vocal authenticity (as inalienable from the local, regional, working-class voice) but also throws into sharp relief the extensive heterophony of other sounds and images from which the album is created.

Cosmopolitanism, national identity and the Englishness of Bishi

Bishi's *Albion Voice* is an active and purposeful artistic renegotiation and articulation of the singer's Englishness and, by extension, an open exploration of the possibilities of national identity in a contemporary, multicultural England. References to England are found not only in the album's title and title track, but throughout the track titles and lyrics, and in the imagery surrounding the recording and performances. That said, hers is by no means the only creative exploration of a hybridized Englishness: the English folk-based project 'Imagined Village' represents another recent, and well-scrutinized musical exploration of a contemporary English identity that is presented as inherently – albeit problematically – multicultural (see Lucas 2013; Winter and Keegan-Phipps 2013: 146–52). *Albion Voice*, however, holds some significant implications for the construction and expression of such an identity, resulting from the unique intersection of the artist's personal subjectivities, performance modes and contexts. First of these is the unusual extent to which Bishi has framed her work – and her Englishness – as so explicitly cosmopolitan. Beyond the specific and vastly disparate soundscapes and literatures invoked over the course of the album, the context in which Bishi's work has been presented also frames it in terms of both aesthetic and social cosmopolitanism. For example, in 2012 music from the album was included in the soundtrack to Julien Temple's documentary film *London: The Modern Babylon*. The explication of an apparently utopian cosmopolis as the imagined context for this music draws us away from the conception of cosmopolitanism as a conditional response – by which creative artists might be equipped and moved to deploy the cultural resources made available through transnational, cultural globalization – and towards a celebration of both the politics and poetics of those conditions. To some extent, then, Bishi performs cosmopolitanism not as an alignment with a transnational genre (e.g. Feld 2012), or as a purely mobilizing structure for the performance of local politics (e.g. Turino 2000; Webster-Kogen 2014), but rather as an aesthetic in itself. When Bishi sings 'bewildering world' (in the chorus and outro of 'Albion Voice'), the word 'bewildering' is accented, elongated and ornamented: the performance, however, is one of an artist in secure control of the multiple contradictions and tropes she calls up. She seems to be embracing the potentially 'bewildering' multiplicity of identities, just as they are embraced in her work though her multiple costume changes, many impersonations of iconic historical English and British national icons, and the multiple Bishis of her kaleidoscopic image projections.

Secondly, Bishi is a rare example of an individual – and, in particular, a woman – presented as author of such musical cosmopolitanism. To a significant extent, Bishi's claim to nationhood through *Albion Voice* is made diffuse by the fact that hers is a very personal claim, rather than seeking to articulate the communally derived consensus of a group (contrasting with e.g. the work of the 'Imagined Village', Winter and Keegan-Phipps 2013: 146–52), or a part of a unified performer–audience movement (as seen in Turino 2000; Feld 2012). There is no indication that she overtly seeks to connect with an audience with specifically shared – or even similar – heritage or experiences, but rather, perhaps, an audience with shared values (inclined towards the celebration of a diverse, inclusive and destabilized view of nationhood) and a shared – cosmopolitanist – aesthetic. Collectivity is nonetheless present, but articulated through the performer's own multiplied voices and images, within the recorded album and during live/ video performances respectively, which effect a significant disruption of the simplistic individual–collective dualism that might commonly be invoked to narrate the formulation or experience of national (or any other) identity.

It is notable, however, that the album finishes with a track ('Ship of Fools') in which collective voices are also achieved naturally, through the employment of two discrete choirs of singers: here, the closing section features a stark juxtaposition between the homophonic chordal accompaniment from a choral group (named in the sleeve notes as Acapella Rising), and the closing refrain, sung in unison by a 'rougher', more vernacular sounding chorus – referred to in the CD's inlay as a 'pub choir'. This final moment of collective voicing points to a third significant element of Bishi's cosmopolitanism: the fact that the hybridities incorporated in the album operate across and between the conventionally opposing constructs of 'elite' cosmopolitanisms – wherein eclecticism is the celebrated luxury of the privileged cultural 'traveller' – and the 'rooted' or vernacular cosmopolitanisms sought by the ethnographers of lived multicultural experience (e.g. Turino, Feld, et al.). The work is, in this way, remarkable for problematizing (if not dissolving) the class-based dualisms that dominate literature on these themes.

Beyond the artistic impact of a standardized voice in the context of a work which celebrates hybridity, discussed above, the foregrounding of RP may seem paradoxical in a work primarily focused on the destabilization of any homogenous narrative of national identity. An interesting answer to this conundrum, however, may lie in the fact that RP's normative impact has long been felt beyond England's shores, and can also be understood as an index of modernist – capitalist globalization, particularly within colonial contexts: Karpf points to the requirement for workers in Indian call centres to master the RP accent (2006: 193). In this way, the voice contributes to a transnational cosmopolitanism. Simultaneously, the album is a more potent exploration of Englishness precisely because the author is not audibly tied (i.e. by a distinctly local accent) to any one region of it.

Bishi's renegotiation of Englishness through this album is also significant since it expands the transnational narrative of cosmopolitan aesthetic borrowing, to evoke not only 'other' places and cultures, but also other (historical) times. Bishi's invocation of 'ancient' – including folk and traditional – cultural materials from England, India and Europe, suggests an inclusive aesthetic that forges *post hoc* connections and resonances, and disturbs those essentializing discourses that commonly articulate cultural uniqueness via the citation of distinct histories. More specifically, however, the interpolation of her own image into a reimagined iconography of the British Empire represents her complete and inalienable immersion in England's present (and future) through a discursive mastery of England's past. In other words, Bishi's work includes explication of the historicity which is now commonly recognized as integral to the oft-cited theoretical framing of Clifford's 'discrepant cosmopolitanism' (1997: 36) but which is rarely evoked so candidly in cosmopolitan cultural outputs themselves.

In the opening section of our discussion we noted that *Albion Voice* is framed by Bishi as an intervention into a vision of popular musical English identity from which, she observes, women and Asians are largely absent. *Albion Voice*, then, can be understood as a reactive exploration of a more cosmopolitan vision of English identity, characterizing the artist's own Englishness as an identity with multiple connections and attachments that are both outward looking and, at the same time, rooted and invested in a sense of national belonging. This chapter demonstrates the scholarly contribution of a detailed textual and contextual analysis in revealing the complexities of such a project: it demonstrates a nexus of artistic mechanisms and semiotic devices, whereby a range of discursive disruptions have effected the (re)framing of cosmopolitanism as simultaneously – and emphatically – personal identity, political message and cultural aesthetic.

Notes

1 For example, as Dyadphonic with Martin Green.

2 'In Sleep' (2014), collaboration with composer Neil Kaczor, commissioned by Science Gallery London.

3 Such as for the silent film *Salome* (1923), commissioned by the British Film Institute.

4 For an overview of the study of cosmopolitanism see Delanty (ed.), 2012.

5 It should be acknowledged that a number of varieties of Jews harp are also found in Indian musical traditions, but these are not so iconic of that part of the world as, for instance, the sitar, and are more readily associated by Western listeners with the musical arcana of the Anglophone world.

6 Britannia's indexical relationship with empire is routinely reiterated in the lyrics of the euphoric anthem *Rule Britannia*, which speaks in no uncertain terms of her military dominance upon the high seas (and, therefore, across the maritime globe).

7 The interval of a flattened second is regularly acknowledged in world and popular music scholarship as mobilizing clear associations with 'the East'. The flattened second degree has been explored, for example, as a signifier of 'Mediterranean tonality' by Manuel (1989: 75), and as a significant feature of Indian classical music by Martinez (2001). More recently, the meanings – including orientalist connotations – of the 'flat 2 [two with a hat … can't render here!]' have been more comprehensively reviewed by Moore (2014).

8 Moy (2007) makes the common claim that 'almost every English singer in popular music sounds, if not actually North American, then at least "transatlantic"' (53). It is true that American pronunciation is still rife in

English popular music but we cannot, however, ignore the enormous upsurge of artists during the first decade of the twenty-first century who have made prominent use of their 'local' accents – specifically the Estuary English of Lily Allen, Kate Nash and Dizzee Rascal.

References

Appiah, K. A. (1997), 'Cosmopolitan Patriots', *Critical Inquiry*, 23(3): 617–39.

Beal, J. C. (2009), '"You're Not from New York City, You're from Rotherham": Dialect and Identity in British Indie Music', *Journal of English Linguistics*, 37(3): 223–40.

Bhabha, H. K. (1994), *The Location of Culture*, London: Routledge.

Bilby, K. (1999), '"Roots Explosion": Indigenization and Cosmopolitanism in Contemporary Surinamese Popular Music', *Ethnomusicology*, 43(2): 256–96.

Binnie, J., J. Holloway, S. Millington and C. Young (eds) (2006), *Cosmopolitan Urbanism*, Abingdon: Routledge.

Bishi (2012), Bishiworld, 4 January. Available online: http://bishiworld.blogspot. co.uk/2012_04_01_archive.html. (accessed 28 July 2016).

Bishi Electronic Press Kit (2008), [Website]. Available online: www.sonicbids.com (accessed 23 June 2013).

Bracewell, M. (1997), *England is Mine: Pop Life in Albion from Wilde to Goldie*, London: HarperCollins.

Cheah, P. and B. Robbins (1998), *Cosmopolitics: Thinking and Feeling Beyond the Nation*, Minneapolis: University of Minnesota Press.

Choudhury, I. (2015), 'Connecting the Circle: Musician Bishi talks about her sound', *Eastern Eye*, 1 May. Available online: https://www.easterneye.eu/ entertainment/detail/connecting-the-circle-musician-bishi-talks-about-her-sound (accessed 22 May 2015).

Clifford, J. (1997), *Routes: Travel and Translation in the Late Twentieth Century*, Cambridge, MA: Harvard University Press.

Cohen, M. (1992), 'Rooted Cosmopolitanism: Thoughts on the left, nationalism and multiculturalism', *Dissent*, Autumn: 478–83.

Coupland, N. (2009), 'The Mediated Performance of Vernaculars', *Journal of English Linguistics*, 37(3): 284–300.

Cruttenden, A. (1994), *Gimson's Pronunciation of English*, 5th edn. London: Arnold.

Delanty, G. (ed.) (2012), *The Routledge Handbook of Cosmopolitanism Studies*, Abingdon: Routledge.

Feld, S. (2012), *Jazz Cosmopolitanism in Acraa: Five Musical Years in Ghana*, Durham, NC: Duke University Press.

Gray, A. (2012), 'Putting The Black in the Union Jack', *Louise Gray*, 23 April. Available online: https://louisegray.net/2012/04/23/putting-the-black-in-the-union-jack/ (accessed 23 May 2013).

Hughes, A., P. Trudgill and D. Watt (2013), *English Accents and Dialects*, 5th edn. London: Routledge.

Karpf, A. (2006), *The Human Voice: The Story of a Remarkable Talent*, London: Bloomsbury.

Liverani, M. (2010), Vogue, 30 September. Available online: http://www.vogue.it/en/vogue-curvy/glam-and-curvy/2010/09/bishi (accessed 23 May 2013).

London: The Modern Babylon (2012), [Film] Dir. Julien Temple, London: BBC Films; The BFI; Nitrate.

Lucas, C. (2013), 'The Imagined Folk of England: Whiteness, Folk Music and Fascism', Critical Race and Whiteness Studies, 9(1): 1–19.

Magaldi, C. (2009), 'Cosmopolitanism and World Music in Rio de Janeiro at the Turn of the Twentieth Century', The Musical Quarterly, 92(3–4): 329–64.

Manuel, P. (1989), 'Modal Harmony in Andalusian, Eastern European, and Turkish Syncretic Musics', Yearbook for Traditional Music, 21: 70–94.

Martínez, J. L. (2001), Semiosis in Hindustani Music, Delhi: Motilal Banarsidass.

Moore, S. (2014), The Other Leading Note: A Comparative Study of the Flat Second Pitch Degree in North Indian Classical, Ottoman or Arabian Influenced, Western, Heavy Metal and Film Musics. PhD thesis, University of Sheffield.

Moy, R. (2007), Kate Bush and Hounds of Love, Aldershot: Ashgate.

Nava, M. (2002), 'Cosmopolitan modernity: everyday imaginaries and the register of difference', Theory, Culture and Society, 19: 81–99.

Regev, M. (2007), 'Cultural Uniqueness and Aesthetic Cosmopolitanism', European Journal of Social Theory, 10(1): 123–38.

Royal Collection Trust (2016), 'Dorothy Wilding', Royal Collection Trust. Available online: https://www.royalcollection.org.uk/exhibitions/the-queen-portraits-of-a-monarch/dorothy-wilding (accessed 28 July 2016).

Royster, F. T. (2012), Sounding Like a No-no: queer sounds and eccentric acts in the post-soul era, Ann Arbor: University of Michigan Press.

Southbank Centre (2015a), 'Alchemy', Southbank Centre. Available online: http://www.southbankcentre.co.uk/whatson/festivals-series/alchemy-2015 (accessed 28 July 2016).

Southbank Centre (2015b), 'Bishi', Southbank Centre. Available online: http://www.southbankcentre.co.uk/whatson/bishi-91435 (accessed: 28 July 2016).

Stokes, M. (2007), 'On Musical Cosmopolitanism', The Macalester International Roundtable 2007. Available online: http://digitalcommons.macalester.edu/intlrdtable/3 (accessed 1 July 2016).

The Nest Collective (2016), 'Bishi', The Nest Collective. Available online: http://thenestcollective.co.uk/artist/bishi/ (accessed 28 May 2016).

Turino, T. (2000), Nationalists, Cosmopolitans, and Popular Music in Zimbabwe, Chicago: University of Chicago Press.

Upton, C. (2008), 'Received Pronunciation', in B. Kortmann and C. Upton (eds), Varieties of English: The British Isles. Berlin: Mouton de Gruyter.

Webster-Kogen, I. (2014), 'Song Style as Strategy: Nationalism, Cosmopolitanism and Citizenship in The Idan Raichel Project's Ethiopian-influenced Songs', Ethnomusicology Forum, 23(1): 27–48.

Werbner, P. (1999), 'Global Pathways. Working class cosmopolitans and the creation of transnational ethnic worlds', Social Anthropology, 7: 17–35.

Wikibin (2008), 'Kashpoint', Wikibin. Available online: http://wikibin.org/articles/kashpoint.html (accessed 28 July 2016).

Williams, R. (1973), The Country and the City, Chatto and Windus Ltd. Reprint, St Albans: Paladin [1975].

Winter, T. and S. Keegan-Phipps (2013), *Performing Englishness: Identity and Politics in a Contemporary Folk Resurgence*, Manchester: Manchester University Press.

Yinka Shonibare MBE (2010), [Website], Diary of a Victorian Dandy, Available online: https://africa.si.edu/exhibits/shonibare/dandy.html (accessed 31 July 2016).

Discography

Bishi (2007) *Nights at the Circus*, UK: Gryphon [Album]
Bishi (2012) *Albion Voice*, UK: Gryphon, [Album]
Marcel Cellier [compiler] (1975) *Le Mystère des Voix Bulgares*, Switzerland: Disques Cellier, [Album]

INDEX

ABC   117
Adorno, Theodor   43
Albarn, Damon   7, 165, 178
Allen, Lilly   5, 7, 208
Almond, Marc   7
Althusser, Louis   107, 115
Americanization   126, 129
Anderson, Benedict   49, 136
Anderson, Perry   127
Angelou, Maya   166
Angry Young Men   25
Archive Fever   38, 67
Arthur Nelson Group, The   94
Arts Council   151
Ashley, Laura   27
Asian Dub Foundation   137
avant garde   163
'avant-pastism'   184

Banksy   31
Barnes, Julian   30
Baschet, Bernard   92
BBC   xiv, 1, 2, 6, 8, 11, 88, 89, 90, 91,
    92, 93, 96, 98, 99, 147, 148, 176,
    178, 179
Beach Boys, The   113, 130
Beatles, The   5, 7, 21–2, 24, 31–2, 41,
    89, 125, 126, 129, 130, 134, 137,
    155, 164
    And I Love Her   41
    I Want To Hold Your Hand   41
    Revolver   170
    *Sgt Pepper's Lonely Hearts Club
        Band* (album)   24, 137
    She Loves You   41
Beatles Story Museum   8
Beck, Jeff   133
Beckenham Arts Lab   39, 46

Beckett, Samuel   36, 42, 44–5, 46, 50
Belbury Poly   8
Belloc, Hilaire   3, 14
Bengali   193, 194, 200, 201, 202
Benjamin, Walter   37–8, 42
Benn, Tony   111, 146
Bevan, Will, *see* Burial
Beyonce   xiv
Bhabha, Homi K.   38
Birmingham   146
Bishi   9, 12, 193–210
    Albion Voice (album)   12, 13,
        193–210
    Albion Voice (song)   194, 196,
        198, 205
    Di Ti Maria   198, 201
    Gram Chara   199, 202
    The Last of England   200
    Indian Queen (photo)   199, 203
    Nights at the Circus   194
Bizu, Izzy   76
Blackadder   30
Blair, Tony   xiv, 136
Blake, James   179
Blake, Peter   129
Blavatsky, Madame   45
Blues   21–2, 25, 27, 69, 78, 163
Blunkett, David   3, 108, 121
Blur   163–5, 169
    Parklife   164
Bomb the Bass   167
Bond, James   23, 60, 170
Bondage (fanzine)   151
Bonham, John   133
Bon Jovi   xiv
Borges, Jorge Luis   76
Boshier, Derek   129, 130
Boulez, Pierre   49

Bowie, David   xiii, 7, 10, 36–50,
      137, 158
   1. *Outside*   45
   Bang Bang   40
   Blackstar   10, 36, 38, 44–7, 50
   China Girl   48
   David Bowie   40, 48
   David Bowie Is... (exhibition)   10
   DJ   40
   Dollar Days   47
   Earthling   40, 47–8
   Five Years   48
   Glass Spider   40
   Hallo Spaceboy   44, 47
   The Heart's Filthy Lesson   40
   Heroes   43, 44, 46, 158
   Jump They Say   41
   Laughing Gnome   48
   Lazarus   44, 46
   Let's Dance   40
   Life on Mars   40
   London Boys   48
   Low   46, 47, 158
   The Next Day   10, 36–40, 42–3,
      44, 46–7, 50
   Reality   40
   *The Rise and Fall of Ziggy Stardust
      and the spiders from Mars*   38,
      40, 48
   Rock and Roll Suicide   40
   Sense of Doubt   40
   She's Got Medals   48
   Space Oddity   40, 44
   The Stars (Are Out Tonight)   43
   Sue (Or a Season of Crime)   47
   Sweet Thing   40
Boyd, Joe   126
Boyle, Danny   5
Bragg, Billy   3
Branson, Richard   148, 157
Brexit   xiv, 2
Bricolage   46–8, 50, 167, 171
Brighton Beach   62
Bristol   9, 12, 162
Britannia   199, 207
British Invasion   19, 22, 23, 126
Britishness   xiii, 1, 13, 20, 71, 88, 126,
      138, 162, 170–1, 194

Britpop   128, 135, 136, 137, 162–3,
      166, 169
Brixton   41, 46
Bromley   xiii
Brooke-Partridge, Bernard   151, 152
Brown, Gordon   77
Brown, James   61, 164
Buckler, Rick   58
Buckley, David   48
Bug, The   178, 180
Burial   8, 9, 12, 174–92
   Ghost Hardware   175
   Rival Dealer   178
   South London Boroughs   175, 186
   Untrue   175, 176, 181, 182, 184
Burroughs, William   40, 50, 113
Bush, George W.   xiv
Bush, Kate   70–2
Butler, Judith   41
Buzzcocks   107, 108, 155

Cabaret Voltaire   9, 11, 106–23
   Crackdown, The   116
   Expect Nothing   120
   Just Fascination   117
   Kneel to the Boss   120
   Methodology   113
Cage, John   50
Callaghan, James   145, 147, 150,
      154, 158
Calypso   29
Cameron, David   xiv, 2, 13, 62
Campaign for Nuclear Disarmament
      (CND)   130
Can   108
'capitalist realism'   8
Caretaker, The   8
Carnaby Street   128, 129, 131, 134,
      135
Carter, Angela   126, 127, 138, 194
Carter Family   78
Cavanagh, David   42
Census (UK   2011)   4
Certain Ratio, A   117
Charge of the Light Brigade   136
Chaucer, Geoffrey   3, 198, 201, 204
Cher   xiv
Chesterton, G.K.   3, 14

Church, Charlotte   xiv
Churchill, Winston   27
Church of England   3
Clark, Paul   134
Clash, The   12, 54, 55, 148, 153,
    155, 156, 158
    The Clash   157
    London's Burning   12, 153
    Police and Thieves   7, 157
    Remote Control   157
    White Man in Hammersmith
        (Palais)   158
    White Riot   12, 148, 157
    White Riot (tour)   157
Cleese, John   29
Clemens, Benjamin   62
Clinton, Bill   xiv
Coburn, Anthony   94, 101
Cochrane, Eddie   78
Cocker, Jarvis   7
colonialism   27, 40, 131, 137, 197
Coltrane, John   47
Colyer, Ken   6
Cook, Georgina   176, 177, 181
'Cool Anglia'   163, 165–6, 172
'Cool Britannia'   xiv, 12, 134, 135,
    162–3
Corré, Joe   8
cosmopolitanism   3, 193, 196, 197,
    200–2, 204–7
    'discrepant cosmopolitanism'   197,
    207
Coward, Noel   21
Creation, The   60
Criminal Justice and Public Order
    Bill   7
Cross of St George   70, 166, 201
Crowley, Alastair   45
Cure, The   167

Daily Mirror   150
Daily Telegraph   3, 135
Dalyell, Tam   13
Daniels, Phil   164
Davies, Dave   20
Davies, Ray   7, 10, 19–31, 60, 63
Davis, Miles   47
Debord, Guy   149

Deleuze, Gilles, and Felix Guattari   43
Depeche Mode   167
Derbyshire, Delia   90, 92
Derrida, Jacques   11, 37–8, 67, 96
Desert Island Discs   xiv, 61
detournement   130, 132
Dickens, Charles   20
Diddley, Bo   164
Difford, Chris   7
Digital Mystikz   175
Disc   131
Dixon of Dock Green   93, 98
Dizzee Rascal   5, 208
DJ-Kicks   176, 185
Doctor Who   11, 85–99
    TARDIS   88, 93, 95, 96, 97
    An Unearthly Child   85, 91, 94,
        95, 98
Donegan, Lonnie   6
Dorset   9, 78
Douglas, Andrew   62
Drabble, Margaret   147
Dublin   131
dubstep   12, 174–92
Dury, Ian   7, 72

Ealing Art School   129
Ealing Studios   97
Eco, Umberto   131
Ed Sullivan show   125
Elbow   177
Electronica   41, 163
Electronishe Musik   89
Eliot, T.S.   27
EMI records   150, 151, 156
Empire, Kitty   71, 77
empire   127, 128, 133, 134, 138, 146,
    198, 199, 206
English   18–32, 36–50, 68–79,
    162–72
English, Michael   129
English Defence League (EDL)   3
Eno, Brian   107, 112
Entwistle, John   131
Epstein, Brian   125
Eric B & Rakim   165
ESG   165
Evening Standard   150, 151

Factory Records   109, 117
Fagandini, Maddalena   89
Fairport Convention   28
Fall, The   116
Fallowell, Duncan   134
Farm, The   167
Faust   108
Fawlty, Basil   30
Fawlty Towers   24
Feld Steven   197
Festival of Britain   135
Field, Frank   3
Fisher, Mark   6, 176, 190
Flanagan and Allen   40
Flying Lotus   176, 177, 178, 185
Folk   24–8, 68, 69–70, 72–3, 79
Foreman, Susan   85, 94, 95
Four Lads, The   78
Four Tet   178, 179
Fox, Kate   20
Foxton, Bruce   58, 59
Freud, Sigmund   98

Gabriel, Peter   201
Gallagher, Noel   xiv, 7
Garage (UK)   184
Gartside, Green   114
Gender   7, 41, 68, 73, 74, 76, 95, 158, 165, 190, 196
Ghost Box Records   8
Gilbert and George   40
Gilroy, Paul   7, 126, 129
Glammore, Matthew   195
God Save the Queen (anthem)   163
Goldfrapp, Alison   164, 166
Gothic Blues   68
Graham, Kenneth   23
Grainer, Ron   92
Gramsci, Antonio   58, 107, 114, 115, 154
Granny Takes A Trip   133
Great Britain   146
Great Exhibition   135
Griffin, Nick   3, 14
Grundy, Bill   150, 151, 156
Gryphon Records   195
Guardian, The   69
Guns at Batasi   136
Gysin, Brion   40

Habermas, Jürgen   150
Hall, Stuart   127, 128, 138, 154
Hancox, Dan   122, 123
Haphash and the Coloured Coat   129
Harden, Matthew   195
Hardy, Thomas   66
Harrison, George   126
Hartnell, William   94, 95
Harvey, P.J.   9, 11, 66–79
    Battleship Hill   78
    The Colour of the Earth   76
    The Devil   72–3, 75
    In the Dark Places   78
    Let England Shake   11, 66–7, 68, 71, 72, 75–6, 77, 79
    Stories from the City, Stories from the Sea   68, 73, 74
    White Chalk   11, 66–9, 72–6, 79
hauntology   8, 187–9
Healey, Denis   111, 146
Heaven 17   108, 117, 121
Heddon Street   38
Heffer, Simon   2
Hendrix, Jimi   133
High Numbers, The   57
Hindess, Barry   114, 115
hip hop   166, 167
Hirst, Paul   114, 115
Hobbs, Mary Anne   176, 177, 178
Hockney, David   129
Hodgson, Brian   90, 93, 95, 96
Höldein, Friedrich   47
Holmes, Sherlock   31, 98
Howell, Peter   111
Human League   108, 117, 121
Hyperdub   175, 178, 179

Image, The   40
Immediate Records   60
imperial   27, 126, 129, 136, 137, 172, 198, 199
imperialism   129, 137
Independent, The   36, 46, 176, 177
independent record labels   156
Independent Television (ITV)   151
India   194, 199, 202, 206
    Indian flag   201
industrial metal   167
Inner Circle   170

Internationale 49
International Monetary Fund
    (IMF) 145
Ireland 138
Irish Republican Army (IRA) 131, 146
I Was Lord Kitchener's Valet 133

Jackman, Hugh 40
Jackson, Michael 166
Jam, The 7, 9 10, 54–64, 71, 136, 137
    All Around the World 58, 59
    All Mod Cons (album) 59, 60
    All Mod Cons (song) 61
    Away from the Numbers 56, 59
    Billy Hunt 60
    Burning Sky 63
    Combine, The 59
    David Watts 60
    English Rose 61
    Eton Rifles, The 60, 62, 63
    Here Comes the Weekend 59
    In the City 56
    In the Crowd 61
    In the Street Today 59
    Life from a Window 59
    Little Boy Soldiers 62
    London Girl 59
    London Traffic 59
    Mr Clean 60
    Private Hell 63
    Saturday's Kids 63
    Setting Sons 62, 63
    Smithers-Jones 63
    Standards 59
    This is the Modern World 58
    Time for Truth 56
    *To Be Someone (Didn't We Have A
        Nice Time?)* 61
James, Richard D. 177, 182, 187
jingoism 62, 129, 145
John, Elton xiv
Johns, Jasper 130
Jones, Colin 126
Jones, David 41
Jones, Mick 153
Jones, Steve 151
Joseph, Keith 110, 111, 121, 146
Joy Division 6, 109, 117
Juke Box Jury 88

Kane, Art 132
Kash Point (club) 194, 195
Kassner Music 21
Kay, Norman 94
Kearney, Martha 148
Kemp, Gary 38
Khartoum 136
King Crimson 75
Kingsley, Reverend James 152
Kinks, The 5, 7, 10, 17–32, 56, 60,
        63, 165
    *Acute Paranoia Schizophrenic
        Blues* 27
    All My friends Were There 29
    Animal Farm 29
    Apeman 29
    *Arthur: (Or the Decline and Fall of
        the British Empire)* 26
    Autumn Almanac 25
    Big Black Smoke 29
    Come Dancing 10
    Dead End Street 28
    Dedicated Follower of Fashion 28
    Exclusive Residence for Sale 29
    Face in the Crowd 29
    Face to Face 21
    Have a Cup of Tea 26
    House in the Country 29
    *The Kinks are the Village Green
        Preservation Society* 21, 23, 26,
        27, 31, 63
    *The Last of the Steam Powered
        Trains* 26
    Low Budget 29
    Mr Pleasant 29
    Muswell Hillbillies 23
    Phenomenal Cat 26
    *Rosy, Won't You Please Come
        Home* 29
    Shangri-La 26
    Sitting in my Hotel 29
    Something Else 21
    Sunny Afternoon 29
    Victoria 26, 27
    Village Green 30
    Waterloo Sunset 29, 42
    Well Respected Man 24
    Wicked Annabella 23, 26
    Yes Sir No Sir 26

Kipling, Rudyard   20
Kirk, Richard H   107, 112, 113,
        114, 116
Kode   9   8, 175, 178, 184, 187, 188
Kraftwerk   158
Krautrock   108
KRS-One   170

Labour Party   3, 145, 146, 147, 158
   New Labour   xiv
Ladbroke Grove   115
Lamar, Kendrick   47
Lambert, Kit   131, 138
Lambert, Verity   92, 93, 95
Lasry, Jacques   92
Latham, Jack   122
Legend, John   xiv
Lennon, John   7, 41
Lévi-Strauss, Claude   185
Libertines, The   71
Lib-Lab Pact   145, 158–9
Life (magazine)   131, 132
Lime Grove   91, 97
Limit, The   108, 121
Lloyd, Harold   51
Lodge, Bernard   93
London   3, 9, 12, 13, 19, 22–4, 31, 32,
        55, 60, 85, 87, 88, 92, 93, 97, 98,
        126, 128, 131, 133, 134, 135,
        136, 138, 162, 179–80, 181, 186,
        190, 193, 194
London: The Modern Babylon   11,
        195, 205
Love, Courtney   70
Lyceum Theatre   108
Lydon, John   55, 138, 148, 151, 153,
        154, 155, 156, 157, 159

McCartney, Paul   25
McCaslin, Donny   46
McCreary, Mary   165
MacDonald, Ian   50
MacGowan, Shane   138, 151
MacInnes, Colin   127
McLaren, Malcolm   56, 116, 149, 154
McQueen, Alexander   40, 48
Madan, Sonya Aurora   201
Madonna   xiv
mal d'archive   37, 38

Mallinder, Stephen   108, 112, 120
Manchester   9
Marley, Bob   172
Marr, Johnny   xiv
Marseillaise, La   49
Martin, George   89
Martin, Ricky   xiv
Marvin, Junior   7
Marx, Karl   107, 111, 115, 118, 119
   Grundrisse   107, 118
Marxism   3, 4, 106–19
Massive Attack   184
May, Theresa   xiv, 2, 21
Mayes, Sean   50
Melly, George   5, 133
Melody Maker   55, 130, 132, 137
Mercury Music Prize   66–8, 76,
        176, 177
Merry Xmas Mr Lawrence   48
Miller, Daniel   6
Miller, Roger   23
Mills, Dick   92
Milton, John   198, 204
minimalist   44, 46–7, 50, 164
Mishima, Yukio   40
Moby   xiv
Mockney   164
mod   xi, 10, 12, 22, 23, 54–65, 128,
        130, 131, 132, 134, 135, 138,
        139, 165
Mojo   137
Mollona, Massimiliano   119, 120
monarchy   1, 3, 128, 136, 138
Moody Blues, The   75
Moon, Keith   126, 131, 132
Moreton, Cole   46
Morris, William   72
Moy Ron   72
Morrissey   7, 137
Motown   22, 165
Murphy, Seamus   68, 72, 77–8
musique concrete   89
Mute Records   6

Nairn, Tom   2, 127
National Front   60, 135, 138
nationalism   2, 3, 5, 7, 50, 69, 127,
        135, 136, 138, 197
National Service   133

Native American Chief   165
Neville, Richard   133
New Labour   162, 164
New Left Review   127
Newley, Anthony   47, 48, 50
Newman, Sydney   88
New Musical Express (NME)   5, 7, 43, 57, 60, 137, 176
New Order   117
New Year's Honours' List   32
New York   132, 134
Niney the Observer   78
Nipple Erectors, The   151
Nirvana   41
Nomi, Klaus   40
Northern Ireland   1, 146

Oasis   xiv, 9, 135, 136, 137
Obama, Barack   xiv
Observer, The   127, 131, 136
Observer Magazine, The   126, 132
Office of National Statistics (ONS)   4, 14
Olympics, London (2012)   5, 14
Oran, Daphne   89
Orwell, George   3–4, 20, 147, 148, 155
Osborne, John   127
Oshima, Wagisa   48
OZ   133, 134

Page, Jimmy   133
Page, Larry   21
Parekh, Bikhu   77
Partridge, Andy   7
Pasnau, Robert   86
Paxman, Jeremy   20
Peel, John   114, 115
Penman, Ian   8, 9, 190
Perry, Katy   xiv
Petridis, Alexis   69
Phillips, Peter   129
Picasso, Pablo   36, 42
Pierrot   40, 165
Pinfield, Mervyn   93
Pink Floyd   7
Plaid Cymru   146
Plasticman   175
Pogues, The   151
Pop, Iggy   40, 158

pop art   129, 130, 131, 138
Pop Group, The   6
Popside   131
postcolonial   4, 126, 127, 128, 129, 170–2, 194
post-imperial   162, 166
postmodern   41, 45, 127, 162, 169
post-punk   5, 6, 7, 106, 107, 108, 112, 114, 115, 116, 117, 121, 122, 123, 158
Powell, Enoch   5, 14
Presley, Elvis   41, 155
Prestige   40
Priestley, J.B.   20
Prince   165
Princess Margaret   129
Private Eye   xv
Profumo Affair   127
prog rock   155
psychedelia   25
psychedelic   129, 137
Public Enemy   166–7, 169
    Black Steel in the Hour of Chaos   169
    Fight the Power   167
    It Takes a Nation of Millions to Hold us Back   167
Public Image Limited   151, 156
Punch and Judy   78
punk   5, 10, 12, 41, 54–61, 64, 68, 108, 112, 113, 114, 115, 116, 117, 138, 145–61, 166–7
Punk London   7, 8, 14
Purple Flag   129

Quadrophenia   62
Quaife, Peter   20
Quaye, Maxine   163
Queen Elizabeth II   7, 12, 126, 145, 150, 159, 199

race   3, 14, 76, 163, 165–7, 171, 204
Radiodiffusion-Télévision Française   89
Radio Italia   89
Radiophonic Workshop   89, 96, 98
Rahman, A.R.   168
Raincoats, The   115
RCA records   90

Ready Steady Go!   130
Rebel Without a Cause   22
Received Pronunciation
    (RP)   203–4, 206
Red Crayola   114
Redding, Noel   133
Redmond, Sean   42
Reeve, Geoff   129
Reggae   168
Reid, Jamie   10, 56, 57, 63
Reith, John   88
Reithian   88, 89, 94, 98
Renaissance drama   72
retromania   7
Reynolds, Simon   37, 38, 116, 121
rhythm and blues   21, 48
Richard, Cliff   6
Rock Against Racism   7, 155
Roddam, Franc   62
Rodgers, Jude   45
Roland TB303   116
Rolling Stone   151
Rolling Stones, The   5, 7, 21–2, 31,
    132, 150, 155
Ross, Diana   xiv
Rotten, Johnny, *see* Lydon, John
Rough Trade Records   108, 109,
    112, 113, 114, 115, 116, 120,
    121, 157
Roxy Music   6, 107
Royal Air Force (RAF)   130, 131, 132
Rukkumani Rukkuman   168

St George's Day   1, 5, 194
St Pancras records   114
Sarne, Mike   48
Saunders, Mark   167
Savage, Jon   113, 116, 126, 145, 153,
    157, 158
Scotland   1, 13
Scott, Walter   26
Scottish independence
    referendum   2, 13
Scottish National Party   146
Screaming Lord Sutch   133
Scritti Politti   107, 114, 116,
    Cupid and Psyche   116
    Early   114
    Jacques Derrida   114

Search and Destroy   113
Second World War   4, 126, 139, 145,
    146, 147, 153
Select (magazine)   135, 137
Sex Pistols   12, 54, 55, 56, 57, 61, 107,
    145–61
    Anarchy in the UK   57, 63, 153
    Anarchy in the UK (tour)   157
    EMI   157
    God Save the Queen   12, 145, 147,
        148, 153, 157–8
    *Great Rock and Roll Swindle,
        The*   16
    *Never Mind the Bollocks, Here's the
        Sex Pistols*   12, 151, 152
    Pretty Vacant   155, 157
Shaar Murray, Charles   60
Sham   69, 155
Sharpe, Cecil   72
Sheffield   106, 107, 108, 109, 111,
    112, 113, 116, 117, 118, 119,
    120, 121, 122
Sheffield University   108, 112, 118
Sherman, Cindy   74
Sideburns (fanzine)   156
silver jubilee   7, 12, 145, 148, 150,
    153, 159
Simple Minds   117
Sinatra, Frank   5, 40
Sioux, Siouxsie   151, 158
Siouxsie and the Banshees   158
Situationists   149
Slick Rick   165
Slits, The   6, 158
Slumdog Millionaire   49
Small Faces, The   24, 165
Smith, Reginald   89
Smiths, The   xiv, 138
Smyth, Frank   23
Sneaker Pimps   170
Sniffin' Glue (fanzine)   55
Specials, The   172
Spencer, Paul   165
Stars and Stripes (flag)   125, 126
Steele, Tommy   48
Stewart, Rod   148
Stockhausen, Karlheinz   49–50, 89
    Hymnen   49–50
Stone Roses, The   137

Stormzy   137
Story, WPC Dawn   152
Strachey, John   127
Stranglers, The   153
Strummer, Joe   153
Suez crisis   127
Suggs   7
Suicide   108
Sun, The   137, 151, 177, 178, 185
Supremes, The   165
Swell Maps   115
'Swinging London'   128, 131, 133,
      134, 135, 138

Tabor, June   198
Tagore, Rabindranath   200
Talmy, Shel   21
Tempah, Tinie   5
Temporary Hoarding (fanzine)   7
Tennant, Neil   7
Terror Danja   175
Thames Television   149
Thatcher, Margaret   14, 146, 158, 159
Thian, Helene-Marie   48, 50
Thompson, E.P.   3
Thompson, Mayo   114
Thompson Twins   117
Throbbing Gristle   113
Time (magazine)   134
Topley-Bird, Martina   165, 168–9
Torquay   24
Tower Bridge   22
Townshend, Pete   12, 125, 126,
      129, 130, 131, 132, 135, 136,
      138, 139
Travis, Geoff   108, 109, 112, 116
Tricky   8–9, 12, 162–72
      Black Steel   166–9, 171
      Brand New You're Retro   165, 166
      Early Bird   163
      Feed Me   169–72
      Maxinquaye   8–9, 12, 163, 165–6,
         169, 170
      Mixed Race   163, 165
      A Ruff Guide   163, 165, 167
trip hop   168, 184
Trump, Donald   xiii, xiv
Two-Tone records   7
Tyne Tees Television   107, 117

U2   xiv
Union Jack (flag)   10, 11, 12,
      40, 48, 57, 58, 60, 62, 63,
      125–39, 201
United Kingdom Independence Party
      (UKIP)   3
Unwin, Paul   121

Valentine, Dickie   6
V&A Museum   7, 10
Van Dyke, Dick   23
Vanity Fair   134
Vaughan, Sarah   165
Vespa   138
Victorian   22, 23, 24, 73, 74, 75, 137,
      186, 199, 204
Virgin records   152, 157
Virgo   175
Visconti, Tony   43

Wales   1, 4, 13
Walker, Adam   3
Waterson, Norma   198
Watson, Chris   107, 108, 116, 122
Watson, Emma   xiv
Weather Report   28
Weller, Paul   7, 10, 54–64, 71
Westdeutscher Rundfunk   89
West Lothian question   13
Westwood, Vivienne   8, 56
Who, The   6, 7, 12, 56, 57, 60, 65,
      126–8, 130–3, 134, 135, 136,
      137, 138, 139, 165
      Dogs   127
      I'm a Boy   56
      Kids Are Alright, The (film)   132
      My Generation (album)   126
      Quadrophenia   164
Wild One, The   22
Williams, Vaughan   72
Wilson, Harold   130, 134
Wire, The (magazine)   175, 176
Wonder, Stevie   xiv
Worthing   199
Wright, Barbara   94, 97
Wuthering Heights   23
Wyatt, Robert   114

X-Ray Spex   153, 155

Yamamoto, Kansai 40, 48
Yeats, W.B. 36, 42, 45–6, 171
   Black Tower 45
   Last Poems 45–6
   Responsibilities 171
Yorke, Thom 178
Young, Jimmy 6

Young Communist League 114, 130
Young Ones, The 30
youth 5, 54, 56, 58, 61, 94, 126, 128,
   132, 147, 154, 170

Zomby 185
Zulu 136

Lightning Source UK Ltd.
Milton Keynes UK
UKHW020030140519
342630UK00007B/46/P